SINO-JAPANESE ENTANGLEMENTS

1931–1932

(A Military Record)

The Naval & Military Press Ltd

Published by
The Naval & Military Press Ltd
5 Riverside, Brambleside, Bellbrook
Industrial Estate, Uckfield, East Sussex,
TN22 1QQ England

Tel: +44 (0) 1825 749494
Fax: +44 (0) 1825 765701

www.naval-military-press.com
www.military-genealogy.com

In reprinting in facsimile from the original, any imperfections are inevitably reproduced and the quality may fall short of modern type and cartographic standards.

FOREWORD

Time has not come yet for writing a history of the fateful events of the past ten months in the Far East in their proper perspective. In the meanwhile, however, it has been thought advisable to have gathered together in a single volume the valuable material from official sources bearing upon the military operations in Manchuria and about Shanghai, that has been printed in some of the pamphlets recently issued at the Herald Press. In this way the only authentic military story, at present available, of the historic crisis in Asiatic development will be saved from the danger of dispersion and secured for easy reference.

Without attempting a comprehensive stock-taking of the situation resulting from the armed conflicts in Manchuria and about Shanghai, I wish to make a brief reference to one or two outstanding features of the picture.

It seems to have been a great surprise to the world to see Japan withdraw her military forces from Shanghai without any hesitation as soon as the safety of her nationals and their property there had been assured. It shows how widely the world had been misled by the Chinese propaganda that Japan was engaged in the conquest of China. It may be recalled that when the situation at Shanghai grew dangerous, General Araki, Minister of War, made it known publicly that, should it become necessary to send a military expedition there, it should be sent quickly and no less quickly recalled the moment it had attained its task of protecting the Japanese subjects there. And that is exactly the procedure the Imperial Government has actually followed in regard to Shanghai. This ought to go far to convince the world that nothing is further from Japan's ambition than to enter upon a career of conquest in China.

As a matter of principle the same is true of our policy in Manchuria. Only the practical application of the principle is necessarily modified in Manchuria by Japan's special position in that region. Japan's position there, as is well known, is strategical and political as well as economic. In addition to vast economic interests Japan has developed there, the course of history has saddled her with a mission which she cannot shirk without danger to her own national existence and to peace in Eastern Asia, if not ultimately to that of the world at large. This is the cardinal principle of our policy in Manchuria. We do not want conquest there any more than in China Proper. All that we want in Manchuria is the maintenance of our special position there, a position which China, in utter defiance of history and treaty obligations, had for years tried by every means in her power to undermine. The inevitable result has been the unfortunate outbreak which forms the subject of the present volume.

Much history has been made in these short ten months. We now see Manchuria an independent state ruled over by the late Emperor of China. It is already as good as informally recognized by Soviet Russia. It is eager to be officially recognized by Japan, and the public sentiment here is overwhelmingly in favour of granting its wish. At the last special session, the House of Representatives unanimously passed a resolution in favour of recognizing Manchukuo, a course which the Press is also united in urging upon the Government. It is, therefore, difficult to see how the Imperial Government could possibly delay much longer to take a step the whole people so clearly and urgently demand of it.

MOTOSADA ZUMOTO

Tokyo, July, 1932.

CONTENTS

	PAGE
CHAPTER I. Manchurian Emergency	1
Events Leading Up To It	7
Outbreak of Hostilities	15
Situation after September 20	19
Disposition of Japanese Troops	23
Concluding Remarks	24
Appendix	27
CHAPTER II. Battle of the Nonni	31
Up to Outbreak of Hostilities	33
Progress of Hostilities	39
CHAPTER III. Battle of Angangchi	45
Ma's Diplomatic Manoeuvring	47
Strength and Disposition of Ma's Army	52
Activities of Japanese Army Prior to Engagement	57
Offensive by Japanese	59
CHAPTER IV. Tientsin Incident	63
CHAPTER V. Chinchow Episode	69
Chinchow Government's Hostile Preperations	71
Reinforcements from Japan	73
Operations in West of Liao-ho	74
Withdrawal of Chinese Army Inside the Great Wall	77
CHAPTER VI. Harbin Campaign	81
A General Outline	83

	PAGE
Northern Campaign of the Kirin Army	84
Conditions in Harbin	86
Northern Movement of the Kwantung Army	88
Anti-Kirin Army in Harbin Well Prepared	93
Entry of the 2nd Division into Harbin	97
Conclusion	99
CHAPTER VII. The Shanghai Affair	103
Conditions Prior to the Outbreak of Hostilities	105
Immediate Cause	107
Happenings after January 21	109
Military Expedition and Statements by the Imperial Government	129
General Ueda's Ultimatum to the 19th Route Army	136
Shanghai Situation Further Explained	138
CHAPTER VIII. Military Operations Around Shanghai	141
The Start of the Military Expedition	143
What was Done to Avert Hostilities	146
Topographical Features of Shanghai Region and Conditions of the Enemy Force	150
Offensive about Kiangwanchen	153
Our Army Reinforced	156
Operations in Liuho, Tachangchen and Thereabout	168
After Cessation of Hostilities	174
Expeditionary Forces Reduced	177
Concluding Remarks	179

	PAGE
CHAPTER IX. The Origin and History of the Anti-Japanese Movement in China	187
Introduction	189
The Guiding Principles of Contemporary China and Anti-Foreign Movement	192
Education and Training in Anti-Foreign Movement	200
History of Anti-Japanese Movement	200
Observation upon Anti-Japanese Agitations	222
Supplement	230

APPENDICES

Japan and China in Manchuria......*Hugh Byas*	293
Japan in Transition ......*Frazier Hunt*	303
The War Minister Speaks Concerning China and Manchuria	311
Interview with "Times" Correspondent	311
Interview with Associated Press Representative	319
Interview with International News Service Correspondent	332

MANCHURIAN EMERGENCY

One of the inspired posters plastered on a wall in the military barracks at Peitaiying, near Mukden. It reads: "Keep a watch at the railway to the west of our barracks."

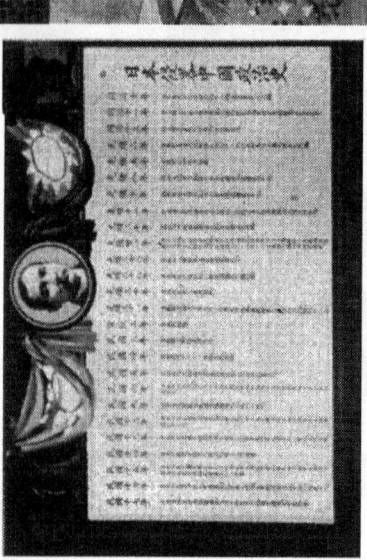

Some of the anti-Japanese posters put on the streets. The left cut gives a chronological record of "Chinese Political History of Japanese Invasion." The picture on the right hand side shows Chinese "sweeping national humiliations" out of their houses.

A pair of inflammatory posters put up on the street. The picture on the left side shows a Korean entering Chinese territory at the point of the Japaese bayonett. The drawing on the right shows the massacre of Chinese people by both Japanese and Koreans.

CHAPTER I

MANCHURIAN EMERGENCY

1. Events Leading Up To It

The Chinese policy toward Japan is best to be seen in the light of a series of more than 300 cases or incidents that have featured the intercourse between the two nations during the past few years. Of the more recent incidents, mention may be made of the question of *agrément* concerning the appointment of a Japanese minister to China, the maltreatment of Korean farmers in the region of Wanpaoshan, mob assaults upon Japanese population at Tsingtao, and the killing of Captain Nakamura by Chinese soldiers, all of which are still fresh in our minds. In Manchuria alone no less than a dozen of such incidents have been noted within a period of but three months after July of this year. Among these may be noted such cases as the wanton detention of Japanese patrol soldiers by 50 Chinese police officers; Chinese soldiers firing upon Japanese guards causing the loss of a life; Chinese bandits attacking 5 Japanese patrol soldiers, killing one of them. In more than a dozen other cases the Japanese civilian population were subjected to persecution or humiliation of one sort or another. Minor cases of open contempt or provocation in which not only civilians but soldiers of Japan have been subjects are almost numberless.

Such attitude of Chinese mind is to be traced to the fundamental idea of the "recovery of national rights," which has been the keynote of China's foreign policy. The Three People's Principles of the late Sun Yat-sen, the abrogation of unequal treaties as expounded by the Kuomintang and the general anti-Imperialistic sentiment form the basis upon which the whole Chinese mentality, official and individual, has in recent years been shaped.

All institutions of learning, from colleges down to elementary schools, employ text-books carrying expressions of contempt or hostility to Japan, or verses of the same tenor which young scholars are taught to sing. Military institutions overlook no opportunity to spread the same feeling in the ranks. An extreme case of the instance was seen when the soldiers at drill, ordered to number off, gave an expression for " Down with Japan! " instead of numbers. This is certainly a form of military training with Japan as China's national enemy.

In the field of civil administration, likewise, the National Government has been responsible for a number of legislative and other acts plainly aimed against Japan. Existing treaty commitments have often been ignored. Attempts have been made to nullify existing agreements with Japan, by purposely evading the issues on the pretext of internal troubles. To the end of nullifying the agreement as to the question of land lease in Manchuria, the Chinese authorities have issued laws whereby any one leasing land to a Japanese may be declared as punishable by death, and no mortgage held by a Japanese subject is to receive official recognition.

Orders have also been issued to cancel all contracts with Japanese people for lease of houses. A special Commission has been organized on the professed ground of guarding against "unpatriotic sales of land." In open violation of the treaties, the governors of provinces have been ordered to stop trading in Japanese goods. Japanese subjects have been refused official permits for inland travels. No opportunity has been suffered to pass without being turned to the furtherance of the anti-Japanese cause. This sentiment of hostility is now reflected even in the address which common Chinese people adopt in daily conversations with Japanese. Where a Japanese was once addressed with all respect due to a person of social respectability he is now often addressed in the low jargon of the street.

Nor does the same spirit fail to display itself among Chinese officials. Dr. Wang Cheng-ting, Minister of Foreign Affairs, speaking before Kuomintang members at Nanking in February of this year, was reported to have openly expressed himself to the effect that, should Japan oppose Chinese recovery of national rights, all that China had to do would be to settle the matter by the grim methods of war. Again, on another public occasion last August, the same Chinese statesman boldly discussed possibilities of driving Japanese population out of Manchuria by warlike methods. Chinese officials, military and others, have of late spoken much about the superiority of their soldiers, pointing out the actual training and abundant experience they have acquired on the field of battle. They have always referred in a contemptuous vein to the Japanese soldiers as men without experience of actual warfare. Such remarks, because often heard not only in military but also other official quarters, gained wide currency. The anti-Japanese attitude of a negative character was thus gradually turned into one of open contempt and defiance. When such a spirit was openly encouraged and was so widely at work, it was unavoidable that a dangerous situation should be precipitated.

Several days before the hostilities broke out in Manchuria, General Wang I-che, Commander of the Chinese Brigade at Peitaiying, which was to become the centre of military operations in the present Mukden campaign, was quoted as having said in the course of a speech on the Manchurian situation, that he would be proud to follow the example of General Han Kwang-yung, who was the author of the Sino-Soviet hostilities of 1930, dying on the field of battle. There were current at the time among the Chinese population rumours of "an imminent expulsion of the Japanese influence" and frequent talks of the "approach of hostilities to be launched by Chinese troops in South Manchuria."

All this by way of showing the attitude of provocative hostility that the Chinese people had been showing in China in general, and in Manchuria and Inner Mongolia in particular, wherever they came in touch with Japanese interests. It was inevitable, under the circumstances, that both the Chinese and Japanese people should come to confront one another with a sharpened sense of antagonism. Fear of an outbreak of some sort had been fast growing in many quarters, when the attack of Chinese soldiers on the South

Col. Doihara, who was for a time in charge of civil administration in Mukden, organized a medical clinic to administer help to the native civilians abandoned in their sick-beds.

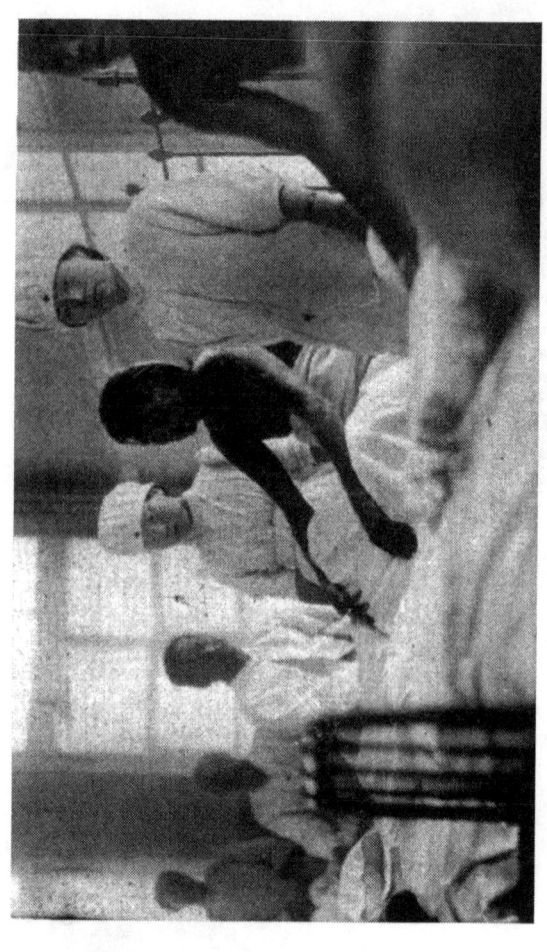

Almost at the first shot fired, Chinese physicians fled deserting their patients in hospital. These civilian patients were removed to the Japan Red Cross Hospital at the first opportunity.

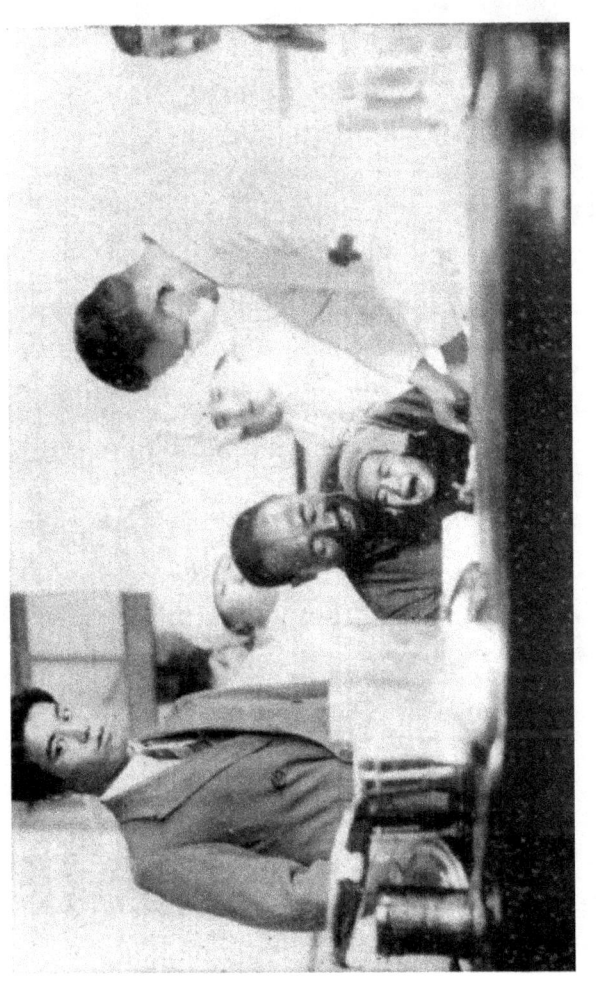

And a Japanese travelling clinic went about like good Samaritans.

The scarcity of foodstuffs became one of the first pressing questions after hostilities ceased in Mukden. Col. Doihara arranged with religious organizations for free distribution of foodstuffs among the poorer classes of Chinese.

Manchuria Railway near Mukden at last threw fat into the long smouldering fire.

2. Outbreak of Hostilities

What gave rise to hostilities near Mukden, was an incident in itself very simple. On the night of September 18 about 10.30 p.m., two or three companies of Chinese soldiers, under direction of a Chinese officer, destroyed the track of the South Manchuria Railway at a point to the southwest of the Chinese military barracks at Peitaiying where some 7,000 soldiers were quartered under the command of General Wang, Commander of the Brigade. These soldiers, having opened fire upon the Japanese soldiers who happened to be patroling the railway, proceeded toward Liutianghu where a Japanese detachment was stationed. Upon the report of this, a company of Japanese railway guards at the Hushihtai hastened to the aid, following the railway line to the south. The Chinese soldiers retired into the barracks at Peitaiying from the southwest side. The Japanese soldiers in pursuit pushed their way to get into the barracks from the same direction until they were brought to a sharp stop by a strong fire directed from the inside. The Japanese company, having occupied a corner on the barrack grounds, opposed the Chinese soldiers who were soon reinforced by machine guns, infantry and artillery. Consequently, the Japanese found themselves in difficulty, Lieutenant Noda falling in the action, until a reinforcement from the Second Battalion of Railway Guards at Mukden arrived under the command of Lieut.-Colonel Shimamoto. These combined forces drove the Chinese soldiers out of Peitaiying toward the daybreak. Inside the barracks large quantities of cartridges and hand grenades were discovered lying about almost everywhere. This is a significant circumstance, because it is a rule in the Chinese army never to supply men with these things except at time of war.

The 29th Regiment of Japanese Infantry under the command of Colonel Hirata stationed in the railway zone near Mukden, and in proximity with the Chinese troops stationed thereabout to the number of some 14,000 men, was naturally apprised of the above incident with little delay. The Regiment was at once put into action against the Chinese troops within the walled city of Mukden.*

Lieut.-General Tamon, Commander of the Second Division stationed at Liaoyang, issued an order at 1 a.m. for a concentration of the main force near Mukden.

Against this force, the Japanese troops in Manchuria were in all not more than 10,400 in number. This force consisted of one division about 5,400 strong, 16 pieces of artillery, and the Independent Railway Garrison

---

* The Chinese troops under Marshal Chang Hsueh-liang numbered 330,000, consisting of 250,000 regulars and 80,000 irregulars. Of these men 110,000 were away on an expedition beyond Shanhaikwan. The remaining force of 220,000, equipped with some 216 pieces of artillery, was stationed in Manchuria, the regions about the city of Mukden being guarded by some 14,000 men with about 40 pieces of artillery. At ordinary times the Chinese garrison within the walled city of Mukden is 3,000 strong.

of about 5,000, whereas the number of Japanese troops sanctioned by treaty is about 17,000. The duty of the Japanese military force in Manchuria is to guard the leased Province of Kwantung and the South Manchuria Railway, extending over a distance of 1,100 kilometres. In performing their duties, they have the right to resort to military action in case of necessity. The safeguarding of some 200,000 Japanese and 800,000 Koreans had also to receive their attention.

Although the Japanese force on such a basis is quite adequate to deal with the bandits for whom Manchuria is notorious, they had quite a different proposition in taking action against the regular Chinese troops of such numerical superiority. The situation of so precarious and perplexing a nature perforce demanded prompt action all along the line. No longer left in doubt as to the situation as regards the hostilities between the two sides, the Japanese military promptly rose to the occasion by concentrating the scattered troops at strategic points and by launching counter attacks wherever possible. Far outnumbered, it was tactical necessity for the Japanese force first to sweep off the Chinese troops in close proximity and next to station themselves at such points as to secure an open field for free manoeuvres. It is natural that the Japanese militarists, well alive to their own situation, should always have on hand plans carefully worked out on such principle.

The main force of the 2nd Division at Liaoyang, largely consisting of the 16th Regiment of Infantry, was immediately set in motion and arrived at Mukden early in the morning of the 19th. They proceeded at once to the district on the east side of the walls. By 8 a.m. or thereabout the Chinese troops had completely been swept off that part of the town. Later joined by the Regiment of Artillery (4 companies with 16 pieces of ordnance) from Haicheng, the main force of the 2nd Division turned upon the Chinese soldiers at Tungtaiying (about 2 miles to the northwest of Mukden), completely driving them off by 2.30 p.m.

Lieutenant-General Honjo, Commander of the Kwantung Military Force, in view of incoming reports, decided to send forth his main force to Mukden to assist in the campaign there. At 3 a.m. on October 19, he set out from Port Arthur for Mukden, requesting at the same time the Second Squadron of the Imperial Navy in port there to dispatch a part of its force to Yingkow for the protection of the Japanese there, and also sending a call to Korea for dispatch of reinforcements.

Lieutenant-General Honjo, arriving at Mukden at noon on the 19th, placed a section of the guard force at Tungtaiying, while the gendarmerie, with the support of an infantry contingent, were put on guard within the walled city. The main force was then concentrated within the railway zone near by.

In the meantime in the direction of Changchun, the 4th Regiment of Japanese infantry under Colonel Nagashima, found itself placed within a line of Chinese military force about 10,000 strong, armed with about 40 pieces of artillery. This Japanese force, as a step in self-defence, began to direct its action against the

Chinese contingent at Nanling with the object of clearing out their base at Kwanchengtze. The Japanese met with strong resistance in that direction, but with the assistance of the First Battalion of the Independent Railway Garrison, they were able to drive off the Chinese from Kwanchengtze after a long action, at about 11 a.m. and from Nanling about 3 p.m. With these points secured, the northern approach to the South Manchuria Railway line was practically closed to attack.

Chinese Treachery at Nanling

In the course of engagement at Nanling, the Chinese treacherously hoisted several white flags and drew the unsuspecting Japanese within 40 or 50 metres, when they opened fire, causing heavy damage to the advancing party.

The casualties on the Japanese side in the fights at the above mentioned places were as follows:—

	KILLED		WOUNDED	
	Officers	Non-com. officers & privates	Officers	Non-com. officers & privates
Mukden & vicinity...	0	2	7	19
Changchun & vicinity.	3	63	3	73
Total	3	65	10	92

3. Situation after September 20

On September 20 the main portion of the 30th Regiment of Infantry and a battalion of field artillery arrived at Changchun from Port Arthur and Haicheng respectively. The Commander of the 2nd Division also moved his headquarters to Changchun the same day to reinforce the line in that direction.

In the city of Kirin general conditions began to show signs of restlessness among the Chinese soon after the outbreak of hostilities at Mukden. Stones began to be thrown upon houses occupied by Japanese. Persistent calls for protection began to come from the Japanese residents there, of whom there were more than 900. There also came the report of the Kirin army moving westward against the Japanese troops. For protection of the South Manchuria Railway on its flank and of the Japanese population in Kirin, therefore, the Commander of the 2nd Division organized a mixed brigade and despatched it to the same city at about 10 a.m. September 21 by the Kirin-Changchun Railway. This manoeuvre removed a considerable portion of the force out of Changchun, but the thinned ranks were strengthened in the following afternoon by the arrival of the 15th Brigade of Infantry from Mukden.

Situation along the Line

In Kirin the Chinese soldiers were evidently thrown into panic at the advance of the Japanese troops. As a result of the parleys which General Hsi Hsia, chief of the staff, came out to conduct, the Japanese entered the city almost without any hostilities about 6 p.m., while the Chinese troops retreated to a distance of 20 Chinese miles (approximately 8 English miles). The 2nd Division, having secured order in this part, again moved its main body of men back to Changchun to strengthen the force there.

In the region of Chientao (Kanto) near the northern frontier of Korea, report of the military clash in Mukden at once began to agitate the Chinese element, until an uprising took place on the 20th. At Lungtsingtsun the Chinese rabble went so far as to set fire to the engine-shed at the railway station. At Yenki a public school was destroyed by fire. Though the socialists are charged with these actions, a state of panic prevails throughout these regions. There are persistent rumours of impending massacres by Chinese. The Japanese and Korean population has been sending out repeated calls to the Commander of the Japanese Army in Korea, though such action has been withheld to date.

The situation in Harbin has been no better, where the Japanese population numbers about 4,000. On the night of September 20 printed sheets were distributed in the city to stir up anti-Japanese feeling. The next morning the local Japanese organized a volunteer militia for self-defence. Urgent calls began to come from these Japanese and from the acting Consul-General there. On the night of September 21 about 9 p.m. bombs were thrown at our Consulate-General, the Bank of Chosen and a daily newspaper office.

Although the Japanese residents not only in Harbin but elsewhere, find themselves under conditions of extreme difficulty and danger, the Japanese Government, desiring to localize the troubles, has decided not to send military force beyond the present line. In other words, the Japanese residents are to be called back in case of necessity.

In the meantime, in the city of Mukden, which was completely deserted by all Chinese authorities soon after the fight, the Japanese military took temporary measures for maintenance of order. However, with the gradual return of peace, the conditions are being restored to what they were before. It is noteworthy that the Chinese populace, who had always been victimized by Chinese military and other authorities, have found under Japanese guardianship such a peaceful order of things as never seen before. Signs of peaceful restoration began to be seen the second day after the entry of the Japanese. On September 21 many shops and commercial establishments began to open, with the financial market again in operation.

As for the Army in Korea, a mixed brigade of some 2,900 men was organized under Major-General Kamura and concentrated at Shingishu on September 19 at 10 a.m., and held in readiness to proceed to places to be garrisoned. At the same time two companies were sent out for advance reconnaissance and other duties.

When the Kwantung Force had advanced to Kirin, the Commander of the forces at Shingishu, in view of the pressing situation, moved his troops, upon his own initiative, across the Yalu on September 21 at 1.20 p.m. to reinforce the Kwantung force. Arriving at Mukden about midnight, it replaced the main force of the 2nd Division, detailing out detachments to Chengtiatun and Shinmin the next day.

4. Disposition of Japanese Troops

As a result of the military actions and manoeuvres described above, hostilities practically came to a close. However, disbanded Chinese soldiers and bandits still continue to be active in the zone of the South Manchuria Railway, causing no small casualties on our side. There are indications of growing activity on their part.

As for the interior parts of the country, there is no means of obtaining information. However, there is reason to think that considerable numbers of Korean settlers have been massacred.

The disposition of the Japanese troops, as it stood at the beginning of October, is as given below, with little sabsequent changes:

In Mukden regions

Headquarters of Kwantung Forces.

The 39th Mixed Brigade.

A part of this force is posted on guard at the railway bridge at Liaoho, east of Shinmin.

In Changchun regions

Main force of the 2nd Division.

A part of this force is dispatched to guard Chengtiatun and neighbouring regions.

In Kirin regions

A part of the 2nd Division.

In addition to these, the Independent Railway Garrison attends to the guarding of the South Manchuria Railway, with its headquarters at Ssupingkai.

A glance at the map of Manchuria will show that Kirin is a point of great importance as a northern approach to the South Manchuria Railway, whence much damage might be inflicted. Chengtiatun and Shinmin are points through which the Chinese would have to pass in order to attack the same railway from the western side. The presence of the Japanese troops between these two points, therefore, is a matter of absolute necessity for safeguarding the same railway, and signifies neither military occupation nor permanent disposition of troops.

5. Concluding Remarks

From the above review, it may be seen that the present Japanese military action in Manchuria began as an act strictly in self-defence. The general situation there made it necessary for the Japanese to extend such action to points essential for self protection. Promptness of action is the first essential in moving small forces against forces of numerical superiority. Failure to forestall would be fatal to a force fighting against great numerical odds, a fact to which the Japanese had to be fully awake to assure their own success. Especially so when the Japanese had to operate with small troops scattered over regions three times wider than Japan Proper.

Digging for mutilated remains of Korean farmers.

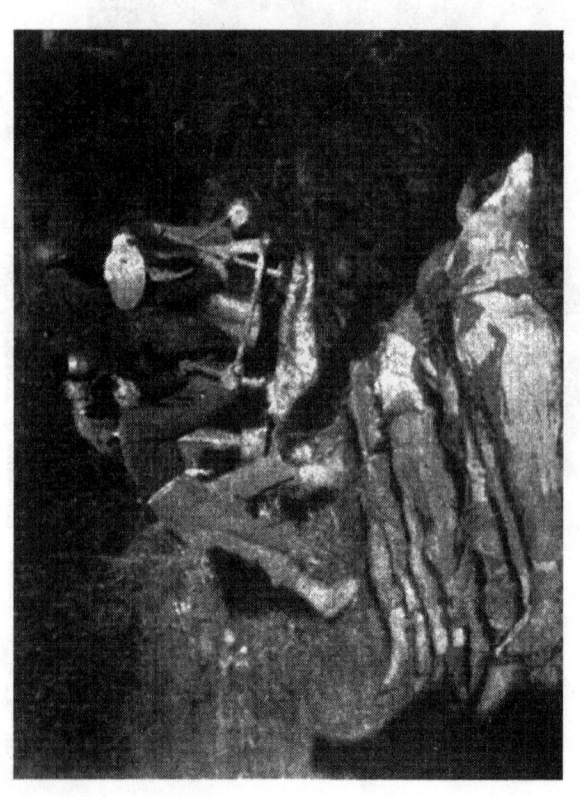

Digging for mutilated remains of Koreans at Kuchiatze, Manchuria.

APPENDIX

Statement by Imperial Government

The Imperial Government, in order to make clear its position as to the Manchurian question, issued on September 24, 1931 the following statement:—

"(1) The Japanese Government has constantly been exercising honest endeavours, in pursuance of its settled policy, to foster friendly relations between Japan and China and to promote the common prosperity and well-being of the two countries. Unfortunately, the conduct of officials and individuals of China for some years past has been such that our national sentiment has frequently been irritated. In particular, unpleasant incidents have taken place one after another in the regions of Manchuria and Mongolia, in which Japan is interested in a special degree, until the impression has gained strength in the minds of the Japanese people that Japan's fair and friendly attitude is not being reciprocated by China in a like spirit. Amidst an atmosphere of perturbation and anxiety thus created, a detachment of Chinese troops destroyed the tracks of the South Manchuria Railway in the vicinity of Mukden and attacked our railway guards at midnight on September 18; a clash between the Japanese and Chinese troops then took place.

"(2) The situation became critical, as the number of the Japanese guards stationed along the entire railway did not then exceed 10,400, while there were in juxtaposition some 220,000 Chinese soldiers. Moreover, hundreds of thousands of Japanese residents were placed in jeopardy. In order to forestall an imminent disaster, the Japanese army had to act swiftly. Chinese soldiers garrisoned in the neighbouring localities were disarmed and the duty of maintaining peace and order was left in the hands of the local Chinese organizations under the supervision of Japanese troops.

"(3) These measures having been taken, our soldiers were mostly withdrawn within the railway zone. There still remain some detachments in Mukden and Kirin and a small number of men in a few other places, but nowhere does a state of military occupation, as such, exist. The reports that Japanese authorities have seized the customs or the salt gabelle office at Yingkou, or that they have taken control of the Chinese railways between Ssupingkai and Chengchiatun or between Mukden and Shinmintun are entirely untrue, nor has the story of our troops having ever been sent north of Changchun or into Chientao any foundation in fact.

"(4) The Japanese Government, at the special Cabinet meeting of September 19, took the decision that all possible efforts should be made to prevent the aggravation of the situation, and instructions to that effect were given to the Commander of the Manchurian Garrison. It is true that a detachment was despatched from Changchun to Kirin on September 21, but it was not with a view to military occupation but only for the purpose of removing a menace to the South Manchuria Railway on its flank. As soon as that object has been attained, the bulk of our detachment will be withdrawn. It may be added that, while a mixed brigade of 4,000 men was sent from Korea to join the Manchurian garrison, the total number of men in the garrison at present still remains within the limit set by treaty, and that fact cannot therefore be regarded as having in any way added to the seriousness of international situation.

"(5) It may be superfluous to repeat that the Japanese Government harbours no territorial designs in Manchuria. What we desire is that Japanese subjects shall be enabled safely to engage in various peaceful pursuits and be given the opportunity of participating in the development of that land by means of capital and labour. It is the proper duty of a government to protect rights and interests legitimately enjoyed by the nation or individuals. The endeavours of the Japanese Government to guard the South Manchuria Railway against wanton attacks should be viewed in no other light. The Japanese Government, true to its established policy, is prepared to co-operate with the Chinese Government in order to prevent the present incident from developing into a disastrous situation between the two countries and to work out such constructive plans as will once for all eradicate cause for future friction. The Japanese Government would be more than gratified if the present difficulty could be brought to a solution which will give a new turn to the mutual relations of the two countries."

BATTLE OF THE NONNI

CHAPTER II
BATTLE OF THE NONNI

1. Up to Outbreak of Hostilities

The first important conflict between the Japanese and Chinese forces in Manchuria after the fightings immediately following the now historic outbreak on the night of September 18, 1931, took place on the Nonni in North Manchuria at the beginning of November. It was occasioned by an act of treachery on the part of a detachment of the Heilungkiang army stationed on the northern side of the river, which, contrary to previous understanding, suddenly opened fire upon a small party of Japanese troops that had been sent there for the protection of the repairs then proceeding on the bridges.

It may be recalled that shortly after the Mukden incident there began a trouble between the Heilungkiang army under General Ma Chan-shan and the army at Taonan under General Chang Hai-peng. Consequently much apprehension was generally entertained as to the safety of the Taonan-Angangchi railway. General Chang was then making preparations for proceeding to Tsitsihar by that railway at the head of his army, with a view to seizing the provincial government of Heilungkiang. On the other hand General Ma, by order of General Wan Pu-lin, concentrated his troops at Tsitsihar to frustrate General Chang's northward expedition. There is reason to believe that the Heilungkiang army was in secret communication with the Soviet army over the border, trying to secure assistance in the form of arms and ammunition.

By the middle of October, General Chang's army had commenced its northward march by the Taonan-Angangchi railway. With its main body stationed at Wumiaotze (north of Tailai), a part of the army advanced to the neighbourhood of the Nonni, when its further progress was stopped by the advance guard of the Heilungkiang army stationed on the opposite bank of the river with some field pieces. Moreover, the railway bridges had been damaged by General Ma's army on the 15th or 16th of October. Under the circumstances General Chang had for the moment to give up any hope of immediate march upon Tsitsihar, and so he retreated with the main body of his army to the neighbourhood of Taoan.

To make the story clear, it must be noted that the Taonan-Angangchi railway was built by the South Manchuria Railway under contract with the Mukden Government. Starting work in March, 1925, it was turned over to that Government in December, 1926, it being opened to public traffic in March, 1927. The amount of money advanced by the South Manchuria Railway Company was ¥17,000,000, of which ¥13,000,000 was the cost of construction and ¥4,000,000 the price of the rolling stock and other forms of equipment. As for the repayment of this money, it was arranged

(1) That the money required for the construction of the railway and its equipment should be paid by the Mukden Government immediately upon the delivery of the railway, and

(2) That in case such payment is not effected within six months after the delivery of the railway, a special agreement shall be made in the form of a loan contract at 9 percent annual interest.

But the Mukden Government failed to carry out any of these terms, even refusing to implement its obligation as originally agreed upon. Its indebtedness to the South Manchuria Railway Company on this score amounted by the end of June, 1931, to ¥26,000,000, principal and interest together. Under the circumstances, this railway may justly be regarded as property of the South Manchuria Railway Company, forming one of its feeder lines. In any case it forms a sufficiently valuable Japanese interest to be protected against damage by any body, Chinese or otherwise. Moreover, the present stoppage of traffic over this railway happened to be at a season when the farm products of North Manchuria were being shipped southward, thus causing no small loss to the railways concerned and also to the farmers in the wide range of territory tapped by those lines.

The Taonan-Angangchi railway authorities and the South Manchuria Railway Company, consequently, made combined efforts, through our diplomatic and military channels, to get the damage to the railway bridges over the Nonni repaired by some responsible Chinese authorities. These efforts, however, failed to bear any fruit, so it only remained for us to undertake ourselves the necessary repairs under the protection of our troops.

It may be interesting to recapitulate some of the facts connected with the fruitless attempts made to get the repairs made by some Chinese authorities:

(1) On October 12, a Japanese member of the staff of the Taonan-Angangchi railway, together with three Chinese colleagues, went to the Nonni bridges to make an inspection of the damage, but they were not permitted to carry out their mission, as a detachment of some 80 Heilungkiang troops brushed aside their identification papers and forced them to turn back at the point of their machine guns. Their train was actually fired upon with field pieces.

(2) On October 21, a Japanese plane reconnoitred along the Taonan-Angangchi railway as far as the Nonni bridges, where it was fired upon by the Heilungkiang troops stationed on the north side of the river. The matter was at once taken up by our military authorities with the Heilungkiang Government through Consul Shimizu at Tsitsihar.

(3) On October 23, Consul Shimizu opened negotiations with the local Chinese authorities concerning the repairs to the damaged railway bridges. The Chinese authorities replied that, as they would undertake the necessary repairs, the Japanese should never interfere with the railway. They, however, refused to say when the repairs would be made.

They further declared that, in case the Japanese attempted to undertake repairs, the Heilungkiang army would prevent it by force.

(4) After repeated negotiations, General Ma Chanshan finally set October 30 as the date for starting repair work. But as a matter of fact, he tried not only to postpone the work but to intimidate us by saying that behind him there was a Soviet army of 50,000 men.

Being now thoroughly assured that the Chinese authorities had no intention of undertaking the required repair work on the bridges over the Nonni, the Directors of the Taonan-Angangchi railway and the South Manchuria Railway Company decided to start the repair work themselves on November 4, and applied to the headquarters of the Kwantung Army for adequate military protection. This decision on their part was necessary in view of the fact that the river was due to be frozen very soon, in which case proper repairs would be impossible. As for the military protection, its necessity was obvious from the proved temper and past conduct of the Heilungkiang army and the bandits who infested the neighbourhood.

The Kwantung Army, thereupon, decided to accept the application for protection, and issued orders for the despatch of a detachment to the Nonni on November 2. At the same time an identical communication was sent to both the Heilungkiang army and General Chang Hai-peng's army, calling their attention to the following points:

(1) That the Japanese army observes strict neutrality as to the civil strife between the two Chinese armies.

(2) That, in order to prevent unforeseen complications, both the Chinese armies should retire to a distance of 10 kilometres from the nearest bridge.

(3) That for the time being the bridges may not be used by either army for military purposes.

(4) In case of any interference with the actions of the Japanese army or any hostile action against it, necessary and efficient measures of self-protection will be taken against the offending army, whichever it may be.

It should be stated that the Nonni at this point has a wide river-bed, measuring about 8 kilometres from one side to the other. It is spanned by five separate bridges, of which the three nearest the southern (i.e. the right) bank were damaged. The railway station at the southern bank is called Kiangchiao, and that on the north bank Tahsing. In order to afford efficient protection to the repair party, it was evident that our detachment should occupy Tahsing on the north side. But a body of Heilungkiang troops was in occupation of that neighbourhood. So the Japanese army requested it to move 10 kilometres further north.

The Japanese detachment detailed for the protection of the repair party consisted of a battalion of infantry (three companies), with a battalion of artillery (two companies) and a company of engineers, under the command of Colonel Hamamoto.

It was called the Nonni Detachment, and its transportation was commenced on November 2.

The troops under General Chang, in compliance with our request, retreated to the south of Wumiaotze. But the Heilungkiang forces, so far from retreating from their positions, were busily engaged in warlike preparations, showing a provokingly hostile attitude toward our detachment. For instance, when a scouting party proceeded on November 2 as far as the second bridge to inspect the actual state of the damage done, it was heavily fired upon by the Heilungkiang troops. Again on the morning of November 3 our scouting party despatched on a similar errand found the third bridge in occupation of Heilungkiang troops with three machine guns which at once opened fire upon it, so that it had to retreat without accomplishing its object.

The disposition of the Heilungkiang army in the neighbourhood of Angangchi on the night of November 4, is shown on Chart 1.

2. Progress of Hostilities

1. November 4.

In compliance with an earnest request of the Heilungkiang army, a party of Japanese authorities, including Consul Shimizu and Major Hayashi, came down to the Nonni from Tsitsihar, arriving at Kiangchao at 8.30 a.m. They were accompanied by General Shih, Chief of Staff to the Heilungkiang army, and a few other Chinese officials. From there General Shih notified the commander of the Japanese Nonni detachment to the effect that the Heilungkiang army had no hostile intention toward the Japanese forces. He left there almost immediately afterward. Thereupon, the Japanese detachment sent a small party (a company) to Tahsing with two national flags, one large and the other small. When it reached a point about 1,000 metres south of Tahsing at about 1.30 in the afternoon, it was suddenly and unexpectedly subjected to a heavy fire from the Heilungkiang troops stationed on the north side of the Nonni, sustaining 15 casualties. It had to fall back to the bridge-head, where it joined the engineer company and waited for the arrival of the main body of the detachment.

It was shortly after two that the detachment joined the advance party at the bridge-head, where it found in front a wide strech of marshy land very difficult of negotiation. To add to its worry, our artillery fire did not reach the enemy's position. A frontal attack being under the circumstances out of the question, the advance party was ordered to outflank the enemy on his left side. It was thus decided to wait for developments.

In the meantime our airplanes bombed the enemy's position, doing considerable amount of damage. But the enemy still continued to bombard our position. By 4.30, however, one of our mountain pieces was with great difficulty brought up to the back of our first line. It at once went into action and succeeded in silencing the enemy's artillery. All this while, the advance party under a heavy fire from the enemy struggled through the marshy land and succeeded in occupying an elevated position about 3 kilometres north-east of Tahsing. But the battle had not shown noticeable development when night descended upon the scene.

The Commander of the Kwantung Army, acting upon the report submitted by a staff officer who had been sent to observe the operations, issued an order tonight for the despatch of another battalion of infantry to reinforce the Nonni detachment.

2. November 5.

The main body of our detachment commenced operations at four in the morning, opened artillery fire at six and started a forward offensive movement shortly after seven. The Chinese occupying a strong position offered a stout resistance, and owing also to the topographical disadvantage, the progress of the engagement was slow. Our troops, however, succeeded in wresting from the enemy an important point about one and a half kilometres east of Tahsing Station at about half past eight. At ten our detachment occupied the enemy's first line of defence. The enemy retreated seven or eight hundred metres back to his second line of defence where he continued to offer a strong resistance. Our artillery experienced great difficulty in moving the guns, so that only three field and three mountain pieces were brought into action by ten o'clock. The result was that it degenerated into a drawn engagement. Not only that, at about three in the afternoon a superior force of the enemy assumed an offensive against the right back of our detachment, inflicting a heavy damage upon it. In consequence, our detachment was forced to reform part of its fighting line, and darkness fell upon it still engaged in a difficult fight.

In the morning the staff officer despatched from the headquarters had reported to the Commander that the Heilungkiang army did not seem inclined to retire, but that it seemed intent upon making a determined resistance. So the Commander ordered two more infantry battalions and three artillery companies to hasten to the support of the detachment. At 7.30 the first reinforcement, Nagura battalion, arrived and at once took up position. But it hardly sufficed to turn the scale decisively in our favour, so that the detachment passed a most anxious night impatiently waiting for the arrival of the rest of the reinforcements.

3. November 6.

Today the command of the detachment was taken over by Major-General Hasebe who had come with the reinforcements. With the arrival of successive units of the reinforcements, the fight assumed a favourable turn. The enemy's units in the rear began to retire northward from about eight in the morning, while a party of cavalry which had been harassing us from early morning withdrew in a northerly and north-easterly direction. The enemy's first line still continued to put up a stout fight, and it was only when an important position was captured by Nagura battalion under artillery support that the enemy began to falter, so that our detachment succeeded in occupying the enemy's position a little after ten o'clock.

At noon our detachment concentrated its strength to the east of Tahsing and took up a suitable position for the protection of the party engaged in repairing the bridges.

The enemy's infantry which fought in the vicinity of Tahsing was not less than 2,000 strong. In addition, a large body of cavalry also took part in the fight. The main body of the retreating enemy halted in the neighbourhood of Angangchi, while a small portion continued the retreat to Tsitsihar.

4. Casualties.

I. On our side:

Killed—1 officer; 35 n.c.o. and men
Wounded—7 officers; 15 n.c.o. and 122 men
Total casualties—180
Aeroplanes damaged—3

II. The enemy left 200 dead, of whom two were Russians.

CHART 1.
DISPOSITION OF THE HEILUNGKIANG TROOPS PRIOR TO OUTBREAK OF HOSTILITIES (NOV. 4. 1931)

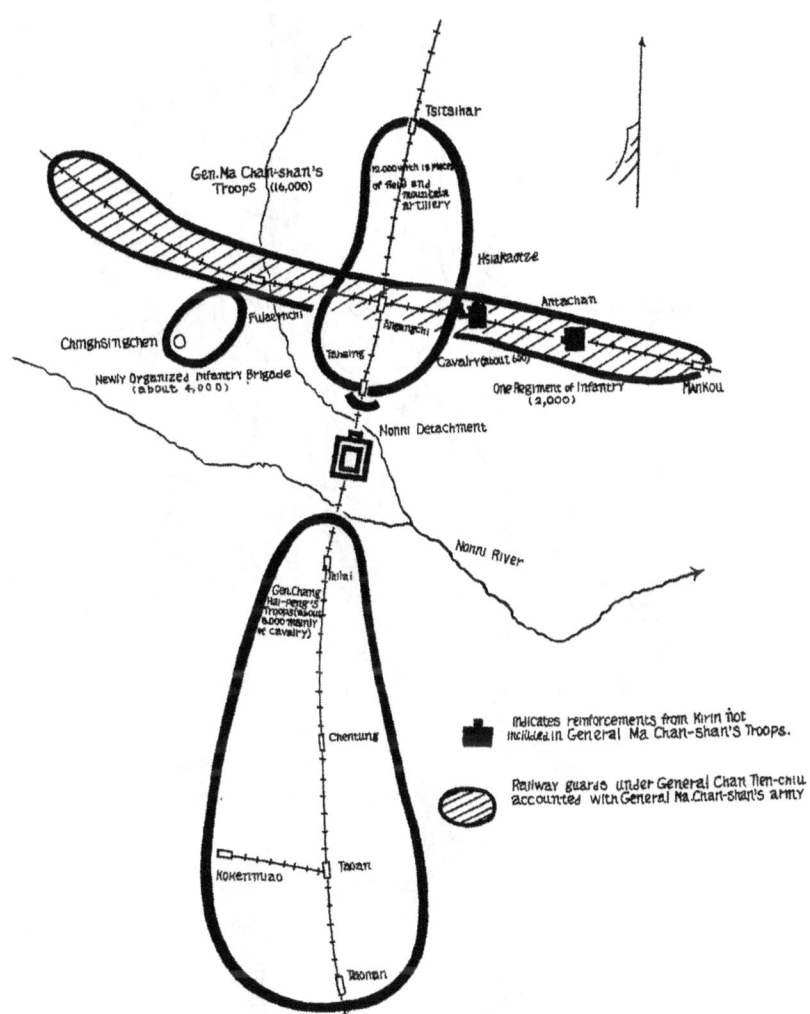

CHART II.

A MAP OF TAHSING AND VICINITY

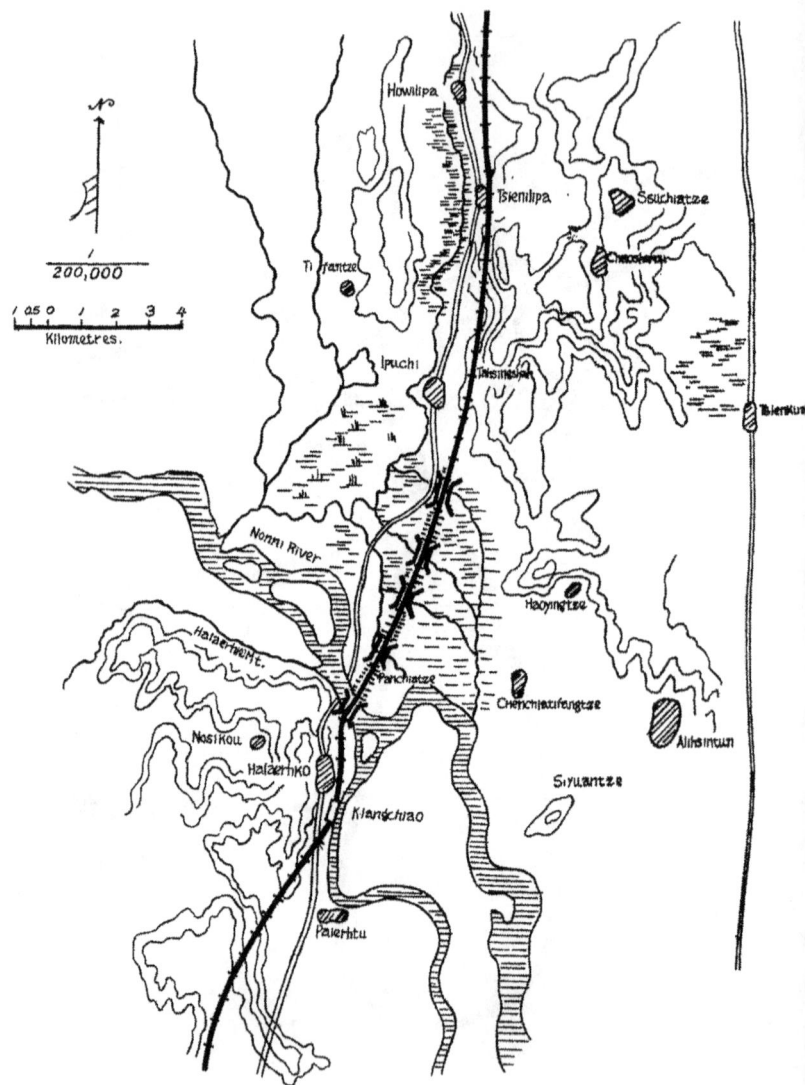

BATTLE OF ANGANGCHI

CHAPTER III
BATTLE OF ANGANGCHI

1. Ma's Diplomatic Manoeuvring

When the Heilungkiang army was defeated at the Nonni on November 6, our detachment which had been joined by the second reinforcements and which was about to be joined by a third party of reinforcements, could have easily launched a strong attack upon the retreating enemy, thereby inflicting such a damage upon him as would probably have fatally crippled him. And our men in the first line were eager to take such a course. But their commander wisely refrained from it for fear lest it might lead to an undesirable complication of the situation contrary to the principle of peace underlying the national policy of Japan.

But unfortunately the praiseworthy forbearance shown by our commander was interpreted by General Ma Chan-shan as a sign of weakness. He accordingly halted his retreating army at a point south of Angangchi only a few kilometres from the Nonni, and constructed a strong position there. Moreover, he summoned there reinforcements from Heiho, Harbin and Manchuli. At the same time he received telegraphic instructions from Chang Hsueh-liang at Peiping, ordering him to utilize convenient opportunity for exterminating the Japanese army.

He was also idolized by his fellow countrymen as a national hero. The result was that General Ma's men were highly elated and longed for further opportunity for distinguishing themselves. They intrigued to create disturbances in the rear of our detachment and also to injure again the bridges over the Nonni. It was thus increasingly evident that another collision between the Japanese and Chinese forces was inevitable in that part of Manchuria.

But the Kwantung army headquarters did not give up the hope of arriving at an amicable under standing with General Ma. So it caused its representative at Tsitsihar, Major Hayashi, to take the matter up with General Ma at that town. Several interviews took place between them on November 3 and thereafter, when the treacherous conduct on the part of Ma at the Nonni and Tahsing was pointed out to him, and he was urged to call his troops back to Tsitsihar, at the same time guarantying the safety of the Taonan-Angangchi railway. But General Ma did not respond to these overtures in a favourable manner or in a spirit of sincerity. On the contrary he seemed to be only anxious to push forward his hostile preparations.

Under these circumstances it was clear that, unless something was done to ease the situation, a dangerous clash would become unavoidable between the Japanese and Chinese armies. So the Kwantung army headquarters, with a view to placing the Heilungkiang army and our Nonni detachment at a safe distance from each other, made the following fair and moderate proposal to the Chinese side on November 14:

(1) Ma Chan-shan should withdraw to Tsitsihar and north of it, at the same time causing the troops concentrated at Tsitsihar and the neighbourhood of Angangchi in connection with the present complication to return to their original positions.

(2) Ma Chan-shan should not send his troops south of the Chinese Eastern Railway.

(3) The Taonan-Angangchi railway will be operated by the administrative bureau of that line, and Ma Chan-shan should in no way interfere with its operation. In case of such interference, the Imperial army will at once take necessary and efficient measures.

(4) Ma Chan-shan should carry out the conditions mentioned above within ten days from November 15.

(5) The Nonni detachment of the Japanese army, after satisfying itself as to the carrying out of the aforementioned conditions, will at once retire to the south of Taoan or Chengchiatun.

Ma Chan-shan was told that his reply to the above communication was expected by noon on November 16. But nothing was heard from him within the required time limit. Not only that, his troops surrounded the Japanese Consulate at Tsitsihar on the pretext of guarding it, and set up military works in the neighbourhood with ordnances trained at the front gate. The Consulate was entirely isolated, all communication with the outside being prevented. Even Chinese servants were not allowed freely to go out and get provisions. So Consul Shimizu and Major Hayashi were obliged to leave Tsitsihar for Harbin on the morning of November 14.

On November 16, at about 10 p.m., a telephone message was received from Ma Chan-shan through Chang Ching-hui, Director of the Harbin Special District, to the effect that he was ready to accept the whole of the conditions proposed by Japan, but that he would formally reply by letter. This was ten hours after the time limit set by our proposal, and instead of being delivered, as it should have been, through a responsible representative of the Heilungkiang Provincial Government, it came through an irresponsible third party. These and other circumstances apparently roused suspicions as to the sincerity of General Ma. It looked as if he was watching the possible change of atmosphere at the Council of the League of Nations, and that his idea in forwarding this belated message through an irregular medium was simply to provide a diplomatic excuse in view of future negotiations, a customary Chinese procedure. Accordingly instructions were sent to the Japanese officers at Harbin to exercise circumspect judgment in connection with this matter.

The promised written answer did not come to the hands of these officers up to 1 p.m. on November 17. So they made inquiries of General Liu, Civil Administrator and Representative of the Heilungkiang Government. It, then, transpired that a telephone message had been received at his office from General Ma to the following effect:

(1) That the Japanese detachment should retire simultaneously with the Heilungkiang army.

(2) That activities of bandits and other circumstances might necessitate the despatch of troops south of the Chinese Eastern Railway for the purpose of preserving peace and order.

(3) That the acceptance of the Japanese proposal would be impossible except on condition that the Japanese army would not permit General Chang Hai-peng's troops to enter Heilungkiang Province.

On the same afternoon Consul-General Ohashi at Harbin also received an answer which was no more reassuring as to the sincerity of General Ma than that addressed to the military mission already referred to.

While thus dilly-dallying with the Japanese army on the spot, General Ma reported to General Chang Hsueh-liang and General Wang Pu-lin at Peiping that he had peremptorily rejected the Japanese proposal. At the same time he caused foreigners at Harbin to send out telegrams saying that he had accepted the Japanese overtures. He evidently intended to play up to the League of Nations Council with a view to turning the scale of diplomacy in favour of his country.

As a matter of fact the Chinese troops on the spot, numerically much stronger than the Japanese, began to show increasing activities from about

November 11, assuming a provocative attitude. Forestalling the arrival of the relief party from the 8th Division, the Chinese forces started offensive movements on November 17. The challenge was accepted by our detachment which at once began action.

Even then the Chinese did not give up their game of diplomatic manoeuvring. At one o'clock on the afternoon of November 18, that is to say two days after the lapse of the time limit for reply, Generals Liu and Chang, speaking for General Ma, forwarded another reply to this effect:

(1) That the forces concentrated in the neighbourhood of Angangchi in connection with the present trouble would be evacuated within ten days.

(2) That as soon as the present trouble was settled no troops would be sent south of the Chinese Eastern Railway.

(3) That the Taonan-Angangchi line being a Chinese railway, it was China's responsibility to protect it, and that it would be operated upon the settlement of the present trouble, Chinese agreeing to the condition that she should offer no interference with its operation.

2. Strength and Disposition of Ma's Army

As already stated General Ma, while indulging in prevaricatory manoeuvres in regard to the repeated overtures of the Commander of the Kwantung Army for peace, was actually engaged in military preparations. He concentrated in the neighbourhood of Tsitsihar the greater part of the Heilungkiang army and of the military guards of the Chinese Eastern Railway, consisting altogether of between 20,000 and 30,000 infantry and cavalry, 30 pieces of artillery, over 10 pieces of trench mortars, and 2 anti-aircraft guns. Of these, the forces concentrated in the neighbourhood of Angangchi comprised approximately 7,000 infantry, 3,000 cavalry, and 20 pieces of artillery. They were encamped along a line which, starting from Tahsingtun, extended through Hsiaohsintun and Sanchienfang to the west of the last mentioned place, with the cavalry placed in front of the left wing. A separate position was prepared facing west at a place to the south-west of Fulaerhchi. The disposition of General Ma's forces on or about November 8 is shown in the accompanying sketch on page 19.

It appears that General Ma completed the final disposition of his troops on November 11, when their activities became particularly noticeable. The following morning his cavalry was sent to the right of the Nonni detachment. Its vanguard now and then appeared in front of our line, thereby occasioning minor conflicts. The situation steadily became serious.

On the night of November 13, a portion of General Ma's army ventured forth to Changhuayuan and Alihsintun, thereby threatening to envelop our detachment.

The relative positions of the two opposing forces on November 14, were as given in the accompanying sketch map on page 20.

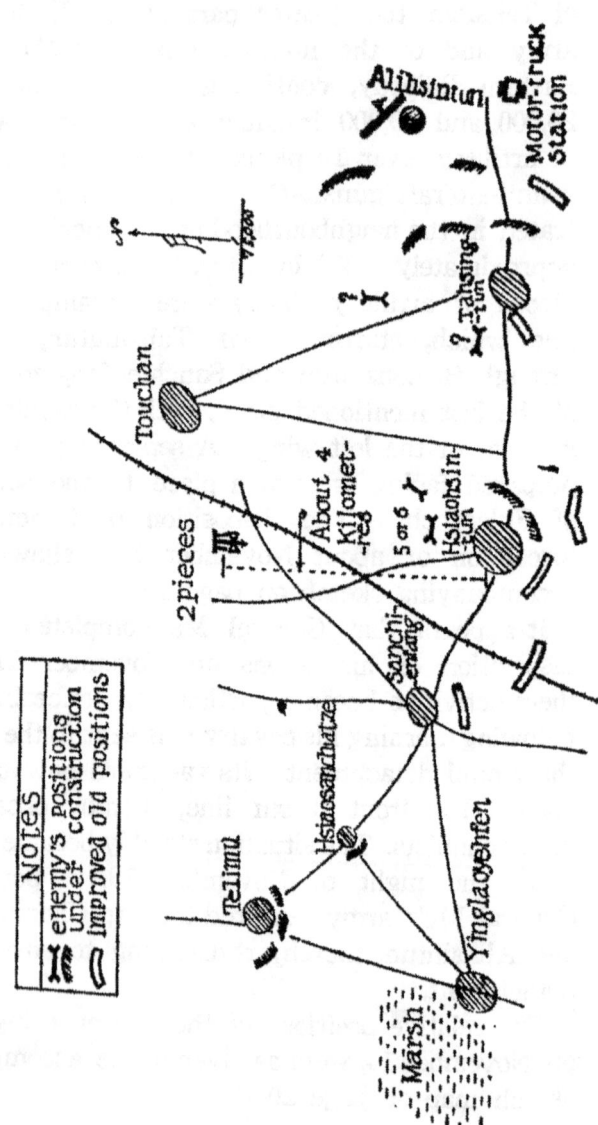

General Line-up of Gen. Ma's Forces South of Angangchi
(November 8, 1931)

The Confronting Fronts near Angangchi
(NOV. 14)

Map showing locations: Fularerhchi, Angangchi, To Tsitsihar, Telimu, Angangchi (Station), Sanchienfang, Hsiaohsintun, Tahsingtun, Tangchih, Wunotoutun, Tsienkuanti, K.K, Howilipa, Nonni Detachment, Changhuayuan, Tahsing, Kiangchiao

Legend:
- Enemy Force
- Enemy Position
- Nonni Detachment

According to the subsequent information brought in by our scouting planes, the Heilungkiang army's line to the east and west of Sanchienfang was steadily extended, its right wing reaching to a point some 1,000 metres south of Telimu. The different positions were connected by deploying trenches. The enemy apparently worked hard at night. His positions at Tahsingtun, Hsiaohsintun and Sanchienfang were soon surrounded with earth works with protected rifle holes, covered spaces, machine gun emplacements, and other appointments, which clearly indicated that this section was his central position. There were altogether four lines up to Tsitsihar. They were as follows:

(1) The line stretching east and west of Sanchienfang, with about 5,000 to 6,000 infantry, about 2,000 cavalry, and about 20 pieces of artillery.

(2) The line extending from Angangchi eastward to Yushutun and Taiwangsanchiatze, with about 1,000 infantry, and about 700 cavalry. Besides, in the neighbourhood of Fulaerhchi there were stationed about 2,000 infantry, and about 1,000 cavalry, with 2 guns.

(3) The line extending westward to Ssuchiatze from Shihwulitun, 10 kilometres south of Tsitsihar.

(4) The line extending westward from the South Barracks, south of Tsitsihar.

The last mentioned two lines were not yet actually manned by troops, but for that purpose there were kept in readiness at Tsitsihar a body of reserves consisting of the students of the branch military academy and the school for non-commissioned officers, the reserve regiments and part of artillery corps.

3. Activities of Japanese Army Prior to Engagement

After the battle on the Nonni, the Nonni detachment (whose main body consisted of $4\frac{1}{2}$ battalions under the command of Major-General Hasebe) remained in the vicinity of Tahsing to protect the repairs of the bridges. By November 10, the repair work had progressed barely sufficient to allow open cars to pass. In the meantime the planes belonging to the detachment were daily engaged in scouting over the enemy's positions, principally at Angangchi. They were every time exposed to the enemy's fire, which was particularly severe on November 9, when fliers were wounded by anti-aircraft guns.

It was probably a mere coincidence but it is noteworthy that on the day (November 11) when it was decided to despatch to Manchuria a contingent from the 8th Division under the command of Major-General Suzuki to relieve the mixed Brigade from Chosen (Korea), General Ma's army, as already stated, commenced to show increased activities, succeeding in nearly enveloping the Nonni detachment. It being increasingly evident that Ma meant shortly to assume the offensive, the headquarters of the Kwantung Army, in order to be prepared for emergencies, ordered the main body of the 2nd

Division to proceed to Tahsing on November 13, when the temporary repairs on the Nonni bridges were completed and the trial passage of a train was successfully carried out.

In view of a possible offensive by the enemy, the Nonni detachment concentrated its main force in the neighbourhood of Tahsing, sending a contingent (two battalions of infantry and two companies of cavalry) to Tsienilipa to watch for developments and beat back the enemy's cavalry that had ventured to the back of our right wing. A party of our cavalry today was attacked by a superior body of the enemy's cavalry in the neighbourhood of Wunotouchan about 10 kilometres north-east of Tahsing, sustaining several casualties. A part of the detachment occupied, after a light engagement, Wunotouchan and an elevated position about 1,500 metres south of Tangti.

The main body of the 2nd Division nearly completed its concentration at Tahsing and the neighbourhood of Kiangchiao. This part of the field passed into the control of the commander of the 2nd Division. The aggregate strength of our forces available for this district was 3,000 men, infantry and cavalry combined, with a little over 20 pieces of artillery.

The Japanese forces were still too small, and as it became evident that Ma's army intended to turn into the offensive before the arrival of our relief party on its way from the 8th Division, it was decided on November 17, as an emergency measure, to summon a part of the air forces respectively belonging to the 3rd, 12th and 20th Divisions.

4. Offensive by Japanese

Ma's army showed a conspicuous activity on November 17, increasing its strength along the whole line, evidently with a view to starting the offensive movement before the arrival of our relief party and the newly summoned air force. Thereupon the 2nd Division decided, as a measure of self-preservation, upon a counter attack. The plan of action was to push the main attack in the direction of Sanchienfang and neighbourhood, and after breaking through the enemy's line and routing him, to launch the main attack in the eastern and north-eastern directions, thus extending the battle front and endeavouring to crush the enemy in the vicinity of his positions. The Japanese forces were disposed as follows:

(1) The right wing (about 4 battalions of infantry) to deploy east of the railway and attack the enemy in the neighbourhood of Hsiaohsintun.

(2) The left wing (about 4 battalions of infantry) to deploy west of the railway and attack the enemy in the neighbourhood of Sanchienfang.

(3) The artillery, of which the main force to take up position to the north of Tangti, while a smaller contingent to take up position respectively at the back of the right and left wings.

(4) The reserve to keep in readiness south of Tangti.

The respective parties started motion half an hour after midnight on November 17, and by 3 a.m. they took up positions 700–800 metres in front of the enemy, preparatory for the attack. It was pitch dark and intensely cold with the thermometre registering 20 degrees below zero and the wind blowing from the north-west at the rate of 15 metres.

About the same time the enemy's infantry began to fire in the dark, and as the eastern sky began to grow grey at about six, more machine guns and rifles came into play. But the Japanese troops did not reply. At six-thirty, our artillery commenced firing to find the range, and at eight started bombardment which was kept up for about an hour, during which time our air forces, in co-operation with the artillery, bombed the enemy's position. As our artillery range was extended, the first line of our infantry started the attack at about nine. Hand to hand fights took place at several points. Unable to stand our furious onslaught any longer, the enemy began to retire along the whole front at about ten-thirty, fleeing along the Taonan-Angangchi railway on both sides of it. Thereupon the 2nd Division pursued the retreating enemy toward Tsitsihar, its main body marching along the railway on the western side and a portion of it on the eastern side. Hotly pursued, the enemy was unable to make a stand at his second line of defence in the neighbourhood of Angangchi, retreating from there northward at about two in the afternoon.

The officers and men of the 2nd Division were thoroughly tired as the result of continued and strenuous exertions for the past several days, and they suffered much from increasing cold and wind, which froze their food and water. But nothing daunted, they pursued the retreating enemy and arrived at a point 4 kilometres south of Tsitsihar half an hour after midnight on November 18. But our troops were in some places badly mixed up with the fleeing enemy, so that there was danger of our own men fighting each other. It was, therefore, decided to concentrate the main body in the vicinity of Tamintun, south of Tsitsihar, where they had a long-needed rest.

At noon on November 19, the main body of the 2nd Division formed in two columns, and leaving the line at Tamintun and Shihwulitun, they entered Tsitsihar at three in the afternoon. The bulk of it was quartered at the South Barracks and the remainder at the North Barracks, leaving the duty of keeping order in the town to the Chinese Director of the Bureau of Public Safety.

The main body of Ma's army seemed to have retreated in the direction of Hailun (120 kilometres north of Harbin and on the Hulan-Hailun railway) and Paichuan. By the nightfall on November 19, there was not visible any important body of Ma's troops, except small insignificant parties, within a radius of 30 kilometres of Tsitsihar.

Our casualties consisted of 31 killed, 104 wounded and 13 missing, besides 300 cases of frostbite.

The Chinese casualties must have been very heavy, but no reliable estimate has been forthcoming.

It is hardly necessary to state that during this engagement the Japanese army took care to respect the property of the Chinese Eastern Railway. It also so arranged the plan of operations as to prevent the Chinese troops from retreating along the railway toward Harbin.

In conclusion it may be stated that this engagement was undertaken by the Kwantung Army simply as a measure of self-preservation. Consequently as soon as Ma's army which menaced our rights and interests had been disposed of, the main body of our troops was withdrawn, without occupying that part of the country.

REAR POSITIONS OF GENERAL MA'S TROOPS SOUTH OF TSITSIHAR

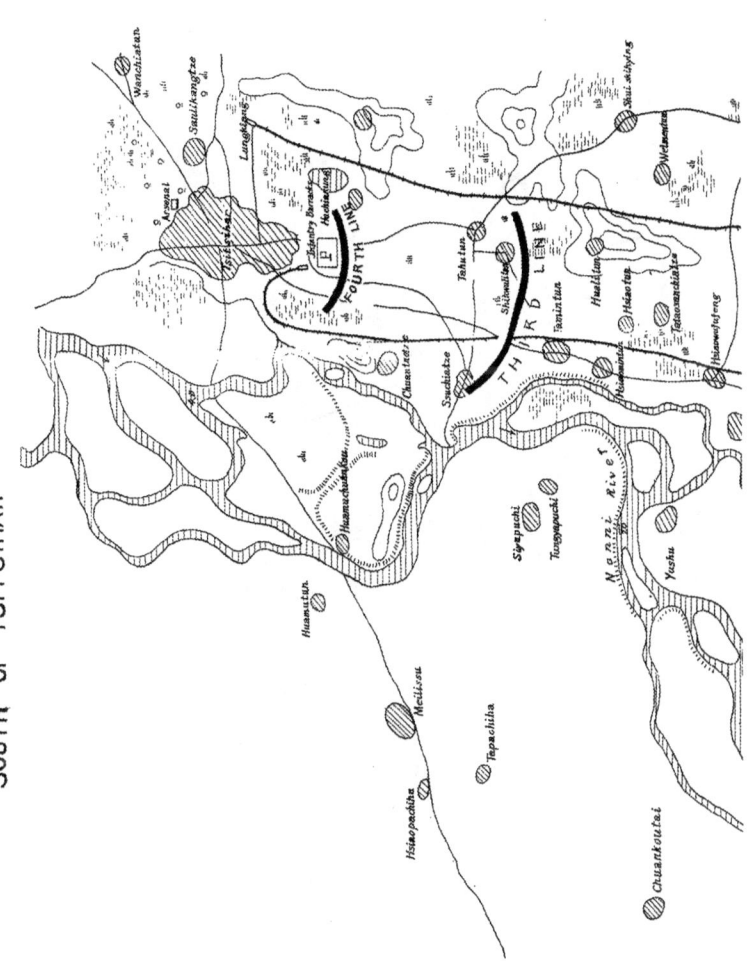

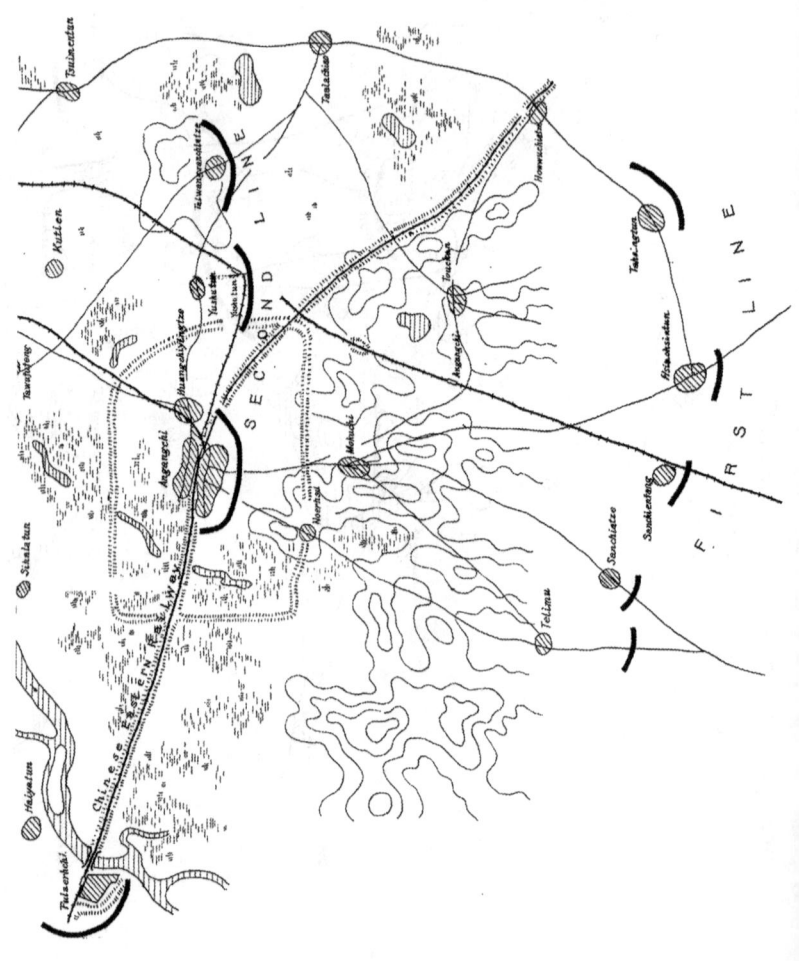

TIENTSIN INCIDENT

CHAPTER IV

TIENTSIN INCIDENT

After the outbreak of the Manchurian trouble, the sentiment among the Chinese at Tientsin grew steadily more and more unfriendly toward the Japanese. The Anti-Japanese Association's activities became better organized. The situation was complicated by the fact that the local Chinese, who had never been particularly cordial toward Chang Hsueh-liang, now grew hostile toward him, whose maladministration they held responsible for the Manchurian catastrophe. In order to check the growing popular antagonism toward him, Chang secretly planned to carry out a policy of drastic suppression against the promoters of the hostile movement against him.

The anti-Chang leaders got wind of this, and with the object of forestalling the approaching danger, they set about organizing a force of plain clothes soldiers, which they styled The Nation Saving Army. On the night of November 8, men of this organization suddenly created trouble in the Chinese city of Tientsin, attacking the guardians of public order.

The Commander of our garrison there made a public declaration of strict neutrality with regard to the clash between the contending Chinese factions.

Measures were at once taken by him for the maintenance of order in the Japanese settlement and the protection of the lives and property of the Japanese residents.

But the Chinese guards stationed in the vicinity of the Japanese settlement fired into a position occupied by our troops, killing two of the latter. Thereupon our troops had to return the fire as a matter of self-defence.

The Commander of our garrison at once communicated with the Chinese authorities, and requested them, with a view to avoid precipitating an unfortunate crisis between Japan and China, to order the contending Chinese factions not to approach within 300 metres of the Japanese settlement. This request was repeated twice or three times, but it was not readily acted upon. As a matter of fact plain clothes soldiers constantly made their appearance, the Chinese troops also firing in the vicinity of the Japanese settlement.

The Chinese authorities continued outwardly friendly, but there is reason to believe that they were secretly fanning the anti-Japanese feeling of their people. In any case the situation became so serious that the other foreign garrisons mounted guard in their respective areas from the 11th or 12th of November.

It transpired shortly afterward that the firing of the Japanese position by Chinese soldiers, which had been alleged to have been directed toward the plain clothes men belonging to the Nation Saving

Army, was really part of a deliberate scheme of harassing the Japanese planned by Chinese officers in high positions.

On this amazing fact becoming known, the Chinese authorities offered a profound apology to the Commander of the Japanese garrison. They also promised to exercise a more effective control over the anti-Japanese propaganda, to remove all military works set up within 300 metres of the Japanese settlement, and not to permit their soldiers to approach within 300 metres of the settlement. But the dangerous practice of firing into the settlement did not cease, and the situation continued to be disquieting. The Japanese garrison, however, remained faithful to its own part of the agreement. It called off part of its guard, restored the traffic in the settlement to its normal condition, and in the afternoon of November 26 it disbanded the volunteer corps.

At eight that evening, the Chinese suddenly opened a stiff firing upon our barracks from a position to the west of it. Our troops did not reply to it, but a remonstrance was at once made to the Chinese authorities against the extraordinary behaviour of their soldiers, demanding the cessation of the firing. They alleged that the firing was directed against the Nation Saving Army and was not meant for the Japanese settlement, but they promised that in any case it would be stopped before half past ten. But the firing did not cease until noon the following day. It was a deliberate act of hostility, so that our garrison decided upon the only course left to it for the protection of the Japanese life and property in the settlement. In other words, it had to accept the challenge and fight the Chinese.

On the morning of November 29, a representative of the Chinese authorities called at the headquarters of the Japanese garrison, and offered to withdraw all armed people from the neighbourhood of the Japanese settlement and also to remove all defence works set up in the Chinese city. This offer being accepted, the armed Chinese police were withdrawn by the evening of November 29, while the defence works were removed the following day.

CHINCHOW EPISODE

CHAPTER V

CHINCHOW EPISODE

1. Chinchow Government's Hostile Preparations

After the battle of Angangchi, Ma's army seemed for a while bent upon an attempt to recover Tsitsihar. But on about December 11 there was concluded a compromise agreement between him and Chang Ching-hui. In the meanwhile matters were steadily improving in the Province of Fengtien. On about December 16 General Tsang Shih-i, former Governor of Liaoning, accepted the post of Governor of Fengtien offered to him by a group of leading inhabitants of the province. It was evident that the movement for reconstruction was growing strong in the three north-earstern provinces with the exception of the south-western corner of Fengtien.

In the neighbourhood of Chinchow, there was stationed a large force of regular troops belonging to Chang Hsueh-liang. Its strength was estimated at about 35,000 men, with a fairly strong artillery equipment. Its main body occupied a strong position on the right bank of the Taling-ho (see Chart IV), while a detachment was stationed in the territory between that river and the Liao-ho. While in this way preparations were being steadily pushed forward with a view to a clash with Japanese forces, the auxiliary troops and volunteers under the control of the Chingchow Government began to show great activities as soon as the Japanese contingent that had been advancing to the west of the Liao-ho turned back. These irregulars tried hard to cause disturbances along the South Manchuria Railway.

Chang Hsueh-liang at first built high hopes upon the support of the League of Nations. But when he found that, Japan's attitude being determined, much could not be expected from that quarter, he made up his mind to fight Japan with the help and co-operation of Nangking. With this object in view, he concentrated to the east of Chinchow a strong army of regulars, 35,000 strong, made up of $3\frac{1}{2}$ brigades of infantry, a brigade and a regiment of artillery. The first line occupied positions extending along Changwu, Paichipu, Taian and Tienchuangtai, with an advanced detachment in the neighbourhood of Fakumen. Besides, as already stated, the territory along the South Manchuria Railway was infested by a strong body of irregulars under the control of Chang Hsueh-liang. It was made up of about 30,000 auxiliaries and about 5,000 volunteers. In addition to these forces, bandits invited from different parts of Manchuria were being organized into units. This was coincident with a general outbreak of bandit activities along the main line of the South Manchuria Railway and the Antung-Mukden line, causing no small damage to Japanese subjects.

It is estimated by competent authorities that the armed forces, comprising the regulars, the irregulars and all other units under the direct or indirect control of the Chinchow Government, exceeded 80,000. Heterogeneous as were their complexions and formations, they were all united in their hostile attitude toward Japan. So unless Chang Hsueh-liang was prepared to change his policy, it was now clear that a clash was inevitable between them and the Japanese army.

2. Reinforcements from Japan

In view of the increased activities of Chinese troops and bandits in Manchuria and of the serious situation at Tientsin, it was decided on December 17 to despatch a specially constituted brigade, together with a force of heavy artillery and a party of rear service men to Manchuria, while a detachment chiefly composed of two battalions of infantry was sent to Tientsin.

By this time the organization of various irregular contingents by the Chinchow Government had made a great progress, so that disturbances of peace and order by these forces now became more widespread and serious than before. Taking advantage of the freezing of the Liao-ho, they crossed that river to its left bank in large force, and a large body of them, 2,500 strong, took possession of the town of Nieuchwang on December 26, while the district to its north and west was in the occupation of several thousands volunteers. These forces, it is needless to say, had penetrated so far eastward with the object of creating diversions in the rear of the Japanese detachment that was operating to the west of the Liao-ho. By recent experience it was wellknown that the fighting capacity of these irregulars was much greater than that of ordinary bandits. Their comrades along the Antung-Mukden line also showed no sign of lessened activities.

Under these circumstances, it became evident that the troops available were insufficient for suppressing irregulars and bandits infesting the territory west of the Liao-ho, in addition to dealing with those threatening the various railway lines. So on December 27, at 6 p.m., Imperial sanction was given to the despatch of the headquarters of the 20th Division and its Yoda brigade to Manchuria to be placed under the orders of the Commander of the Kwantung Army. All these forces in due time arrived in Manchuria.

3. Operations in West of Liao-ho

The disturbances caused by the routed soldiers and bandits in the territory west of the Liao-ho, and which threatened to spread to regions nearer the South Manchuria Railway lines, having become very serious, the main body of the Kwantung Army was ordered to suppress these marauding bands of Chinese peace breakers. The Japanese army started on its important expedition on December 28, the

Kamura Brigade proceeding along the Peiping-Mukden Railway and the Tamon division along its branch line. The main part of that division left Tienchuangtai on December 28, and proceeded along the route assigned to it, always taking care to exercise proper pressure upon such Chinese troops and auxiliaries as may happen to be in the neighbourhood. It reached Tawa at dark, and the following day it continued its march. At two in the afternoon its vanguard occupied Panshan after a slight fighting. The Chinese force occupying that place was about 500 strong, made up of regular troops belonging to the 19th brigade (654th regiment) who were in cooperation with auxiliaries. The division reached the neighbourhood of Huchiawupu on December 30.

The Kamura brigade left Hsinmintun on December 30, and proceeding along the main line of the Peiping-Mukden Railway, reached Tahushan at nightfall. On the way it met and dispersed some parties of marauders.

On December 31, the Kamura brigade reached the neighbourhood of Koupangtze. As for the Tamon division, a part of it reached Koupangtze, while its main force reached a point to the south-east of that place on the same day.

On January 1, the Kamura brigade proceeded in the direction of the Taling-ho and reached Shihshanchan at noon, while the train that carried its vanguard arrived at the railway bridge over the Taliao-ho at 3 p.m. The Tamon division was occupied in concentrating its forces in the neighbourhood of Koupangtze.

The Chinese forces that took part in the engagements east of the Taling-ho, comprised two regiments of the 19th brigade, nearly the whole of the 20th brigade, a portion of the 3rd cavalry brigade and volunteers. The casualties they sustained are estimated at 2,000.

At daybreak on January 2, the Yoda brigade, now forming part of the Muro division, advanced by the Peiping-Mukden Railway to the rear of the Tamon division. That night the Kamura brigade was quartered in villages between Shuangyangtien (8 kilometres east of Chinchow) and Talinghotien, while the Yoda brigade stayed at villages between Shihshanchan and Koupangtze. The Kamura brigade, which had been restored by the Commander of the Kwantung Army to the Muro division, was charged with the task of occupying Chinchow.

The vanguard of the above mentioned brigade entered Chinchow early on the morning of January 3, while the headquarters of the division arrived there at 10.40 the same afternoon. The commander of the division was welcomed on arrival at the railway station by a large crowd of important people, including the heads of the various Government and municipal offices and leading citizens. The streets were lined by dense crowds of happy looking people, while the houses on both sides were adorned with Japanese flags.

On January 4, it was as a whole quiet and peaceful at Chinchow and neighbourhood, but at night a party of our patrols was fired upon by bandits. Lieutenant-General Muro ordered a detachment, whose main body was composed of a battalion commanded by a colonel, to advance west of Chinchow. It proceeded this day as far as Lienshan.

On January 5, the Muro division despatched a detachment each to Ichow and Suichung. A part of the detachment sent to the latter place continued its march southward on the following day to keep order in the region west of Suichung. Its advance party, on reaching Tsienso (about 20 kilometres east of Shanhaikwan), established a definite contact with the Japanese garrison at the latter place.

A troop of cavalry belonging to the above mentioned detachment was sent to Chinsi, and at about noon the next day it put to rout a party of about 80 soldier bandits at a point about 10 kilometres west of Chinchow.

4. Withdrawal of Chinese Army inside the Great Wall

On the night of December 29, that is to say before our army reached the Taling-ho line, the Chinese army in and round Chinchow began to evacuate by the Peiping-Mukden Railway. It appears that a part of the army withdrew in the direction of Jehol. As to the forces that retreated within the Wall, a brigade each seems to have been concentrated at Lanchow, Changli and Tangshan.

The Chinese detachment that had stayed behind at Suichung commenced evacuation on the morning of January 5, while those stationed at Shanhaikwan and in the region east of it also withdrew inside the Wall on the night of January 5.

This was a pitiable ending of the rather grandiose attempt which Chang Hsueh-liang had made for the recovery of Mukden. In view of the powerful pressure which self-styled patriots brought to bear upon him and also to the necessity of saving his face, Chang Hsueh-liang had no alternative but to keep up some show of spirit, although he may not have felt much confidence in the success of further resistance. Under the circumstances, evacuation without resistance was probably the wisest thing for him to do. There is, however, reason to believe that Chang Hsueh-liang's motive in ordering a peaceful evacuation was probably not so simple and harmless as it may at first sight appear. At any rate, the Japanese army had to face an aftermath which proved anything but pleasant or easy to deal with. It is customary with a Chinese army when defeated, to leave behind it troops of inferior quality, so that they may combine with local bandits for the purpose of harassing the enemy's rear. At all events that has been exactly what happened in the present case. The suppression of banditry in the evacuated region has subsequently proved a rather costly affair to the Japanese army.

The extinction of the last vestige of Chang Hsueh-liang's authority in Manchuria undoubtedly marks an epoch in the history of that country. It was a definite step in the consolidation of the influences in favour of peace and progress in Manchuria. It was undoubtedly in recognition of this fact that the Emperor chose this opportunity for honouring the Japanese army in Manchuria with a Message graciously acknowledging the heroic services which His Majesty's troops had rendered in different parts of Manchuria and exhorting them to continue their valuable exertions with a view to strengthening the foundation of peace in the Far East.

CHART IV. CHINESE TROOPS AS STATIONED ON THE RIGHT SIDE OF THE TALING–HO
(towards the end of December)

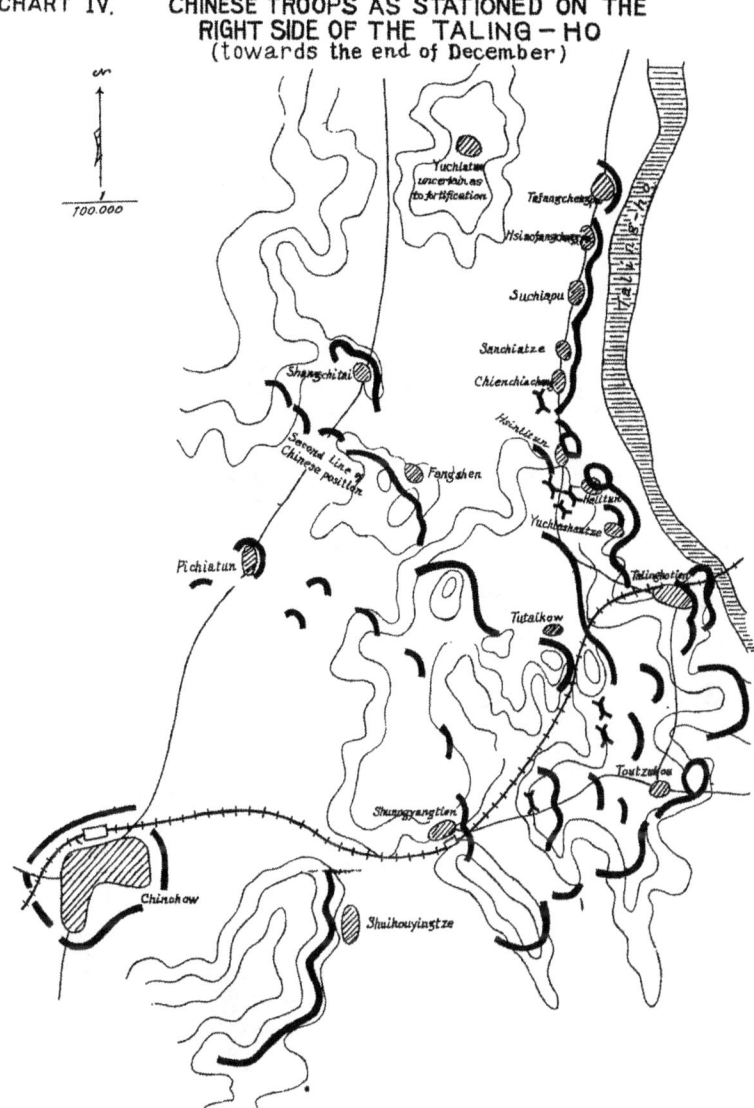

Regular Troops:—
35,000
Artillery 68 pieces: heavy guns 32; field pieces 36
Other troops under the direction of the Chinchow Government were an independent detachment of 30,000, chiefly formed of bandits; 6 battalions of volunteers, about 5,000; 10 squads belonging to cavalry guards of Liaoning and Mongolian frontiers; all of which were daily being augmented in number.

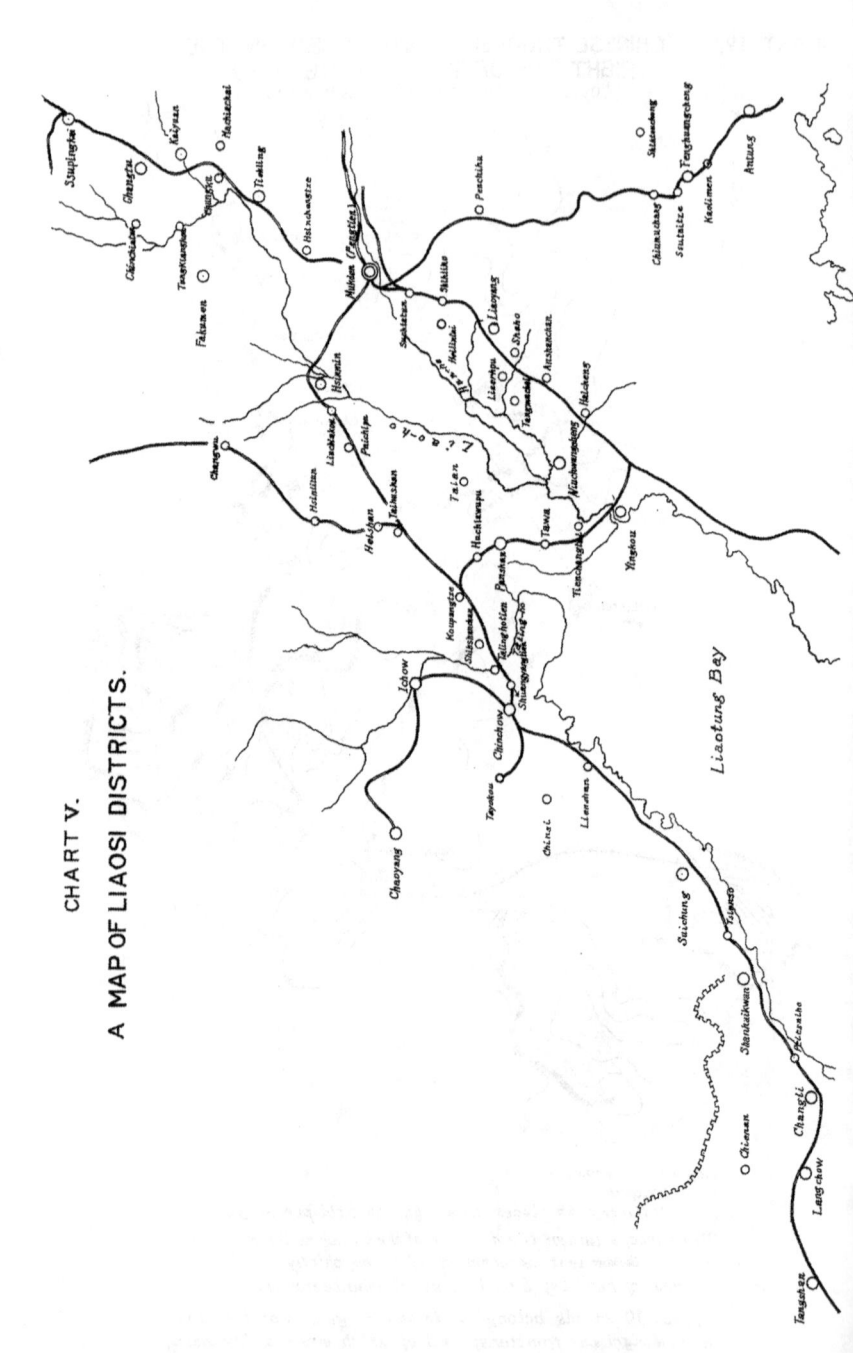

CHART V.
A MAP OF LIAOSI DISTRICTS.

HARBIN CAMPAIGN

CHAPTER VI

HARBIN CAMPAIGN

1. A General Outline

The clash brought about on January 27 between the Kirin troops, commanded by General Hsi Hsia, and the anti-Kirin forces plunged the city of Harbin and neighbouring districts into a state of confusion, which was intensified by a series of atrocities committed by the anti-Kirin troops. They looted a number of Korean dwellings, attacked the office of a Japanese owned newspaper, the "Taihoku Shimpo," killed a Japanese military officer, and kidnapped Japanese civilians. The Japanese population in Harbin, numbering 5,600, was placed in a state of extreme danger. The chairman of the Japanese Residents Committee repeatedly appealed for despatch of military troops. The Commander of the Kwantung Army, in view of the situation, was finally moved to send to Harbin a detachment of troops in order to guard peace and protect the Japanese residents.

In the meanwhile, the anti-Kirin troops continued to conduct themselves with bold insolence, making no secret of their hostile disposition toward the Japanese. Wanton deeds were committed to harm Japanese, and malicious propaganda conducted against them. The second Sungali railway bridge was destroyed by fire to impede the transportation of our troops. In the vicinity of Shuangchengpu, our advance forces encountered armed resistance. Under the circumstances, our military forces were obliged to take action against them. The enemy forces holding positions to the south of Harbin were consequently routed. Our troops entered the city of Harbin on February 5.

2. Northern Campaign of the Kirin Army

The downfall of Chang Hsueh-liang after the outbreak of the Manchurian trouble ushered in a new era of hope for the thirty million people in that country. The situation has since been fast maturing for the birth of a new state where justice and righteousness should hold domain. In the province of Kirin a new government was set up with Hsi Hsia at its head, with the object of replacing the old corrupt system by a new and better one. The populace has hailed the new regime with enthusiasm, even many of the men who had served under the former military power having sworn allegiance. The only case of defection was a group of military men who were formerly under the command of General Chang Tso-hsiang, head of the Kirin government under the old regime. These men, still receiving directions from Chang Hsueh-liang and Chang Tso-hsiang in Peiping, set up a provincial government at Pinhsien, a point northeast of Harbin, and refused to take orders from the new administration at Kirin. Repeated invitations having failed to win the allegiance of these men, the Kirin government was at length compelled to use force.

The military forces of the Kirin government, starting their operations on January 5, directed their way northward, meeting with but weak resistances. Having routed the enemy forces along the route, they took possession of Yushu on January 18. Thence they set their eyes in the direction of Harbin, the centre of political and economic activities as well as communication in North Manchuria.

Alarmed over the situation thus precipitated, the anti-Kirin men in Harbin met in council. With the exception of the chairman, Cheng Yun, practically all leaders, such as Li Chen-sheng, Feng Chan-hai, Li Tu, Su Te-chan and others, in consultation with Chin Hsuan-wu, representing Hsi Hsia, adopted a resolution to the effect

(1) That their military forces would surrender themselves to Hsi Hsia, who should provide them with military expenses, and

(2) That the Pinhsien government would be abolished.

General Chang Tso-hsiang in Peiping, hearing of this, sent to Cheng Yun and Chang Tso-chou on January 20 instructions to the effect that the military troops, under the circumstances, should place themselves under the command of General

Chang Ching-hui, Governor of the Heilungkiang Province, while the Pinhsien government should declare itself subject to the Command of the Harbin Special Area, a post which General Chang Ching-hui also held. It was plain beyond question that Chang Tso-hsiang's intention, in issuing such instructions, was to preserve his former troops in the name of the Heilungkiang governor. All efforts at peaceful settlement having failed, Hsi Hsia decided to settle the matter by armed argument. His troops were again put in motion on January 21, one part advancing on Harbin through Shuangchengpu and the other by way of Acheng.

3. Conditions in Harbin

The Kirin troops at first found little to impede their progress northward. They ousted the troops under Feng Chan-hai, occupying Lalin, and reached the vicinity of Acheng two days later. Having arrived in the outlying district south of Harbin on January 25, a portion of their forces was set to clearing the regions about Acheng and south of Shuangchengpu, their plan being to enter the city of Harbin the next day.

However, in anticipation of the disturbances that might be caused within the city by military operations, the Kirin troops sent to demand General Ting Chao, in command of the anti-Kirin forces, to remove his troops out of town toward Pinhsien, with which the latter refused to comply. On the contrary, General Li Tu, Commander of the 24th brigade stationed at Ilan, a point 60 kilometres northeast of Harbin, suddenly entered China Town (Puchiatien) of Harbin in the morning of January 26, at the head of two of his battalions. Falling in with the soldiers under Ting Chao and Hsing Chan-ching, they were soon in control of the Chinese quarters and lost no time in plundering, causing a panic throughout the city. The resident Japanese population, of which 4,000 were Japanese proper and 1,600 Koreans, were at once exposed to serious danger. The Japanese residents quickly rose to the situation organizing volunteer forces to protect the Japanese colony, and aiding their nationals to flee from China Town. One Japanese and three Koreans were killed in flight by soldiers belonging to Ting Chao's army. Several Korean females were kidnapped.

The Kirin troops, who had been withholding themselves, could no longer stay behind, almost in sight of such disturbances in Harbin. They resumed their march to save the city from confusion, only to come into conflict south of China Town with the soldiers under Ting Chao, Li Tu and Chang Tso-chou. It was then that a Japanese scouting aeroplane which had been despatched to survey the conditions in and about Harbin, particularly with regard to the Japanese residents there, was compelled by some mechanical trouble to alight on a farm to the south of Harbin. Captain Shimizu, of artillery, who was aboard the machine, was killed by cavalry men belonging to Ting Chao's army.

Whereupon our official representatives in Harbin took up the matter with General Ma Chan-shan who had arrived at the same city on January 27 in order to offer his service for mediating between the Kirin and Chang Ching-hui army on the one hand and the anti-Kirin troops on the other. The murder of our scouting officer and residents was reported to General Ma, as cases chargeable against soldiers under Ting Chao and Chang Tso-chou, demanding his serious attention. In the night of the same day, however, the "Taihoku Shimpo," a Japanese owned newspaper, was attacked and looted by Chinese soldiers. Disturbances became worse in the Chinese quarters. On January 28 the Chinese Chamber of Commerce and other Chinese associations jointly petitioned for despatch of Japanese troops.

The Japanese residents in Harbin, on instruction from their Consul General, began on January 28 to gather at prescribed points in the town, and organized volunteer forces for self-protection. The Koreans in Puchiatien, numbering more than 1,500, were brought under protection on the primary school premises near the River Front.

4. Northern Movement of the Kwantung Army

The Kwantung Army, being well aware of the lawless character of Chinese soldiers turning into marauders after a defeat on the field of battle, decided to despatch for the protection of the Japanese residents a detachment formed of two infantry battalions under Major-General Hasebe.

The first difficulty then experienced was railway traffic. The employees of the southern branch of the Chinese Eastern Railway had practically all of them deserted their posts. What was more, the Kirin authorities had a number of carriages under detention with the object of transporting its own railway guard forces to Harbin. Undue delay was caused through these and other circumstances, so that it was not before the night of January 28 that by recourse to temporary measures three trains were at length formed and sent northward. Their progress was next impeded by a portion of the Chinese 22nd brigade, stationed along the southern branch of the Chinese Eastern Railway, which, in an attempt to interfere with our military expedition, destroyed the second bridge across the Sungali River on January 28, causing further delay in transit. Temporary repairs being made the next day, the military trains forced their way across the river.

The Kirin army, on the other hand, in consideration of the damage to be caused to the civil population in Harbin by bombardment, retreated some distance from the city, suspending its fire for the time being. The anti-Kirin forces, however, continued to increase their ranks by the enrollment of bandits. Their troops were being steadily concentrated about Harbin, stationing the main force on a line running from the southwestern end of the city to Old Harbin, while another portion took its position on the east side of Harbin. They openly declared themselves in readiness to meet the Japanese in armed conflict. From their manifest temper and bold movement it was concluded that fighting was in sight and unavoidable. The Commander of the Kwantung Army issued an order on January 29 to Lieutenant-General Tamon, Commander of the 2nd Division, to advance his main force to Harbin and protect the Japanese residents there.

The detachment under Major-General Hasebe, overcoming a series of troubles on the railway, pushed its march northward, until it arrived about 5 o'clock in the afternoon of January 30 at Shuangchengpu where it passed the night. Early in the following morning toward daybreak an enemy force (the main body of the 22nd brigade), some 2,000 of infantry and several pieces of artillery, raided our camp under cover of darkness. They advanced at a time within a distance of only 20 metres from our position, but were finally repulsed, after a sharp engagement, about 10.30 o'clock in the morning, with heavy damage, one of their units being almost completely annihilated. Our casualties were 13 dead and 35 wounded.

In view of the character of resistance to be expected, the Commander of the Kwantung Army ordered the troops in Tsitsihar to reinforce the troops near Harbin.

In the evening of January 31 the Kwantung Army

addressed an ultimatum to Ting Chao, Li Tu, Li Chen-sheng and other leaders of the anti-Kirin army, accusing them of their aggressive operations of the same morning, and demanding them to resign their positions in token of their allegiance. It was also notified that, in the event of their failure to comply therewith, the Kwantung Army would take action against the whole anti-Kirin army as its enemy. The anti-Kirin leaders were informed at the same time that inasmuch as the Soviet authorities had given their agreement to offer no interference with military transportation on the Chinese Eastern Railway, the Japanese would not infringe upon the rights of the same railway, and hoped that the anti-Kirin army would likewise guard themselves against any step likely to cause complication in the same respect.

As for the management of the Chinese Eastern Railway which at first showed an unfavourable attitude as to the transportation of the Hasebe detachment, they were informed that "our army being forwarded for the sole purpose of protecting our nationals in Harbin, they should offer no interference with our military transportation." To this the Soviet representatives gave formal agreement on January 30. Nevertheless, the railway still continued to be destroyed between Harbin and Shuangchengpu and also in the rear of the Hasebe detachment, considerably impeding the northern progress of our troops. The 2nd Division, under the circumstances, managed to do the best it could with a limited quantity of rolling stock at its disposal, while it began on February 1 to transport soldiers in motor cars that had been concentrated at Changchun. Continuing its progress under such unfavourable conditions, the main force succeeded in concentrating near Shuangchengpu in the morning of February 3.

With regard to the expedition of military troops to Harbin, the Kwantung Army issued on February 1 the following notice:

"The Japanese army has been despatched to Harbin for the sole purpose of protecting our nationals and maintaining the public peace in the same city. Not only common civilians but even men of military affiliations will be left free if they refrain from any hostile action against our army. The general populace are advised to feel themselves secure and follow their peaceful pursuits. As for the Chinese Eastern Railway and all other institutions owned by a third nation, the Japanese army shall offer no interference, taking a strictly neutral attitude. Although the Japanese army will remain true to its aforesaid policy of justice and fairness, it will promtly deal with any act of hostility or any attempt to interfere with its work. Civil as well as military people are hereby advised to repose confidence in the Japanese army and properly shape their conduct in accordance therewith.

    Commander of the Japanese Army"

5. Anti-Kirin Army in Harbin Well Prepared

The anti-Kirin army stationed in and about Harbin, which had assumed for itself the name of the "Self-Protection Army" under the leadership of General Li Tu, commander of the 24th brigade, issued on January 31 a notice which may be regarded as a sort of ultimatum running in substance as follows:

"Whereas the Japanese acts of aiding and abetting internal troubles, and their seizing of railway trains, even killing and wounding railway employees, show the course they are bent on following with forcible means, defying the dignity of our nation, we have decided to mobilize all available troops for the purpose of a combined armed resistance. Our end being clear, we hold ourselves above thoughts of success or failure. We hereby announce the formation of the Self-Protection Army, praying for the support of all our brethren—"

In the meantime Chang Hsueh-liang had ordered Ting Chao and Ma Chan-shan to hold Harbin in their hands, while he strove to strengthen his own position by enlisting the support of Soviet Russia through Mo Te-hui who was in Moscow in charge of Sino-Soviet negotiations. On the other hand, the Pinhsien government which had been formed by a handful of men, finding its geographical position unsuitable for administrative purposes, set up in Harbin what they called the Kirin Committee of

Peace. Ting Chi as chairman was put in charge of military, administrative and financial affairs, to the end of attaining under one head an internal solidarity against our army. Ting Chi, anticipating the eastward advance of our troops from Tsitsihar, ordered the guards of the western section of the Chinese Eastern Railway to destroy the railway. Consequently, the railway and other means of communication were cut off between Harbin and Tsitsihar on the night of February 2.

In the rear of our line, the railway guard force (1 company of the Independent Railway Guards) at Lalinchia, a point about 25 kilometres south of Shuangchengpu, was assaulted on February 1 by a Chinese force of 1,000 men. The next day our company of railway guards at Changchiawan, about 70 kilometres north of Changchun, was attacked by Chinese soldiers numbering about 400. The assailants were repulsed in each case with heavy damage.

On or about February 3, the anti-Kirin army about Harbin, which had steadily been adding to its ranks, had swelled to a force of some 13,000 to 14,000 soldiers, who were disposed as shown in the sketch on page 53.

The Right Area (about Kuhsiangtun): about 1,000 men; 6 pieces of field artillery.

The Central Area (between Intendantskaya and Hospital Street): about 3,000 men; 2 pieces of artillery; light wire entanglements before the line, and dwelling houses provided with defensive work.

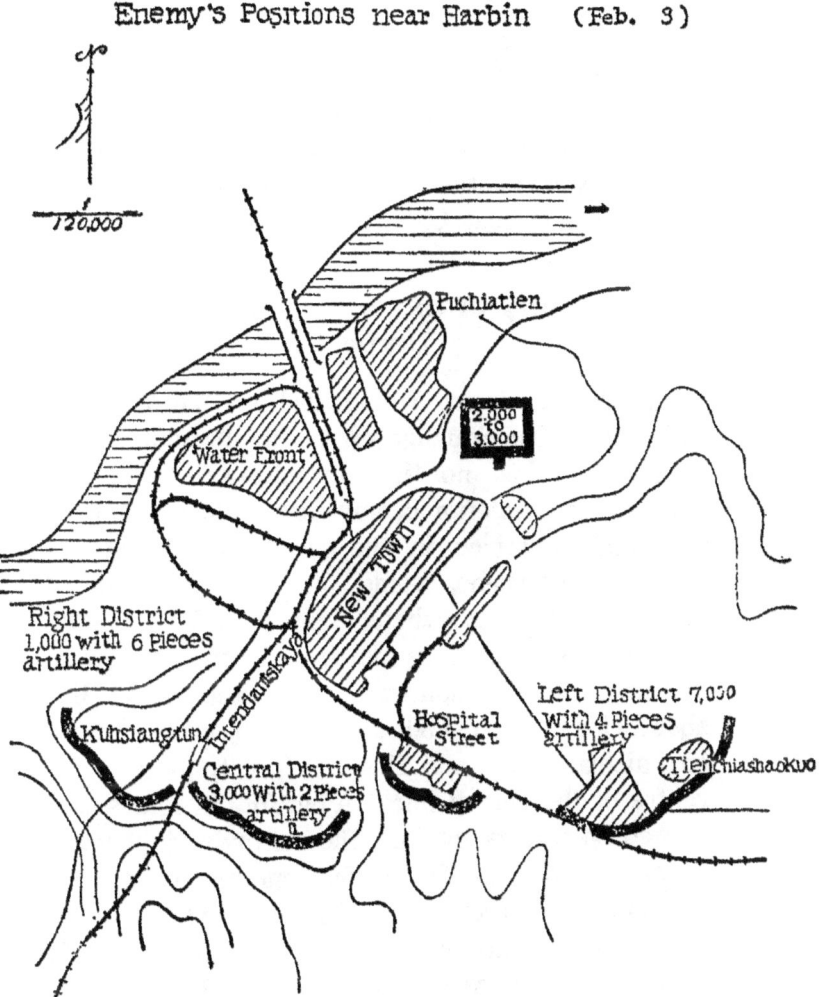

Enemy's Positions near Harbin (Feb. 3)

The Left Area (about Old Harbin): some 7,000 men; 4 pieces of artillery.

The Cavalry Force: Several hundred of cavalry men under the command of Feng Chan-hai.

The above, altogether about 11,000 in number, formed the first line.

The Reserves: Reserve forces numbering 2,000 to 3,000 were stationed at Machiakou on the east of Harbin and near Old Harbin.

6. Entry of the 2nd Division into Harbin

The 2nd Division, which had concentrated its main force near Shuangchengpu in the morning of February 3, lost no time to advance northward. Pressing upon inferior enemy forces along the way, our soldiers arrived in the evening on the line of the Weitangkou-ho, some 50 kilometres north of Shuangchengpu, where they passed the night. Resuming the march northward the following morning, the Division came upon the enemy line about 11 a.m. At 3.30 p.m. our objective was set on Paichiawupeng and Hospital Street, forming the centre of the enemy line. A part of our forces then started operations against the enemy's right wing, advancing within 400 to 500 metres from their position, where they passed the night. On the same night another part of the Division, making a night raid, occupied a sector of the enemy line near the monument standing in honour of two Japanese heroes in the war with Russia, near the southeast end of Hospital Street.

The 2nd Division resumed the offensive in the morning of February 5. When the enemy line began to show signs of wavering at about 10 a.m., our troops intensified their action until they took possession of the enemy's position around noon. Toward 3 p.m. the enemy forces, completely routed, were fleeing from Harbin towards Pinhsien and elsewhere.

The city of Harbin had been restored to peace. The Japanese residents had been freed from the grip of terror. They, with Russian and even Chinese population, came forth to receive the entry of our army into Harbin with heartiest ovations.

In this connection it is important to note that our military forces, in conducting their operations in this campaign, took every precaution to prevent disturbances to foreign residents, and directed with scrupulous care their rifle and artillery fire, and every other offensive action so as to avoid the railway and other public institutions in the city.

The Self-Protection Army, having abandoned Harbin, moved its main force in the direction of Pinhsien. A section of their troops have since gone as far as Hulan, north of Harbin, while the other toward Acheng, south of Harbin. An independent detachment (affiliated bandit soldiers) under Kuan Chung-hai directed its course to Acheng. Ting Chao and Li Tu are thought to have fallen back to Hulan,

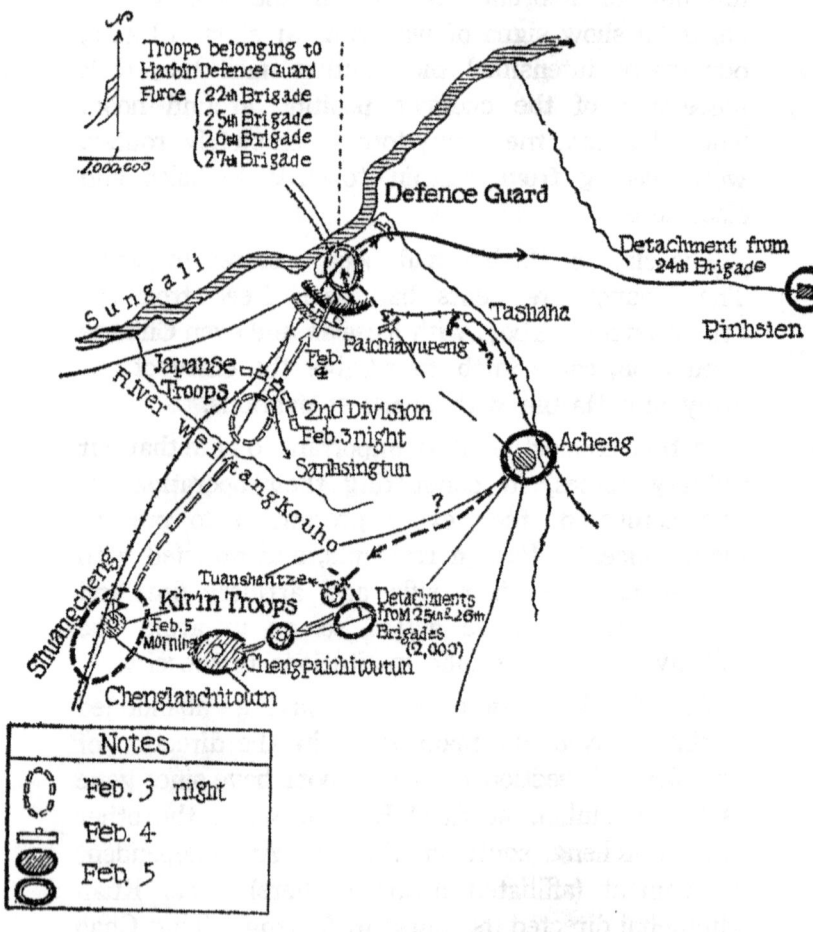

and Feng Chan-hai to Pinhsien, where they are no doubt collecting their routed ranks.

Through the military operations near Harbin lasting 5 days from February 4, our casualties were 31 killed and 65 wounded. While the enemy's casualties are not definitely known, they have beyond doubt suffered considerably heavier damage.

The progress of military operations in this campaign is shown in the sketch on page 56.

7. Conclusion

The trouble in Harbin, which called for the above military action, was occasioned by internal disagreement within the Chinese military camp, with its centre at Harbin. The trouble sprang up just when Manchuria, with the suppprt of her military and other influential elements, was paving the way for the creation of a new independent state comprising Liaoning, Kirin, Heilungkiang and a part of Mongolia whence the old regime had been driven off. The disturbances caused in this way threatened the lives and property of not only our own people but many other resident nationals there; but they were put an end to by the prompt and timely action of our army. In a way, the above campaign has served to clear North Manchuria of what had still remained of the old military power, thus removing an obstacle that had stood in the way of bringing the new state into being, materially clearing the atmosphere for the outlook for future.

We are pleased to add in conclusion that Soviet Russia and her representatives on the management of the Chinese Eastern Railway, properly appreciating the rightful policy of Japan, adopted a fair-minded attitude toward our military operations in and round Harbin.

Japanese Casualties

The Japanese casualties ascertained since the outbreak of the trouble up to February 9, all of the military force, are 353 dead and 761 wounded, the total number being 1,014. These casualties are shown in detail in the list below:

	Dead (including those who died afterwards)			Wounded in Military Action			Grand Total
	Officers and Ranking Officers	Sub-Officers, Non-Commissioned Officers, Privates	Total	Officers and Ranking Officers	Sub-Officers, Non-Commissioned Officers, Privates	Total	
Kwantung Army	6	90	96	12	157	169	265
2nd Division	8	174	182	25	400	425	607
Mixed Brigade	11	62	73	10	152	162	235
Gendarme Force	—	2	2	—	1	1	3
Tientsin Garrison	—	—	—	—	4	4	4
Grand Total	25	328	353	47	714	761	1,114

THE SHANGHAI AFFAIR

CHAPTER VII

THE SHANGHAI AFFAIR

1. Conditions Prior to the Outbreak of Hostilities

Middle and South China has always been known as the centre of anti-Japanese movement. This became more conspicuous following the Manchurian clash, especially in Shanghai. The Chinese newspapers one and all flared into a highly provocative mood, filling their pages with writings calculated to stir up public feeling. On September 22 a mass meeting was held in Shanghai as a demonstration against Japan. A great number of people representing political, commercial, industrial and educational lines attended the meeting which resolved

(1) That an appeal be made to the central Government to put revolutionary diplomacy in play.

(2) That civil strife be abandoned to put up a united front against Japan.

(3) That war be declared against Japan.

(4) That economic boycott be strictly enforced against Japan.

(5) That any one opposed to anti-Japanese measures be made liable to capital punishment.

(6) That absolutely no foodstuff be sold to Japan.

(7) That the Chinese workers in the Japanese cotton factories go on strike.

Those present at that meeting constituted themselves into an organization under the style of "The Anti-Japanese National Salvation Society" to be put under the direction of the Shanghai Municipality, so that unity of action might be ensured. Then anti-Japanese activities broke out afresh on all sides, assuming forms of extreme intensity. An increasing number of Japanese people were assaulted with violence. The Anti-Japanese National Salvation Society, with all its malicious activity, was now a factor no longer to be ignored.

Such being the case, the Imperial Government addressed a note to the Nationalist Government at Nanking under date of October 9, 1931, pointing out that the anti-Japanese agitations now seen in all parts of China constituted nothing less than an instrument of national policy under the direction of the Kuomintang headquarters and that it was unarmed but none the less hostile. The Chinese authorities were for the same reason requested to check all such activities, and take adequate steps to protect the lives and property of the Japanese nationals. Warning on this matter has since been repeatedly addressed to the central as well as local Chinese authorities.

The Chinese officials, however, never had any idea of paying heed to such request. As a matter of fact, they were disposed to look even favourably upon lawless conduct on the part of their people as expressions of patriotic sentiment. Sure of official connivance, the agitators became bolder and more reckless, as was seen in the killing of Japanese nationals in Canton, Tsingtao and Foochow, or in the case of a Japanese official who was subjected to a very humiliating insult. Then came the most inexcusable, in Japanese eyes, of all offences, namely, that committed by a Chinese newspaper of Shanghai, the "Min Kuo Jih Pao," which, when reporting the recent attempt in Tokyo on the Imperial life, expressed its regret that the bomb had "unfortunately missed the mark."

Of all places Shanghai was most conspicuous for the violence and pertinacity of anti-Japanese activities. It was there that the Anti-Japanese National Salvation Society and a number of other organizations of similar complexion enjoyed an unstinted prosperity.

2. The Immediate Cause

On January 18 about 4 p.m. two friars belonging to the Myōhōji, a Buddhist temple of the Nichiren sect on Kiangwan Road, were proceeding near Yinhsiang Creek in company with three of their religious followers, when they were held up in front of a Chinese bathtowel factory called "San Yu" by a group of workmen in the employ of the same factory and those belonging to the volunteer force organized by its working staff. These men, though quite unprovoked, with a cry of "Down with the Japanese!", fell upon the friars and their companions in presence of Chinese police officers who simply stood aside, looking indifferently on the whole procedure. The Japanese suffered more or less heavy wounds, requiring two to four weeks to heal, one of the Buddhist friars dying on January 24. This incident, coming as it did, on top of a series of Chinese provocations as described above, naturally roused deep indignation among the Japanese population. Representative residents, at a meeting hurriedly called, decided that nothing short of armed forces could give them adequate protection. They lodged, on the one hand, a strong protest with the Mayor of Shanghai and, on the other, laid the matter before the Japanese authorities calling for their serious consideration.

This procedure, however, failed to satisfy a hot-headed section of the Japanese population. Thirty-two members of the Shanghai Seinen Doshikai, an association headed by one Yoshizo Mitsumura, went in a body to the said San Yu factory about 2 o'clock in the morning of January 19 and made an assault upon the place, and set fire upon one of the buildings used as the employees' dormitory, which was partially destroyed. The assailants then had trouble with Chinese police officers, two of whom were killed and two others wounded. The casualties on the Japanese side were one killed and two wounded by the shots fired by the officers.

The feeling ran very high among the Japanese

residents, particularly of the younger generation, and a mass meeting was held on the same day. Some of the speakers on the occasion expressed themselves not content with such protection as might be expected from the warships, and proposed to appeal for a miliatry expedition. After the meeting was closed, a party of some 500 men proceeded from there to the Japanese Consulate-General and the headquarters of the Naval landing force, parading for demonstration on the way. In the course of this procession through the streets, these men smashed window glass at some Chinese shops displaying anti-Japanese posters. Some of the men under excitement had a clash with British police officers who tried to interfere.

3. Happenings after January 21

On January 21, about 11 a.m. Consul-General Murai paid a visit to General Wu Tieh-cheng, Mayor of Shanghai, and handed to him a note of protest concerning the assault on the friars' party and, pointing out the gravity of the incident, asked him to agree to the Japanese demand consisting of the following four points:—
 (1) Apologies by the Mayor of Shanghai;
 (2) Arrest and punishment of the assailants;
 (3) Payment for the victims' consolation and expenses for their medical treatment;
 (4) Immediate dissolution of the Anti-Japanese

National Salvation Society and all other anti-Japanese associations.

Mayor Wu expressed his agreement to all points except (4), concerning which he said he would have to go to Nanking for due authorization by the central Government before he could reply.

Rear-Admiral Shiosawa, Commander of the First Expeditionary Squadron, issued the same day the following statement:

"The Commander of the Japanese Squadron earnestly hopes that the protest lodged with the Mayor of Shanghai by the Japanese Consul-General concerning the assault on the friars by members of the Anti-Japanese National Salvation Society will promptly be complied with, and its terms satisfactorily carried out. In the event of such compliance being refused, we are determined to take such steps as may be necessary for protection of the interest of the Empire."

The Japanese residents, on the other hand, made clear their determination to hold another mass meeting on January 23, in case their official representatives should fail to take a strong enough attitude to satisfy them, and organize an armed force to attack the headquarters of the Anti-Japanese National Salvation Society. From Chinese sources reports came to the effect that students would organize volunteer forces and attack the Japanese telegraph office and cotton factories With such ominous portents in the air, the Emergency Committee of the Japanese residents held their meeting on the night of January 21 and decided two points; namely, first that they should see that an ultimatum with a time limit would be sent, demanding dissolution of the Anti-Japanese National Salvation Society; and secondly, that in the event of China refusing to comply, they should appeal for armed action.

The Chinese newspapers in Shanghai, making free use of such scarehead lines as "Shanghai in Danger," "Japanese Ronin Over-ride Shanghai," etc., gave exaggerated and often distorted accounts of the Japanese attack on the San Yu factory and the Japanese demonstration along North Szechuan Road. Some of them even went so far as to say that these offences had been committed by Japanese ronin on instigation by the Japanese naval men, insulting the name of the Imperial Navy and adding to the Chinese excitement. In certain western parts of the city, handbills printed with "Kill Japanese on Sight" were distributed on the streets. Within the International Settlement Japanese school children began to be assaulted. There were 8 cases of the kind on January 22, and more than a dozen on the day following.

The Japanese naval authorities, in protest against the accusation so falsely made against them, sent a note to the "Min Kuo Jih Pao," a daily paper most conspicuous for anti-Japanese expressions, and responsible for the offensive remark about the attempt on the Emperor's life, and demanded

(1) That a half-page space should be given in

the issue of January 23 for printing apologies for the article in question.

(2) That the offender should appear in person at the headquarters of the Japanese landing force to tender his apologies.

(3) That in case the paper failed to agree to these terms, the Japanese naval force would take such steps as might be deemed proper.

The same Chinese newspaper in its issue of January 23 carried an evasive statement to the effect that it was not the only paper that had printed an article of the kind. This Chinese refusal to comply with our demand only served to aggravate the situation which was already bad enough.

At the mass meeting held the same day the general feeling ran high. The Japanese residents had their ardour curbed only by the promise given by the consular authorities that they would without fail secure a satisfactory settlement of the matter with the least delay. The residents under the circumstances decided to hold themselves in abeyance pending further official negotiation. But the temper manifested on the occasion left no doubt as to their determination to wrest satisfaction from the Chinese authorities by whatever means within their power.

The trouble between the Imperial Navy and the "Min Kuo Jih Pao" was now turned over to the Executive Committee of the International Settlement, in accordance with the latter's offer. The Municipal Council of the International Settlement then decided to close down the "Min Kuo Jih Pao" and order all anti-Japanese associations within the Settlement to disband.

In view of the serious situation in Shanghai, the the cruiser *Oi* and four destroyers were ordered January 21 to proceed from the Kure naval port to Shanghai, where they arrived in the evening of January 23, to be followed by the aircraft carrier *Notoro* the next day, each at once placing herself on the guard.

The Chinese military authorities now made declaration to the effect that, should the Japanese navy send without reason its men into Chinese quarters, they would resist with their utmost force. The Association of Shanghai Chinese Citizens, an organization formed of local commercial and student population, held an emergency mass meeting on January 24 and decided

(1) To oppose dissolution of anti-Japanese associations;

(2) To object to the landing of Japanese naval men;

(3) To appeal for a concentration at Shanghai of Chinese military, naval and aerial forces; and

(4) To organize forces for self-protection.

A state of siege was proclaimed in Woosung in the north, in Lunghua in the south, and elsewhere, prohibiting Japanese traffic outside the International Settlement. Furthermore, in the northern and southern parts bordering the International Settlement defence works began to be set up with sandbagged emplacements and wire entanglements.

On the night of January 24 a volunteer band consisting of members of the National Salvation Society visited the Japanese Consulate-General in the French Concession and set fire to the building. However, the fire was discovered in good time by a guard and put out after destroying only shatters on two windows. A memorial service was held the same day in honour of the Chinese police officers killed in the San Yu incident, and the people present on the occasion issued in the name of the Funeral Committee a resolution demanding

(1) An indemnity of 50,000 silver dollars for each of the dead, and 10,000 for each of the wounded;

(2) Trial of the Japanese offenders in Chinese Popular Court;

(3) Apologies by the Japanese Consul-General;

(4) Absolute guarantee by the same Japanese official against recurrence of the kind in the future.

Mr. Murai, the Japanese Consul-General, again held an interview with Mayor Wu to request a reply to his note of protest. The Mayor, still persisting in his evasive efforts, asked the Consul-General to wait until January 30 inasmuch as the task of checking the anti-Japanese agitations was difficult and necessarily required time.

Mr. Murai, for his part, gave it to be understood that the situation permitted of no further delay, and requested for Chinese reply with the least possible delay. He notified the Mayor that in case no satisfactory reply was forthcoming, the Japanese would be compelled to take self-protective measures.

On the same day the Nationalist Government at Nanking, at its meeting, decided concerning the Shanghai case—

(1) To take effecfive steps in self-defence should the Japanese troops seize public institutions;

(2) To offer absolute protection for the patriotic movements, (an appellation by which the Chinese call any anti-Japanese activity);

(3) To control, however, any movement calculated to harm the lives and property of Japanese;

(4) To order the troops to hold themselves under restraint.

On the same day more than 30 anti-Japanese associations in Shanghai, such as, Anti-Japanese National Salvation Society, Citizens' Association, Native Product Encouragement Society, Emergency Relief Society, etc., jointly sent their representatives to the Municipal Office and presented their demand including the following points:

(1) A strong protest should be lodged with the Japanese authorities concerning the San Yu case, demanding the offenders to be punished, the damage indemnified, and apologies tendered, with adequate guarantee for future;

(2) Unreasonable Japanese demands should all be rejected;

(3) The Japanese landing party should all be withdrawn from ashore within three days;

(4) The Government should promptly despatch military forces for self-protection;

(5) The demand for suppression of the patriotic movements should be rejected;

(6) The volunteer corps should be provided with arms;

(7) A true account should be made public as to the San Yu workmen's alleged assault on Japanese friars.

The Executive Committee of the International Settlement, in accordance with its previous decision, caused the "Min Kuo Jih Pao" to be closed on January 26. The employees, however, betook themselves to a certain place within the French Concession where they are continuing the publication of their paper.

Mayor Wu, reporting to the Nanking Government January 26, stated that an armed police force of 8,000 strong and two divisions of regular soldiers having been placed on the guard, with naval and aerial forces in readiness for emergency, the city of Shanghai would be safe whatever the Japanese might attempt. From this it may be seen how the Chinese authorities had been making military preparations, while they pretended a disposition to amicable settlement.

The Chinese troops stationed in and about Shanghai had in the meanwhile vigorously pushed preparations against the Japanese. By January 26 defensive works had nearly been completed in the Chapei district and western portions of the city. Another line of defence had been built from Chapei down to Woosung, generally running parallel to the Shanghai-Woosung railway, with machine guns and anti-aircraft ordnances mounted at places. The Chinese military men were now displaying an attitude which left no doubt as to their determination on armed argument with the Japanese, regardless of their municipal authorities. Such being the case, when reports were set abroad, alleging that the Chinese authorities had decided to comply with the Japanese demand, the student organizations were at once extremely agitated. The Anti-Japanese Association of Shanghai Middle Schools was the first to raise its voice, expressing its disapproval of the Mayor at its meeting on January 26. Other associations echoed its voice. The Industrial Association also began to show activity.

Mayor Wu, however, realizing from the determined attitude of the Japanese that his evasive tactics would no longer cope with the situation, issued orders to the Police Bureau on January 27 to break up the Anti-Japanese National Salvation Society, liberate the Japanese goods under seizure and stop all anti-Japanese agitations.

In the evening of January 27 Consul-General Murai sent a note to Mayor Wu, requesting for the belated Chinese reply, setting a time limit at 6 o'clock next evening.

Next morning about 8 o'clock a Chinese seemingly of the Anti-Japanese National Salvation Society appeared near the Japanese Consulate-General and fired his revolver, breaking one or two window panes and throwing into the building what seemed like a bomb, though it failed to explode.

This same day the anti-Japanese associations, in order to express their objection to the Mayor's proposal to break up the Anti-Japanese National Salvation Society, held an anti-Japanese emergency meeting at the athletic field near Hongkew Bridge. Although this assembly was stopped by the police, it adopted a resolution against the Mayor's order. A crowd of no less than 5,000 then proceeded to swarm round the Municipality toward the evening, openly airing their disapproval of the Mayor's policy. There were unmistakable signs of the situation fast passing out of the Mayor's hand.

Nevertheless, Mayor Wu, for his part, finally notified his compliance with the Japanese demand this day at 3.15 p.m. But being no strangers to the customary ways of the Chinese, the Japanese did not lessen their vigilance, being determined to see Chinese fulfilment of the promise through, and standing on guard against contingent moves on the part of some lawless elements.

In the International Settlement the Municipal Council, in view of alarming signs seen among the Chinese soldiers placed near the boundary, proclaimed martial law over the Settlement at 4 p.m. the same day. It was consequently arranged that the Powers, possessing military guards, should each take over its defence area, according to the pre-arranged plan. The Japanese landing forces, therefore, began just after midnight to set out to take

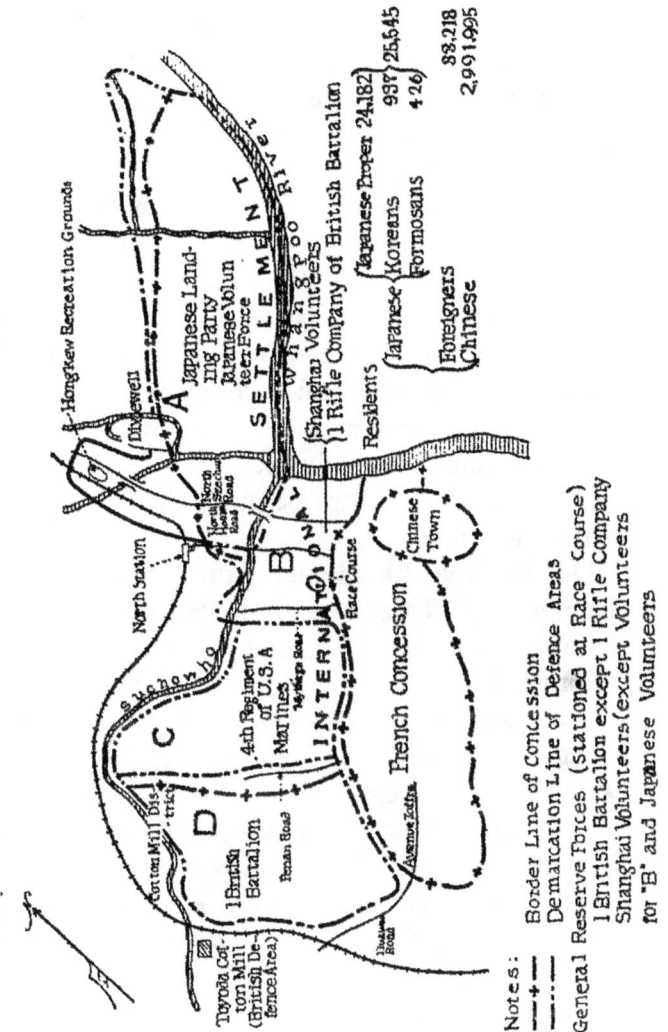

Defence Areas of International Settlement at Shanghai

their positions along either side of North Szechuan Road which had been assigned to them, as shown in the sketch map on page 15. But the Japanese bluejackets were suddenly fired upon by regular Chinese soldiers (of the 78th Division), and forced to return the fire.

Hostilities thus began without any provocation on our part and despite all Japanese efforts to avoid them. It goes without saying, therefore, that responsibility in the case rests with the Chinese who deliberately challenged our men into action.

The clash at this point developed into sharp street fighting wherever the Chinese offered stubborn resistance. But the Japanese had generally made their way to the assigned line by 6 o'clock in the morning.

This day the 19th Route Army, commanded by General Tsai Ting-kai and stationed as shown in the sketch on page 17, openly declared its hostility by proclaiming that "it will under blood oath fight the Japanese to the last man if it has to dye the Whangpoo River red with its soldiers' blood." The Commercial Association also declared the same day "a general strike of the whole city by way of protest against the Japanese soldiers invading Chinese territory," and forced all shops to close, those in the fighting areas, of course, closing of their own will.

At the first line, the Chinese taking the offensive, fire was exchanged all the day long. The Chinese soldiers, with reinforcements steadily arriving, kept

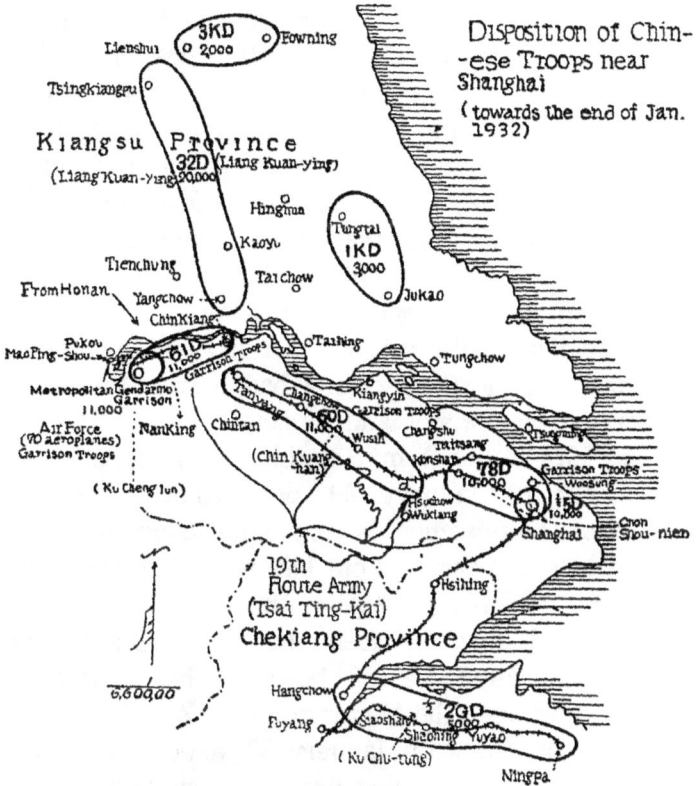

up an aggressive front, to which the Japanese properly responded. In view of the situation fast growing worse, the British and American Consuls jointly offered their mediation. Consul-General Murai, accepting their offer, concluded a truce agreement with the Chinese authorities, according to which both sides were to suspend aggressive action in status quo after 8 o'clock in the evening (January 29). But the Chinese first line and mufti-soldiers not only kept up their fire after the appointed time, but they even intensified it as darkness gathered. It was not before about 11 p.m. that their action began to slacken, though the mufti-soldiers continued their activity with unabated vigour. The Japanese colony had to pass the night under extreme worry and anxiety.

The 19th Route Army, again issuing a notice in the night of January 29, declared: "We are soldiers. Self-defence is our only concern. We will hold our ground to our last man and last shot, and thus raise the prestige of the Chinese soldiers." From this it may be seen that the Chinese had never had any idea of heeding the agreement arranged between the Mayor and our Consul-General.

In the morning of January 30 about 5.30 a.m., the Chinese again opened fire, contrary to the truce agreement, upon our first line and also on our back, continuing it for about one hour. The Japanese then sent a note to the Chinese through the British and American Consuls, accusing them of their faithless conduct and notifying them that they would be forced to take action necessary for self-defence unless the Chinese showed better faith.

What should be noted in this connection is that when the truce agreement was made on the night of January 29, the Chinese at once began to show an attitude of provocative insolence. The next morning all Chinese newspapers of Shanghai carried fictitious accounts, giving an impression, for obvious purposes, as if the Japanese had been ousted in the engagement. The papers reported

(1) That the Chinese soldiers had shown their superiority on all sides, taking possession of the headquarters of the Japanese naval men as early as 5 o'clock in the afternoon and driving what remained of the Japanese back into the International Settlement;

(2) That the Municipality had rejected the Consul-General's proposals for truce;

(3) That the main body of the 19th Route Army, which had been despatched to Shanghai, had received heartiest ovations from the inhabitants all along the way;

(4) That the Japanese casualties had amounted to 800 from officers down, they being carried homeward by warships;

(5) That the Chinese had shot down four Japanese airplanes.

This information had strong influence on the unthinking common people whose insulting attitude toward the Japanese became even more pronounced. Such Chinese temper was further to be roused by the Citizens' mass meeting which was followed by similar meetings of commercial and industrial people, each passing resolutions expressed in fiery language.

The Nationalist Government issued under date of January 30 a telegraphic message announcing the temporary transference of the capital from Nanking to Loyang, Honan Province. The statement ran as follows:

"The Government, with a view to be liberated from threats of violence for free execution of its duties, has decided to transfer the capital temporarily to Loyang.

"The administrative chiefs of provinces and the leaders of military troops are requested to unite in the spirit of harmony in discharge of their duties so that the people throughout the country may rest assured of peace and safety.

"Our nation should meet its national crisis with fortitude and coolness of mind, and overcome it by pursuing the path of righteousness, giving violence no chance to run rampant."

It appears that the Nationalist Government, leaving Ho Ying-chin, chief of Military Administration, in charge of all affairs of peace and order in Nanking, and Lo Wen-han, Minister of Foreign Affairs, in charge of diplomatic affairs, departed for Hsuchow.

It was not certain, however, whether Chiang Kai-shek, who, by the way resigned his post last December only to return to Nanking a month later practically to resume his powers, had taken the above step really from his determination on armed conflict with Japan, or from a desire to keep himself away from the scene of trouble and thereby save himself from direct responsibility. But it was at least certain that he had no intention to put forth his effort to bring about an amicable settlement of the situation. What is more, Chiang Kai-shek's attitude, such as it was, had imparted to the 19th Route Army and the anti-Japanese associations in Shanghai, each equally inspired with bellicose ideas, a definite impression as if their central Government had come to decision 'to declare war on Japan, thereby intensifying their belligerent spirit.

Early in the morning of January 31 about 1.30 a.m., the Chinese soldiers again opened fire upon the Japanese cordon. About 4.30 a.m. they began to direct rifle fire from their positions near the North Station upon our line and the British volunteer corps. This was followed by a desultory exchange of fire on the first line throughout the day, while the mufti-soldiers showed increasing activities in our back, the Japanese Consulate-General being repeatedly fired upon.

The Command of the 60th Division which had been stationed at Suchow was transferred to Shanghai January 31. A volunteer force of some 2,000 men, formed by members of the National Salvation Society, and another of some 500 student volunteers had by this time been supplied with arms and joined the first line. The Chinese press continued their feverish effort to fabricate news in the anti-Japanese cause. They invariably printed stories of overwhelming military successes of the Chinese army, in some cases even reporting the sinking of several Japanese warships.

In the afternoon of January 31 Consul-General Murai and Rear-Admiral Shiosawa, Commander of the First Squadron, had an interview with General Tsai Ting-kai, Commander of the 19th Route Army, with a view to arranging for a truce on a new basis. Discussions were made on the Japanese proposal that the Chinese troops should withdraw some 1000 meters from their present position, while the Japanese would retire to the line they had held prior to the outbreak of hostilities, turning the intervening area to the guard of a third nation. But the Chinese insisted that the Japanese quarters outside the International Settlement should be placed under military guard of a third nation. The negotiation on the occasion, therefore, failed to reach any agreement beyond what had been covered by the previous truce parley. The Chinese, still continuing their activities contrary to the previous truce agreement, not only went on firing into the Settlement but even shifted the same night their troops toward Yangshupu, the Japanese quarters in the eastern part of the town, and, in concert with mufti-soldiers, repeatedly launched offensive operations against our line. The Japanese, however, responded in each instance to the extent of repulsing the assailants, without resorting to any offensive action, true to the truce agreement.

The plain clothes soldiers now even intensified their activity within the area under Japanese military guard. A large number of Japanese as well as Chinese residents moved away to seek shelter within the former British Concession, south of Suchou Creek. There was also a great exodus of home-bound Japanese.

The 19th Route Army, having practically completed concentration of its main body near Shanghai, now began to make aggressive efforts, with reinforcements continually arriving, to envelop the area guarded by the Japanese. They repeatedly directed offensive action against our line, causing fires at places.

The Nanking Government, presumably, alarmed over the unexpectedly great shock its telegraphic statement of two days ago had given not only to the people of the country but abroad, especially the League of Nations, issued a statement February 1 in the name of the Foreign Minister, saying that reports of its alleged intention of declaring war on Japan were groundless.

On the other hand, various associations in Shanghai, such as the Commercial Association, the Bankers' Association, etc., had been encouraging the 19th Route Army by presenting money and goods for their consolation. The volunteer corps organized by students and the National Salvation Army formed by industrial workmen had by February 1 reached the number of 12 units, about 4,000 strong. All of these had joined the fighting ranks.

The Commercial Association then demanded the Municipal Council of the International Settlement to disarm the Japanese troops within the Settlement. Organizations of various descriptions went on raising funds for the benefit of the soldiers. The working men of Shanghai, following the example of the commercial people, went on a general strike on the first day of February.

The next day the Chinese again opened offensive fire, to which the Japanese replied, though their artillery, in consideration of the position of the International Settlement, was not put into play. Rifle fusillades, however, continued till the evening. The Chinese positions in the meantime had daily been strengthened on all sides. At North Station an armoured train mounted with 6 field pieces was now stationed.

On the Chinese side the fighting spirit soared higher. Volunteer forces were formed one after another, and sent as quickly to the fighting line. On February 2 the Commander of the 19th Route Army again issued a notice by telegraph, saying that " they, being now united in the purity of heart and the purity of blood, will offer resistance and gladly lay down their lives to the last man in the cause of their Republic." General Cheng Ming-su, Vice-Chairman of the Administrative Committee and also Minister of Communications in the Nationalist Government, who had resigned his post as Commander of the 19th Route Army in favour of General Tsai Ting-kai only to continue his activities behind the scenes, now resigned his posts in Nanking, asking to be returned to his military command. He personally visited the front to inspire the officers and men with encouraging words.

4. Military Expedition and Statements by the Imperial Government

The Japanese landing party, since the outbreak of the trouble, had constantly kept themselves on duty day and night, with little rest and even less sleep, in order to protect the lives and property of their nationals, numbering some 30,000, in the face of the enemy force a dozen times as large as their own. In spite of all their efforts to the contrary, the situation went from bad to worse, plunging the Japanese residents into great jeopardy. But there being a limit to the number of men to be drawn on the navy for land operations, the Imperial Government decided to despatch, with Imperial sanction, military forces to Shanghai to safeguard the Japanese nationals and their vast interests and fulfil our international duty by properly guarding that part of the International Settlement which had been assigned to our charge. Under pressure of time, therefore, an advance force was despatched to Shanghai February 6 on board men-of-war.

The Imperial Government, with reference to the military expedition, issued a statement just after midnight on February 6, explaining its policy as follows:

"It is the immutable policy of the Japanese Government to ensure by all means in their power the tranquility of the Far East and to contribute to the peaceful progress of the world. Unfortunately, of late years the internal discord and unsettled political conditions prevailing in China, coupled with rampant anti-foreign agitation, have given cause for serious concern to all the Powers, especially to Japan, which because of her geographical proximity and the vast interests of hers which are involved, has been made to suffer in a far greater degree than any other. While the Japanese Government, in their solicitude for neighbourly amity, and international good understanding, have exerted every effort to maintain a conciliatory attitude, China, taking advantage of our moderation, has resorted to frequent infringements of our rights and interests, to various acts of violence towards Japanese residents and to an intensification of the vicious anti-Japanese movement, which is without a parallel elsewhere, as it is under the direct or indirect guidance of the Nationalist Party, which is identified with the Nationalist Government itself.

"It is in these circumstances that the Shanghai Incident has broken out. It is similar to the numerous outrages and insults that had previously been perpetrated at Tsingtao, Foochow, Canton,

Amoy and elsewhere, in that they are all characterized by Chinese contempt for Japan and the Japanese by acts of physical violence. The Shanghai Incident only happens to be the most flagrant case. On January 9, a vernacular journal, the *Minkuo Daily News* published an article, insulting the honour of our Imperial House. Shortly afterwards, on January 18, a party of Japanese priests and their companions, five in all, were the subjects of an unprovoked attack by Chinese desperadoes. As a result, three of the victims were severely wounded and one was killed. The shock of these events was sufficient to explode the long pent-up indignation felt by the Japanese residents in Shanghai, who had suffered for many years past from, and had exercised the utmost restraint in the face of, increasing Chinese atrocities and affronts.

"Noting the extreme gravity of the situation, the Japanese Consul-General, under the instructions of the Government, and in order to do all that was possible to prevent, by a local solution of the question, any aggravation of the case, presented to the Mayor of Shanghai on January 21 a set of four demands, including one for the dissolution of anti-Japanese societies. At three o'clock in the afternoon of January 28, the Mayor's reply acceding to the above demands was received. The Japanese authorities, hoping that the tension might then relax, decided to wait and watch the performance of their promise on the part of the Chinese.

A Sketch Showing Military Operations in and about Shanghai

However, soldiers belonging to the 19th Army, then concentrated in the vicinity of Shanghai, began, for reasons connected with internal politics, to display signs of recalcitrance toward the Nanking authorities, and appeared to be making hostile preparations in spite of the Mayor's acceptance of our terms, thus creating a new source of danger. In the meantime Chinese soldiers in civilian costume and various lawless elements had stolen into the International Settlement, creating a source of danger to the quarters in the vicinity of the Municipal Offices. Many alarming rumours were in circulation and the residents were plunged into an agony of terror, the police of the Chapei district having taken flight. Thereupon, on the 28th, at 4 o'clock, the authorities of the settlement proclaimed a state of siege, and the armed forces of the Powers were ordered out to duty in accordance with a plan that had been previously agreed upon. It was when the Japanese landing party was proceeding to their assigned sector in Chapei that the Chinese opened fire upon them, precipitating a conflict between Chinese and Japanese armed forces, of which the present situation is the outcome.

"As is clear from what has been said, the incident of the Chinese assault upon Japanese priests and the incident of the armed Sino-Japanese conflict were entirely separate affairs. With regard to the armed collision, as it was entirely contrary to every intention of ours, and as the British and American Consuls-General offered a tender of their good offices, the Japanese authorities sought to effect a cessation of hostilities, and in fact, succeeded on the 29th in arriving at an agreement for a truce. But on the following day the Chinese, in contravention of their pledge, opened fire once more. At a conference summoned on the 31st, it was agreed that the opposing forces should cease from all hostile action during the progress of negotiations for the establishment of a neutral zone. However, the Chinese, resuming the offensive, are continuing the concentration of troops in the neighbourhood of Shanghai. So far, the Japanese navy, desiring, in view of the international character of Shanghai, not to aggravate the situation, has refrained from taking any drastic action, while the Chinese, spreading news of Japanese defeats, are maintaining even greater vehemence in their actions.

"In the existing state of affairs in China, uncontrolled and uncontrollable, and in view of historical precedents in such cases, we can have no assurance as to the possible behaviour of the vast armies congregated in the Shanghai area, should unscrupulous politicians care to incite them. Our landing party, opposed to Chinese forces outnumbering them by more than ten to one, is being wearied to exhaustion, while the predicament of the Japanese residents, facing imminent danger as they do, is beyond description. In order to meet the absolute necessity of at once despatching adequate military reinforcements, (as there are obvious limitations to the naval units which can be landed), so as to put an end to the menace of the Chinese army, to restore Shanghai to normal conditions and to relieve the inhabitants of all nationalities from the strain of fear and disquiet, the decision was taken to order the necessary military forces to Shanghai.

"It should be stated that this despatch of a military force carries no more significance than the despatch of the naval landing party in accordance with the practice on several previous occasions, and that the Japanese Government are prompted by no other motive than that of discharging their international duty of safe-guarding the large number of Japanese nationals, and the Japanese property worth many hundreds of millions, involved in the affair.

"The expeditionary force has been therefore limited to the strength absolutely required for the above purposes, and its action will be guided solely by the policy of protecting the commom interests of all the Powers. Unless the Chinese, by continuing hostilities or by obstructing our army in attaining the above ends, compels us to take necessary action, there is of course no intention whatever that it should enter upon an aggressive campaign. The Japanese Government have already declared that they cherish no political ambitions in the region of Shanghai nor any thought of encroaching there upon the rights and interests of any other Powers. What they desire is to promote the safety and prosperity of that region by co-operation with other Powers and mutual assistance, and so to contribute to the peace and well-being of the Far East."

5. General Ueda's Ultimatum to the 19th Route Army

Lieutenant-General Ueda, Commander of the 9th Division, handed to the Commander of the 19th Route Army the following ultimatum on February 18 at 9 p.m.

"Prompted by an ardent desire to fulfil my duties through effective steps for peace, I have the pleasure of communicating to your army the following conditions:

"(1) Immediate cessation of belligerent acts on the part of your army, and complete evacuation of the present first line, before 7 o'clock on the morning of February 20; and complete withdrawal of your army to areas 20 kilometres northward (including the Lion Hill Fort), from the boundary lines of the International Settlement, running from the western bank of the Whangpoo and the northwestern extremity of the International Settlement across a line between Tsaochiatuchen, Chouchiachiaochen and Pusungchen and including lines between the eastern bank of the Whangpoo, Lannitu and Chaochialouchen, before 5 o'clock on the afternoon of February 20. The fort in the area designated and other military preparations are to be removed, and no new preparations are to be undertaken.

"(2) After your army begins withdrawal, our army will take no action of shooting, bombing or chasing against your army, an exception being scouting by airplanes. After withdrawal of your army, the Japanese army will maintain only the area in the neighbourhood of Hongkew, facing the streets on which the Municipal Council Building is located, including the area around Honkew Park.

"(3) After withdrawal of the first line of your army, the Japanese army, with a view to ascertaining completion of withdrawal, will despatch a committee of investigation, accompanied by armed guards, into the area evacuated. This commission will carry the national flag of Japan for identification.

"(4) Your army is to offer perfect protection to the lives and property of Japanese nationals in the neighbourhood of Shanghai outside the area of evacuation. In case the protection herewith designated is not fulfilled, the Japanese army will take proper measures. Your army is also to suppress all kinds of activities by plain clothes soldiers.

"(5) Measures of protection for foreign nationals in and about Shanghai, including those in the area evacuated, must be decided through separate negotiations. As regards the suppression of anti-Japanese activities, the pledges made by General Wu Tiehcheng, Mayor of Shanghai, to Mr. Kuramatsu Murai, Japanese Consul-General, on January 28, must be put into effect. On this point negotiations must be held between diplomatic officials of Japan and your administrators in Shanghai.

"In case the foregoing points are not carried out by your army, the Japanese army will be obliged to take free action against your army. Any responsibility arising from such outcome must be borne by your army."

6. Shanghai Situation Further Explained

Enlarging further upon the situation in Shanghai, which called for our military expedition for the reasons set forth in the foregoing official statement, the military authorities have given out the following explanation:

"The Chinese military forces at present stationed near Shanghai, are the 19th Route Army commanded by Tsai Ting-kai. Their first line is taken by the 60th Division, about 11,000 strong, under the command of Shen Kuang-han, while the second line is held by the 61st Division under Mao Ping-shou, also about 11,000 strong. The third line is taken by the 78th Division under the command of Chu Shou-mien, which numbers about 10,000, having suffered heavy damage in its engagements during the early stage of the conflict.

"In the areas between Chenju and Suchow the 3rd Guard Division is stationed, while in Nanking and vicinity the 1st Guard Division is concentrated. In addition to these, twenty-two units of the newly organized anti-Japanese Forlorn Hope Corps and a certain aerial force, have already joined the fighting ranks.

"What must be noted is that these soldiers have been trained into an acutely anti-Japanese mentality by the militarist leaders who have their own purposes to serve, and that their arrogance has been pampered by the support of the unthinking populace. These men are, therefore, as self-confident as hostile toward the Japanese whom they are determined to fight to the bitter end.

"The international population in Shanghai, according to nationality, is as follows:—

International Residents in Shanghai

(As Returned at the end of December 1931)

Nationality	Population
British	9,700
American	3,607
French	1,533
Italian	314
German	1,900

"And the guard forces maintained in Shanghai by these Powers are as follows:—

International Guards Landed in Shanghai

(As Estimated February 6, 1932)

Nationality	Military	Landed Naval Force	Total
British	3,400	3,200	6,600
American	3,200	3,000	6,200
French	2,400	1,000	3,400
Italian	2,000	—	2,000

"It must be noted that the Japanese residents number several times as many as any of these nationals. Besides, many of the Japanese have their dwellings and businesses outside the International Settlement. In proportion to the population to be protected, our naval landing force is far too small, as may be seen in comparison with the other nationals. Our landing force, in fact, is hardly sufficient even to take care of the guard area assigned to it by international arrangement, to say nothing of safeguarding our nationals outside the Settlement. There can be no question that our naval landing party had to be reinforced by military forces.

"In short, it will be seen that the present military expedition has been undertaken to the sole end of preventing disturbances in Shanghai from spreading further. It is obvious that only by a speedy restoration of a normal state of affairs in the same city, can its residents of various nationalities be freed from the grave fears and danger in which they equally stand."

MILITARY OPERATIONS
AROUND SHANGHAI

CHAPTER VIII

MILITARY OPERATIONS AROUND SHANGHAI

1. The Start of the Military Expedition

The Imperial naval force, which was landed at Shanghai upon the outbreak of the trouble there, to protect some 30,000 Japanese residents and their property, was to find itself confronted by a Chinese army numbering more than ten times as large as itself. Our naval men, in their continuous struggle against such tremendous odds, had to fight under extremely trying conditions, day and night, with little rest or sleep. Inspite of such efforts, however, the situation in Shanghai went from bad to worse, plunging our resident population into a state of unbearable uncertainty and danger. But there being a limit to the number to be drawn upon the Navy for service ashore, the Government decided early in February to despatch, with Imperial sanction, a military force to Shanghai to assure the safety of our residents there and also to perform our international duties of guarding the Settlement.

There was organized an expeditionary army with the Ninth Division as its main body. In addition a mixed brigade was despatched from the

Twelfth Division. The latter force, for the time being placed under the Commander of the Third Squadron later to be put under the Commander of the Ninth Division upon his landing in Shanghai, boarded vessels of the Second Squadron and left Sasebo at 11 a.m. on February 6. In the following afternoon these men began to make a landing at a point some 3 kilometres south of Woosungchen. Towards 5.30 p.m. the first-line troops were advanced on the southern side of Woosungchen to face across the creek a hostile force garrisoning the Woosung forts, while our main force was concentrated near the railway station. After a survey of the field, it was decided for tactical reasons to suspend the offensive movement for the time being, and keep a watch on the opposing line.

The Ninth Division began to board ships at Ujina on February 9. The first portion, under cover of the bombardment made by the convoying ships for restraining the forts, proceeded past Woosung in the evening of February 13. A portion of these troops was taken to the railway wharf south of Woosungchen, while the main body was brought up to the wharf in Shanghai.

First Statement by Commander of the Ninth Division

Lieutenant-General Uyeda, Commander of the Ninth Division, upon his arrival at Shanghai, issued prior to his landing a statement which rendered into English reads as follows:

"I have this day arrived here charged with the duties of safeguarding the subjects of our Empire resident in and about Shanghai. The provocative Chinese attitude toward our landing party has placed the Settlement in a state of danger and uncertainty. Our nationals are now subject to extremely trying conditions of life. In directing the action of the Division under my command, I intend to cooperate with our Navy and save our nationals from their present difficulty with the least delay. While it is our aim to attain our object as peacefully as possible, any interference with the action of our Division will be disposed of promptly and with decision. With regard to the Powers with which we are to work, we shall aim at a friendly cooperation in our efforts to rescue the Settlement from the present menaces. As for the general populace of China who will offer no interference with our Division or its performance of duties, we are ready, being aware of their difficulty well deserving of sympathy, to show full regard for the peaceful tenor of their lives."

The Ninth Division began to land its first contingent at 7 a.m. on February 14. A part of these troops was stationed at a Chinese village about 6 kilometres east of Kiangwanchen, while the main body was quartered in the Japanese factories in Yangshupu, an eastern section of the International Settlement. On the following day, February 15, a portion of its forces, replacing the landing party, took over the guard of North Szechuan Road. The second contingent, arriving at the wharf in the morning of February 16, completed its landing the same day.

2. What was Done to Avert Hostilities

The Ninth Division thus completed its concentration near Shanghai by February 16; but being still hopeful of an amicable settlement, the Commander caused his Chief of Staff to arrange an interview with the Chief of Staff of the Nineteenth Route Army. At this meeting our advice was offered as to possible means of effecting a peaceful settlement. The conference, however, disclosed a wide divergence of views, and our suggestions, which were offered in a spirit of fairness, failed to win a favourable response. The Commander of the Ninth Division, still reluctant to forego his hope of settling the situation by means other than arms, addressed on February 18 at 9 p.m. a note to the Commander of the Nineteenth Route Army, asking for his reconsideration.

General Uyeda's Note to the Commander of Nineteenth Route Army

The Note which Lieutenant-General Uyeda addressed on the same occasion was to the following effect:

"Being most earnestly desirous of performing by peaceful means the duties I am charged with, I wish to submit the following with the hope that it may meet with your favourable consideration:

" (1) You will at once cease hostilities, completing the evacuation of your first line by 7 a.m. in the morning of February 20. Your army will then withdraw by 5 p.m. in the afternoon of February 20 to areas, excluding the Lion Hill Forts and 20 kilometres from the boundary line of the International Settlement as follows: in the area lying on the west side of the Whangpoo, to the northward of the line to be drawn from Tsaochiatuchen at the northwestern point of the International Settlement to Chouchiachiaochen and Pusungchen; and in the area lying on the east side of the Whangpoo River, to the northward of the line from Lannitu to Changchialouchen, a line largely running through the heart of Shanghai from east to west. The forts and other military works within the designated areas should be removed not to be replaced by new preparations.

" (2) The Japanese army will make no shooting, bombing, or movement in pursuit, excepting reconnoitring by aeroplane, after your army have begun to withdraw. Upon evacuation of your army the Japanese army will confine itself to the maintenance in Hongkew of the area about the street on which the Municipal Council building is placed, including the locality round Hongkew Park.

" (3) Upon the complete withdrawal of your first-line troops, the Japanese army will despatch under armed guard a committee of investigation to go over the evacuated area. The same committee will carry the Japanese national flag for identification.

"(4) Your army will offer full protection to the lives and property of Japanese nationals resident near Shanghai outside the above areas of evacuation. In case such protection should fail, the Japanese army will take such measures as may be considered proper. Your army will also put an effective stop to all activities of the plain-clothes soldiers.

"(5) As for the protection of foreign residents, other than Japanese, around Shanghai, including the above areas of evacuation, negotiation shall be made on some future occasion.

"(6) With regard to the suppression of anti-Japanese activities, the pledge given by Mayor Wu to Consul-General Murai on January 28 must be strictly put into effect.

"On this point the Japanese diplomatic officials will approach your civil authorities in Shanghai for separate negotiation.

"In case the foregoing points fail to be carried out, the Japanese army will be obliged to take free action against your army which should hold itself responsible for whatever consequences."

Commander of the Nineteenth Route Army Replies

Replying to the above note, General Tsai Ting-kai, Commander of the Nineteenth Route Army, sent a note at 8.15 p.m. on February 19, which ran in substance as below:

"We beg to acknowledge receipt of your note despatched at 9 p.m. on February 18. Our army, being responsible directly to the National Government, holds itself subject only to its order. We have reported the points contained in your communication to the National Government which, we trust, will transmit its reply directly to your Minister through the Foreign Department. While I am as yet in receipt of no official instruction, the National Government, according to Rengo news, has instructed Commander Tsai and Mayor Wu to reply to you to the following effect:

"(1) The Chinese army will withdraw to 20 kilometres from the boundary line of the International Settlement:

"(2) The Japanese army will likewise withdraw 20 kilometres:

"(3) As regards the permanent disarmament of the forts at Woosung and Paoshan, we refuse to comply with the Japanese proposal."

In such circumstances the Commander of the Ninth Division was obliged to conclude that the Chinese had no intention of agreeing to his proposal, and decided to follow the only course now open to him.

3. Topographical Features of Shanghai Region and Conditions of the Enemy's Forces

(A) Topographical Features

The country round Shanghai, which is a level plain made of the sandy mud carried down by the Yangtze, forms a veritable canal zone with Kiangwan Canal, Woosung Creek, Whangpoo River and hundreds of other creeks running in all directions between lakes and rivers. There are great facilities for water transport; but as for land traffic and especially roads over any speakable distance, there are absolutely no paths except those made along the wider creeks or canals used by men towing boats. The minor creeks are spanned at places by bridges hardly negotiable by anything heavier than cattle. Besides, these waterways are such that soldiers could never wade through by foot, and, therefore, form very serious obstacles to movement of organized forces. Military operations under such conditions were by necessity hampered to a very serious degree.

What is more, the towns in the neighbourhood of Shanghai are encircled by heavy brick walls which proved not only unclimbable but even formed effective barricades against field artillery fire. Smaller villages, though without such walls as a rule, are in many instances girdled by waterways. These villages generally have no defence work to guard the whole communal areas, but there are walls built by family groups which live closely together behind them for self-protection. These walls offered considerable facilities for resisting the offensive fire.

(B) Conditions of the Enemy Forces

The Chinese force which the Ninth Division upon its landing had to face at the front was the Nineteenth Route Army, commanded by Tsai Tingkai, which roughly consisted of the following:—

Soldiers and arms	60th Div.	61st Div.	78th Div.	Total
Number of soldiers	11,000	12,500	10,000	33,500
Number of rifles	9,000	10,500	8,000	27,500
Machine guns	24	28	20	72
Mountain artillery	8	10	6	24
Trench mortars	10	20	10	40

Note:—Each Division consists of 6 *Tuan*, one *Tuan* corresponding to one Japanese regiment.

It may also be noted that the main forces of the Guard Divisions at Nanking and Hangchow were at the time still placed at Sungkiang, Nanhsiang, Kunshan and also westward of these places. The dispositions of these troops were as shown in Chart I.

With regard to these enemy positions, further

details mentioned below were learned as a result of open hostilities.

The construction of the enemy's positions near Shanghai had been started before February 12. It was apparently planned from the start that Kiangwanchen and Miaohsiangchen should form the first line of defence. The Chinese positions at the former town and northward were each constructed strongly with a village as its basis and effectively guarded on the flanks by a series of strong emplacements for machine guns. These preparations may further be described as follows:

(1) Shelter Trenches

These trenches consisted of standing fire trenches with traverses and also of double bottomed trenches which were not of uniform strength. As a rule the trenches were narrow but fairly deep, occasionally lightly sheltered by wooden boards or panels, and iron sheets.

(2) Covered Machine Gun Emplacements

The machine gun emplacements were generally covered. The protective covers were fairly strongly built with thin iron sheets and brick. The mounds or Chinese graves, wherever found, were utilized for defensive purposes. Concrete and brick buildings were seldom overlooked, not a few of them being provided with loopholes.

(3) Outer Trenches

The outer trenches before the enemy's positions generally seemed to have been made by utilizing ways. At some points d'appui there were formed special outer trenches 4 metres wide at the top and 2 metres deep.

(4) Barricades, etc.

Points d'appui were invariably guarded by light wire entanglements made by use of standing trees, wooden beams of houses and so forth joined by a network of barbed wire. These were mostly built to a depth of about 4 metres, some of them being movable. Palisades were also seen at some places.

(5) Armour-Sheltered Positions

As for positions protected by armour, there was nothing specially noteworthy except those with light protective covers of iron for use of commanding officers.

4. Offensive about Kiangwanchen

(See Accompanying Chart)

What should particularly be noted about the present operations is that the Japanese army, in the first place, openly set the date for commencement of its general offensive, thus sacrificing tactical advantages, and, in the second, it directed its action by only frontal attacks. These tactical moves were deliberately chosen, despite the obvious disadvantages, in consideration of serious eventualities otherwise likely to involve the other Powers in Shanghai. If, for instance, attack was made on the enemy's flank from the north, his force might have fallen back in disorder into the International Settlement to imperil the civilian population there. Operations from the southern side were likewise out of the question because of the existence of the French Concession. The Japanese forces in the circumstances were obliged to fight under the worst given conditions.

(A) Fighting on February 20

At 7 a.m. on February 20 the Chinese first line showed no signs of withdrawal, but even displayed their hostile disposition by firing upon our aeroplanes. Nor had the National Government sent its reply. The Ninth Division, therefore, launched its offensive action at 7.30 a.m. with its troops disposed as below:

The Woosung Detachment (two infantry companies as unit).

> Placed south of Woosungchen; this detachment covered the rear of the right flank of the Division.

The Mixed Brigade (less the Woosung Detachment).

> By advancing through the area southwest of Woosung, this brigade directed its action againt the enemy's positions northwest of Kiangwanchen.

The Right Column (6 infantry battalions and one battalion of mountain artillery as unit).

> This column attacked the enemy about Kiangwanchen from the east side.

The Central Column (approximately 4 battalions

of infantry and one battalion of mountain artillery as unit).

> This force attacked the enemy to the south of Kiangwanchen.

The Left Column (the landing party as unit).

> These troops held their positions in Chapei, keeping watch over the opposing front.

Field Artillery and Aerial Force.

> In the earlier stages of fighting these forces chiefly cooperated with the Right Column.

The Third Naval Squadron at the same time cooperated with the Ninth Division in support of the Woosung Detachment by bombardment of certain strategic points and manoeuvring in the direction of Liuhochen.

Our first-line troops continued to move forward at each point, by driving off small enemy forces on their way, until they reached at 10 a.m. the line from north to south of the Kiangwan race course. Then our Right Column routed the enemy force, two to three thousand strong, occupying the strong positions along a line from north to south of the eastern side of Kiangwanchen. A portion of this column entered the same town at 1 p.m.

Toward the evening the Mixed Brigade in the right wing advanced to the northwest of Kiangwanchen, reaching the line of Peisungchai, Chinfengchai, and Maochiachai. The main body of our Division had in the meantime moved eastward from the areas north of Kiangwanchen along the railway line, until it advanced to a line on the east side of Fangpin, 1 kilometre south of Kiangwan.

By midnight of the same day it had been learned that the enemy's first line occupied the fortified positions on a line extending from near Miaohsiang to the neighbourhood of the North Station, Shanghai, across the creeks on the west side of Kiangwanchen. A hostile force placed in the centre of Kiangwanchen was still offering stubborn resistance. There was a massed force of Chinese in the neighbourhood of Tachangchen. The areas about Woosungchen were still held by the enemy. It was also learned that the enemy's second line of positions was placed along a line from north to south touching at the east end of Tachangchen, while his third line, close behind, on a north to south line running at the western end of the same town. In the light of such knowledge the Commander of the Division transferred the main body of the Central Column to the area between the Right Column and the Mixed Brigade, in preparation for the operations of next day. He also made the following changes in dispositions of our forces:—

The Woosung Detachment.

>This was to continue its duties as before.

The 24th Mixed Brigade.

>Prepared for the offensive against the enemy force in front.

The Right Column (approximately 3 battalions of infantry and one battalion of mountain artillery as unit).

This body prepared for its offensive by advancing to a line extending southward from Paiyangtsun to Sunchiachai and beyond.

The Left Column (approximately 6 battalions of infantry and one battalion of mountain artillery as unit).

Prepared for the offensive against the enemy at Kiangwanchen and northward.

One Infantry Battalion.

Prepared for the offensive against the enemy south of Kiangwanchen.

The Main Force of Field Artillery.

This was placed near the Kiangwan Race Course chiefly to act in cooperation with the Right Column.

The Landing Party.

Was to guard its present positions.

The Reserve Force (approximately 2 battalions of infantry).

This was stationed on the east side of the Kiangwan Race Course.

(B) *Fighting on February 21.*

At 8 a.m. on February 21 our Division opened action with artillery fire, to be followed by assaults on the enemy at Kiangwanchen.

About 9.30 a.m. the enemy forces in the centre of Kiangwanchen began to show signs of wavering under our fire. A part of our Left Column was then charged with the task of clearing the enemy from the streets, while the rest advanced on two sides of the streets, moving forward along a north to south line at the western end of the town.

In the evening of February 21 the enemy firmly held their ground from near Chichialiu, about 6 kilometres northward from the west end of Kiangwanchen, to the eastern ends of Siwan and Miaohsiang, and southwardly, to the villages along a small creek running from north to south at the western extremity of Kiangwanchen. Our first line closely pressed against these positions.

(C) *Fighting on February 22*

At daybreak our Division started operations against the enemy's positions north of Kiangwanchen. At 6.40 a.m. or thereabout the 24th Mixed Brigade captured the hostile positions in the neighbourhood of Miaohsiang; and later, broke through the opposing line extending northward from Howkuochiachai, about 600 metres north of the western end of Kiangwanchen. But what with a number of plain-clothes soldiers now overriding the field of battle, demanding our serious attention, and a series of creeks and narrow paths impeding our progress, considerable difficulty was experienced in employing our troops to full advantage. Our progress for the day was as far as the lines described below, a portion of our troops being posted in Kiangwan and southwestward to keep a watch over the enemy's positions.

Main Body of the 24th Mixed Brigade: near the western point of Miaohsiang.

Right Column: at the western end of Maochiachai and Pusi.

Left Column: near Shouchiashe and Shunchiachai.

Main Force of Mountain Artillery: near Liangyinchai north of Kiangwanchen.

Main Force of Field and Heavy Artillery: near Kiangwan Race Course.

The defeated enemy soldiers stopped in the villages close before our line.

As a result of the day's engagements near Miaohsiang, it was definitely ascertained that the 18th Guard Division under Chiang Kaishek had joined the Chinese first-line.

At midnight on February 22 an enemy force of about 3 battalions made an assault on the rear of the right flank of our 24th Mixed Brigade at Nansunchai and eastward. The assailants, however, were repulsed with heavy damage. The same night also saw a series of counter-attacks north of Chapei and bombardments by Chinese artillery, which were in each case overcome.

It was also in the course of this day's fighting that three Japanese privates met with their end in a manner that was to be acclaimed by the whole nation as mirroring national heroism of the highest order. Below is a brief account of the same incident.

The enemy's positions about Miaohsiang were well protected as the mainstay of his left wing. No less than a score of days must have been spent on their preparation. Protected by a system of barbed wire and outer trenches, they really presented propositions of considerable difficulty. Besides, the wire entanglements happened to have escaped the punishment of our artillery fire. It became necessary in the circumstances that our engineers should undertake to open up paths through these areas of wire entanglements for the charge of infantry men which was set for an early morning hour of February 22. It was therefore planned to accomplish it by improvising for the purpose long explosive tubes, on which work was started in the evening of February 21.

A small squad of engineers, to whom the task of breaking down the wire entanglements had been given, made arrangements with the infantry troops which were to charge through the opened paths. These engineers then betook themselves close to their objective points about 5 a.m. and waited for the appointed time. In early hours of the seventeenth day of the lunar month, the moon was still out, though more often veiled by morning mists. So they could command a view to a distance of not more than 30 or so metres ahead.

The explosive squad under Sergeant Umada was divided into three parties each of three men. Intending to complete their work of destruction in the dark, they put up a smoke screen under cover of which they crawled on. But they had not approached within 30 or so metres from their objective when their presence was discovered. A heavy fusillade was poured upon them. But our men hurled themselves forward in their resolute attempt.

They were all killed or disabled. Whereupon the task of destruction fell upon the second squad under Corporal Uchida which had been holding itself in reserve. Private Sakue's first party and Private Kitamura's second party each prepared for their duties. It was plain that the enemy, now well on their guard, would give them no time to ignite the explosive after placing it in the entanglement. These men, therefore, decided to drive the explosive home in a way which, counting all chances of success in their favour, still meant their own destruction as sure as that of the entanglements. Having ignited the fuse, they carried the heavy explosive tube between them and ran for the wire entanglement. The second party of Private Kitamura managed to withdraw itself to some distance in time. The first party of Private Sakue and two others, however, with no thought of withdrawal, carried on their duties until their end. Corporal Uchida in command was also wounded. Thus there were opened up two passages, each about 10 metres wide. Sergeant Umada, in command of the first squad, who had sent his three parties with unsuccessful results, now leaped forth and hurled more than a dozen of hand grenades upon the enemy line. In the moments of confusion thus created he rushed single-handed into the wire defence and cut open a passage by means of hand shears. Three pathways thus having been made, the infantry charged through to capture a sector of the Miaoh-siang line.

(D) *Fighting on February 23-24* (Chart II)

A tactical change was now thought advisadlé in the light of the experience gained during the past few days. The enemy, in fortifying their positions, seemed to have overlooked no creek, village or dwelling house of any strategic value. At each important point a barricade of one sort or another had been put up. In consideration of these points and also our numerical strength put into play, the Ninth Division decided to drop the idea of making operations on the general line at the same time. They decided on a new line of tactics in which our bombardment, especially from the air and by heavy artillery, after full preparation on well elaborated schemes, was to be concentrated on the enemy's strategic points one after another until a complete destruction should be wrought all along and the field opened up for more extensive and freer operations. On the two days February 23-24 our troops generally remained at their positions of the previous night, making preparations for the proposed offensive.

The enemy, however, made around sunset on February 23 counter attacks against the front of our Mixed Brigade and the front of our Left Column. About 8.30 p.m. they attacked the neighbourhood of the radio station of the Divisional Headquarters.

These sectional counter-attacks were repulsed in each instance.

From the information in hand from various sources, it was gathered that the enemy's positions at this stage were roughly as shown in Chart II.

(E) *Fighting from February 25 to 29*

On February 25 our Division launched the second general offensive. The 24th Mixed Brigade was charged to maintain the captured positions about Miaohsiangchen. The Right Column was the first to start action, opening the fire at 6.30 a.m. by heavy artillery and from the air, concentrating it upon the enemy line in front. At 10 a.m. these forces captured the hostile positions to the north and south of Chinchiachiang. By this time the enemy line to our south or to the southwest of Kiangwanchen, began to waver with some numbers already in retreat to the west. Our Division then had its artillery fire concentrated upon the enemy in and about Howkuochiachai and Tsienkuochiachai in front of our Left Column, which had by 4 p.m. completely captured the enemy's positions in these areas.

The routed enemy ranks were being concentrated at Erhshihsanyuan, a point about 2 kilometres northwest of Kiangwan, when a force of Inspecting Soldiers or "shock troops in the rear," who are charged to encourage or punish the soldiers of their own side in retreat, happened to appear on the scene on their eastern advance. These two groups had an armed clash the while our aeroplanes and artillery went on to inflict heavy damage upon them. However, the ruthless barrier set up by the Shock Troops in the rear at least had the effect of causing the routed soldiers to heel about and advance eastward for the recovery of their lost positions. These men reappeared before the villages now in our hands. But almost completely demoralized, they were no longer capable of brisk action. Of the enemy force, too, which had been offering a stubborn resistance from within Kianwanchen, some began to retaeat toward 4 p.m.

On the other hand, fresh enemy troops began to move forward about noon from two directions, one from the west, and the other from Lotienchen, both proceeding towards Tachangchen.

During the offensive of this day the Navy accorded very effective aid. Cooperation between our infantry and artillery likewise being effected to satisfaction, our men succeeded in wresting all of the objective positions from the enemy. Though we were unable to develop our fighting capacity to the full for numerical and topographical reasons, our army this day inflicted on the hostile line damage of serious material and moral significance.

On the following day, February 26, at 6.20 a.m., a company under Sub-Lieutenant Wakabayashi, of the Seventh Infantry Regiment, made a surprise attack at Yenchiachia, on the northwest side of Kiangwan. By an adroit movement at a dead angle of their arms, these men succeeded in capturing the Chinese position, guarded by four machine guns.

At 2.10 p.m. on February 27 our Division occupied the western end of Kiangwanchen, thus taking the whole enemy line extending from Miaohsiangchen to the western end of Kiangwanchen. Our work was now to be directed to preparation for the offensive against the enemy's second line near Tachangchen.

5. Our Army Reinforced

At the time of despatching the Ninth Division to Shanghai there was no knowing as to the attitude of Chinese troops other than the Nineteenth Route Army. It was not until February 22 that it was ascertained as a result of engagements that the enemy's ranks had considerably been swelled by addition of the Guard Divisions under Chiang Kai-shek. Now taking into reckoning the topographical elements to be overcome and the numerical strength of our side, the existing situation suggested possibilities of our Division coming to a deadlock on the field of battle. A speedy reinforcement was plainly necessary in order to dispose of the Chinese opposition for an early settlement of the situation. It was therefore arranged to form an expeditionary army in the Shanghai region by addition of the Eleventh and Fourteenth Divisions, together with some special forces from elsewhere. General Yoshinori Shirakawa was placed in command of this army. The transportation of these reinforcements was prepared with the least possible delay.

The Commander of the expeditionary army, accompanied by his staff, sailed from the home waters on February 27. Arriving at the mouth of the Yangtze on February 29, he effected arrangements for the Naval cooperation for the landing of the troops. The Commander, taking all the circumstances into consideration, deemed delay impermissible. A general offensive was set for the next day, March 1, and instructions were issued accordingly. The Ninth Division was ordered to advance, according to its prearranged plans, to a line from near Changchiachiao, west of Miaohsiangchen, to Hsimawan about 2 kilometres to the south of Kiangwanchen via Tahsingchiao, some 2 kilometres west of Kiangwanchen. The main body of the Eleventh Division, freshly arriving, was to make a landing early in the morning of March 1 on the shore of the Yangtze in a northwesterly direction of Liuhochen, with the instruction to take possession of the last named place with the least possible delay so as to be in readiness for later offensive moves on Tachangan and Chenju.

General Shirakawa, the Commander, landing at Shanghai at 1 p.m. on March 1, at once issued a statement.

Commander Shirakawa's Statement

"I have this day arrived in Shanghai in command of the expeditionary forces and charged with duties of according protection to the Japanese residents in and about Shanghai, in cooperation with the Imperial Navy.

"Japan's solicitous efforts to make an amicable settlement of things has met with no success. Since our Ninth Division was called forth for armed operations, the Chinese have been increasing their military preparations, leaving no doubt as to their determination on armed action. Our Empire under the circumstances is compelled to make such an increase in its expeditionary forces as necessary for the attainment of its original objects. However, being without hostile designs and solicitous to avoid any unnecessary complications, our army is ready to suspend hostilities at any time, if the Chinese withdraw their army, in compliance with our request.

"As for the civil population of China, we shall show them due regards as our friendly neighbours. Regarding the nationals of other Powers, we shall, needless to say, remain in friendly harmony with them, showing full respect for their rights and interests.

"Upon my arrival in Chinese territory in command of the Imperial army, I declare, in pursuance of our present object, my intention that our warlike operations will be confined within the least possible area, with always in view an early restoration of orderly conditions, so as to ensure the safety of our nationals and restoration of peace in the Far East.

General Yoshinori Shirakawa,
Commander of the Expeditionary
Army to Shanghai

March 1, 1932.

6. Operations in Liuho, Tachangchen and Thereabout

(See Chart III)

(A) Positions of the Chinese Armies Prior to Action

The Chinese troops were generally disposed as shown in Chart II, except the 60th and 61st Divisions which Tsai Ting-kai had concentrated near Tachangchen, evidently determined to hold the second line there at all costs. At the first line in the area of Chapei a great number of volunteers had been placed, while the 89th Division had been distributed in the rear toward Chiating and Nanhsiang.

The Nineteenth Route Army had originally been full of spirit, with fairly good fighting capacity. When, however, the number of casualties steadily mounted they became more and more demoralized. Soldiers of the Guard Divisions who had had but little experience in actual warface were heavily punished by our fire from the first hour of their appearance at the front. The damage was so heavy that these men was soon to lose their fighting spirit. Besides, their clash with the "shock troops in the rear" from the Nineteenth Route Army at Erhshihsanyuan on February 25 caused a fatal discord between the leaders of these two armies. The attitude of the Nineteenth Route Army men parading themselves as the only laurel-winners in the fight were also the cause of an eventual collapse of their solidarity. Besides, the Chinese soldiers took after February 28 to looting and plundering in the neighbourhood of their quartering places. At Tachangchen and Woosungchen the whole villages seemed to have been sacked.

What with the pressure given by our army and internal discords and trouble, the Chinese, when informed of our reinforcements, felt that further fighting would be futile. The Chief of Staff of the Nineteenth Route Army and Wellington Koo notified us on February 28 through the British Naval Command that, "if the Japanese would withdraw within the International Settlement the Chinese army was ready to evacuate beyond 20 kilometres." The same day Wu Tieh-cheng, the Mayor of Shanghai, likewise had a message of a similar purport conveyed to us by Yin Chao-chen. The Chinese first line nevertheless went on fighting, showing no signs of withdrawal.

On February 29 Wang Chin-wei (Wang Chao-ming) sent us a messenger bearing a proposal for withdrawal of both armies, who, however, emphatically stated that "the voluntary evacuation of the

Chinese troops as stated by Wellington Koo would never accord with the will of the people. The Nationalist Government would consider nothing short of the evacuation of both armies on terms of equality."

(B) *Fighting on March 1*

The Ninth Division, including the 24th Mixed Brigade, and reinforced with three infantry battalions from the Eleventh Division landed the previous day, resumed action early this morning. Placing the fresh troops between its two regiments, the Division directed its attack on the line between Miaohsiang and Kiangwan. The situation generally turning favourably, our men captured the enemy's positions about 4 kilometres in front and 2 kilometres in depth. At the close of the day our first line was advanced to the line of Miaohsiangchen, Tienyuan, Ssuchetou and southwards. In course of these engagements, Colonel Hayashi, commander of the Seventh Infantry Regiment, was killed in action about 1 p.m., while assaulting a point to the west of Kiangwanchen.

On the same night the Ninth Division advanced all along the front, reaching the line of Paoyuhsiang, 500 metres northwest of Miaohsiangchen; Huchiawan, to the west of Miaohsiang; Tahsingchiao; Maochiahsiang; Yangchiachai, 3 kilometres to the southwest of Kiangwanchen.

The main body of the Eleventh Division, receiving a close cooperation from the Navy, began to make a landing at 6 a.m. on March 1 in the face of the enemy's machine guns. The hostile force in this region consisted of about one battalion. The landing place was guarded by a Chinese force, about 100 strong and equipped with 3 machine guns. However, our troops were completely landed during the forenoon with no more casualties than one engineer officer and private killed. These forces started their southward march after noon to come at 1 p.m. to a clash with the enemy at Chienchingying which was taken at 5 p.m.

The destruction by our navy of the Woosung fortress at the mouth of the Whangpoo gave material help to the transportation of our military forces. When the Twenty-Second Regiment of Infantry and a small force to fill up the Twenty-fourth Mixed Brigade were landed at Woosung, the Chinese were misled to think that the main body of our reinforcements was first to be concentrated at this point, and their attention was consequently diverted in these directions. When, therefore, a portion of the Eleventh Division was landed up the Yangtze, the Chinese forces were given a surprise, and turned in rout.

The region selected for the above landing was swept by a violent northwesterly wind during the night. Rough waters gave promise of difficulties of landing. But just before the time set for the landing the wind turned to the south, a dead calm settling over the Yangtze water. Under these favourable conditions and with a perfect aid of the Navy, our military forces were able to effect such a successful landing in the face of the enemy as has seldom been recorded in the military annals of the world.

(C) *Fighting on March 2*

The Ninth Division resumed action early this morning, and advanced to a line north to south of Tachangchen. The enemy retreated in a rout all along the front. Making unbroken pursuit, the Ninth Division advanced at 4.30 p.m. to the line of Wanchai, 3 kilometres north west of Tachangchen; Laojenliu, about 2 kilometres west of Tachangchen; Chunghsiang, about 1 kilometre south of the same town; Sanchili, to the south of the same; Wangchiachai, about 2 kilometres west of the Chenju Railway station. Later toward sunset our first-line forces advanced as far as Hsiaonanhsiang, about 1,500 metres northeast of Nanhsiang and Chenju.

Our landing force in Chapei also swung into pursuit of the enemy.

The main force of the Eleventh Division, starting from near Chienching early in the morning, advanced on Liuhochen which was taken by 4.30 p m. It then went on in pursuit of the enemy toward Chiating.

Throughout these engagements, the air forces of our Army and Navy operated in full and effective cooperation with the troops on land, assailing the enemy in retreat at many points, and carrying out their destructive work to the full.

(D) *Fighting on March 3*

The Ninth Division this day reformed its ranks by concentrating its main portion at Nanhsiang, and a portion at Chenju. The Eleventh Division turned in the afternoon on the enemy at Chiating from two sides, directing its main force forward from the direction of Loutang, and another portion, which had been landed south of Woosung, from the direction of Nanhsiang. These troops took the same town at 5.30 p.m.

Early this morning men of our landing party, supported by an infantry force, effected a landing in front of the Woosung fortress and took it by assault.

In the afternoon of March 5 the Commander of the Expeditionary Army issued an order to his troops to suspend action so long as the Chinese should refrain from hostilities, and to remain in the present positions.

The Statement by General Shirakawa

"The Imperial Army, in concert with the Imperial naval forces, made every effort to discharge the duties of protecting the Japanese nationals through pacific measures. Our ardent desire, however, was frustrated by the Chinese Nineteenth Route Army, which led to hostilities.

"Now the Chinese troops have withdrawn to the distance originally demanded by the Japanese army, with the consequence that safety of the Japanese residents has been insured and peace restored in the Settlement.

"I hereby declare that so long as the Chinese troops do not resume provocative operations the Imperial army will suspend all armed action."

7. After Cessation of Hostilities

(A) *The Japanese Army*

On March 4 our troops were generally reformed on the line of Chiliaokou, Chiating, Nanhsiang and Chenju. The Eleventh Division advanced a part of its men to Hakkon, 10 kilometres to the northwest of Chiating, while a force from the Ninth Division was sent forth to Huangtu, 10 kilometres west of Nanhsiang, each for the purpose of keeping guard.

On this day a section of our forces took possession of the Lion Hill Forts.

From the outbreak of hostilities to March 17 the casualties of the Japanese Army were as follows:

	Killed	Wounded	Total
9th Division	503	1,274	1,777
24th Mixed Brigade	151	417	568
11th Division	64	96	160
Others	—	1	1
Total	718	1,788	2,506

Compared with what was experienced in the European war where armies assailing strongly fortified positions generally suffered a loss of 50 per cent of their numbers, our damage was remarkably small. While a large measure of credit is due to the good work of the Ninth Division and 24th Mixed Brigade, the landing of the Eleventh Division up the Yangtze, as a restraining movement, had good effects upon the decision of the day.

(B) *The Chinese Army*

The Chinese army seems to have withdrawn its main force toward Soochow, and a section toward Sungkiang, having suffered very heavy damage. It is reported that the number of their casualties since the outset, together with those who are missing, amounted to about 40,000. Small forces are still to be found at places near Taitsang and Kunshan, but there is no longer a single force of any considerable strength east of Soochow.

(C) *Conditions in Shanghai*

In the Settlement of Shanghai the news of our victory and the subsequent statement by the Commander of the Expeditionary Army were received with great rejoicings by our nationals. On March 4 the Japanese shops in Hongkew were all opened. The whole male population voluntarily offered their services to assist in the work in the rear. Most of the Chinese shops in the Settlement were also opened. The refugees in the direction of Yangshupu, guarded by the Japanese, began to return to their homes. Our army further addressed an assuring message to these inhabitants, advising them to return to their peaceful pursuits.

(D) *Chinese Propaganda*

The Chinese press throughout the country had been filled with information of malicious and often ridiculously absurd characters. Chinese recoveries of Liuho, Nanhsiang and Chenju; complete annihilation of the Japanese army; repatriation of the routed Japanese troops; death of General Shirakawa and consequent hoisting of the national flag at half mast at the consulate; sinking of two Japanese warships— these are representative of the type of news printed in the Chinese newspapers. By propagating such misinformation the Kuomintang hoped to cover the reverses their army had been meeting with on the field of battle. They represented the retreats of their military forces as voluntary movements made necessary through the menaces on the flank, failure of the reinforcements to arrive, inferiority in military equipment and numerical strength, and all sorts of imaginable reasons.

The public was so misled in some instances that they fired off firecrackers in celebration of an imagined military success of their soldiers. It may also be of some interest to see, for instance, what would be the Japanese casualties according to the Chinese reports given out from the end of January to March 3. By adding up these figures we see that Japan is represented to have lost 33,470 men, 29 aeroplanes, 6 warships and 15 tanks or armoured cars.

The common people, kept in ignorance, still seem to believe in such versions of Chinese military successes. In fact, most Chinese seem more favourably disposed toward the Nineteenth Route Army than the Nanking Government which, through the machinations of the Cantonese political influence, was incapacitated to render adequate support to the Nineteenth Route Army in hours of need. The movement against the Kuomintang still remains under the surface.

8. Expeditionary Forces Reduced

In view of a steady restoration of peace and order in and about Shanghai, the Imperial Government issued on March 14 an order recalling home the Eleventh Division, 24th Mixed Brigade and certain special forces.

On the same occasion our military authorities expressed themselves to the following effect:

"As set forth clearly when our military forces were sent to Shanghai, our object in exercising our right of self-protection was first to safeguard the lives and property of our nationals there, and secondly to restore peace and order in the International Settlement in cooperation with the other Powers. In order to attain these objects, the commanders of our armed forces there tried all in their power to confine the disturbances to narrow areas and settle them by amicable means. But the Chinese were not only totally lacking in sincerity but even assumed the offensive against us, causing, much to our regret, bloodshed and slaughter. But due to the august virtue of our Generalissimo and the gallant performance of duties by our troops and the effective cooperation of our navy, we have achieved a glorious victory over the Chinese, inflicting decisive damage upon them. The situation having thus been securely established, we are now able to withdraw a part of our expeditionary forces.

"However, the general situation there is still fraught with serious eventualities. Military bands still remain at places, and plain-clothes soldiers are still engaged in secret activities of various sorts, so that careful vigilance is required. The situation in such circumstances is far from reassuring. There are also probabilities, if current rumours be true, that the Chinese military authorities, with an eye to strengthening their positions both internally and externally, may after all decide upon a continuation of the anti-Japanese agitation or upon instigating their people again into armed action with slogans of recovering their lost territory."

Incidentally, our military authorities stated at the same time that rumours that our troops had been despatched to Formosa in connection with the Shanghai trouble were utterly groundless.

9. Concluding Remark

Our military expedition, after a series of successful operations, has accomplished its primary object. The comparatively slow progress seen in the earlier stages of the fighting was largely to be accounted for by the impediment caused by the topographical difficulties of those regions, offering favourable condition for defence and proportionately bad conditions for offence. There was also too great a difference in the numerical strength of the two opposing armies. Our action then was planned so as to keep our casualties as low as possible. Our men throughout showed superb and resolute courage in meeting all situations. In addition to the fightings continued practically day and night, our men had to experience considerable hardships through lack of drinking water, poor supply of food through absence of hands to transport, annoyances caused by plain-clothes soldiers, and difficulties of keeping communication with the rear.

It must also be noted that the present Shanghai incident stood against a background of inglorious strifes among the militarist politicians of China. The plan for causing disturbances in Shanghai was really conceived when the Cantonese were ousted in their struggle with Chiang Kai-shek. Schemes had subsequently been elaborated. It was the idea of these men to instigate the Nineteenth Route Army into action to the very end of complicating the situation, hoping thereby to place Chiang Kai-shek in a political impasse and thus to acquire for themselves the ruling power of the whole country. These men purposedly propagated misinformation as to the strength of our army so as to inspire their soldiers and others with proper courage and antagonism. However, even with military forces far superior in number, the Chinese were forced to suffer heavy damage and lose ground in every encounter. They are now at pains to shove the responsibility for each military failure to anyone but themselves. Under the circumstances the political situation in China is pregnant with uncertainties and far from settled.

Nor can we be blind to the efforts the Chinese are now making to draw the League of Nations Powers into the Shanghai imbroglio, apparently intent upon following their traditional policy of playing one Power against another.

But no matter however the military situation in China may change and however her political conditions may be aggravated, our army will follow its unchanged line, as set forth in the statements of the Imperial Government. Needless to say, it shall never be our purpose to acquire new interests or extend them by armed force, or harbour territorial designs. Our action will strictly be confined to the exercise of the inviolable rights of national self-protection, as may be seen from the statement our commander made at the first opportunity, ordering a cessation of hostilities,—a point which is no doubt clear not only to the Chinese nation but to other friendly peoples as well.

What seems certain about this present question of Shanghai is that the settlement of the situation is not to be hoped for unless the National Government of China show good faith in extirpating the anti-Japanese education and likewise all agitation against Japan, awakening fully to the necessity of Sino-Japanese friendship. It is our earnest prayer that sanity will soon come to rule over China that she may see a peaceful and orderly state of affairs throughout her land.

10. Japan's Troops Withdrawn Far Ahead of Truce Terms

The Imperial Government, with full reliance on the efficient work of safeguarding Shanghai by friendly Powers, decided on May 11 to withdraw the entire expeditionary force, far exceeding the terms of the truce agreement signed the previous week. On the same day the War Office issued the following statement:—

"Relying upon the activity of the representatives of friendly Powers concerning perpetuation of peace in Shanghai and upon the effectiveness of the armistice agreement recently concluded, Japan has decided to withdraw home the entire strength of the expeditionary force in Shanghai and then to watch calmly the future situation. Imperial sanction has been granted on May 11."

11. The War Minister's Explanation

On the same occasion Lieutenant-General Sadao Araki, Minister of War, gave the following statement for publication:—

"The Chinese army's challenge of the Japanese bluejackets on duty in defence of the International Settlement in Shanghai precipitated a conflict between the two forces, resulting in the disturbance of peace and order in the vicinity of the city. Under the circumstances, the Imperial army was mobilized for the protection of Japanese residents, effecting a landing on the lower reaches of the Whangpoo River on February 7. Since that time, the Japanese expeditionary force has been making every effort to accomplish its aims.

"The Japanese army, at first, hoped to settle the conflict amicably, in order to avoid unfortunate bloodshed and in order to carry out its obligations to the world at large, but the Chinese army was influenced by anti-foreign sentiment and not only refused to accept Japan's rational demands but menaced the Imperial army by strengthening its preparations for war. We were thus obliged to draw the sword of righteousness.

"The objects of Japan's military operations was the defence of the International Settlement and the protection of the Japanese residents of Shanghai. It was, therefore, necessary to drive the Chinese army back a certain distance, as it was threatening peace and order in the vicinity of Shanghai. This was accomplished as the result of the offensive started at the beginning of March.

"The Japanese army had then secured a full opportunity to effect a complete destruction of the Chinese forces; but restricting its sphere of activity, it refrained from an annihilating drive. This attitude of the Japanese army was a manifestation of the consciousness of the Imperial army that it was acting from the simple motive of establishing peace.

"In the meantime, other nations concerned and the League of Nations urged the conclusion of an armistice agreement between Japan and China on condition that a round table conference would be held by all nations concerned for the purpose of arranging to maintain peace in the vicinity of Shanghai, which was quite acceptable to the Imperial army. It is most gratifying, therefore, that that an armistice agreement was concluded on May 5, after more than two months of negotiations, through the good offices of the British, American, French and Italian representatives.

"The scope of the armistice is limited to the cessation of hostilities between the Japanese and Chinese armies. The agreement does not include any provisions concerning the establishment of permanent peace in the Shanghai area. Nevertheless, by the terms of the stipulation the Chinese army are to remain at a certain distance from Shanghai and refrain from hostile acts in the neighbourhood of the city, and if any doubt arises as to the fulfilment of these terms, the question is to be decided by the British, American, French and Italian representatives on the joint committee.

"In the light of such points secured by the same agreement, providing that China faithfully observes provisions and the representatives of the friendly Powers perform their duties correctly, there seems no fear of disturbance of peace in the neighbourhood of Shanghai by the Chinese army for the time being. All the more so, since the interested Powers will see to it that a round table conference is called, following the conclusion of the armistice, in order to establish terms for maintaining peace in the neighbourhood of Shanghai.

"Due to these considerations, the Imperial army, relying on the representatives of the neutral Powers concerned for the establishment of permanent peace in the Shanghai area and the smooth operation of the armistice agreement, it has been decided to withdraw the entire Japanese army back to Japan and to observe developments in the situation of Shanghai with a calm attitude."

12. Evacuation

In accordance with the above the statement, the Japanese Expeditionary Force began its withdrawal of the first line on May 16, continuing it in the order given below:

May 17; from Tachangchen:

May 19; from Kiangwanchen:

May 23; from Chenju and Chenju Railway Station:

May 24; from Yinhsingchen and Lion Hill.

May 25; from Paoshanhsien, Woosungchen, and region of Woosung Forts.

Then on May 31 the last of the Japanese army boarded the transport on the homeward journey.

13. Japanese Casualties

The total casualities suffered by the Japanese army throughout the fighting around Shanghai, and those suffered in Manchuria from September 18, 1931, to June 13 of the present year are officially announced as follows:—

Japanese Casualities

	Killed	Dead Afterwards	Total	Wounded	Grand Total
Kwantung Army	481	72	553	1,274	1,827
Expeditionary Force to Chientao region	7	4	11	29	40
Garrison in China	2	—	2	4	6
Troops sent from Korea	4	1	5	19	24
Expeditionary Force to Shanghai	541	95	636	1,789	2,425
Grand Total	1,035	172	1,207	3,115	3,322

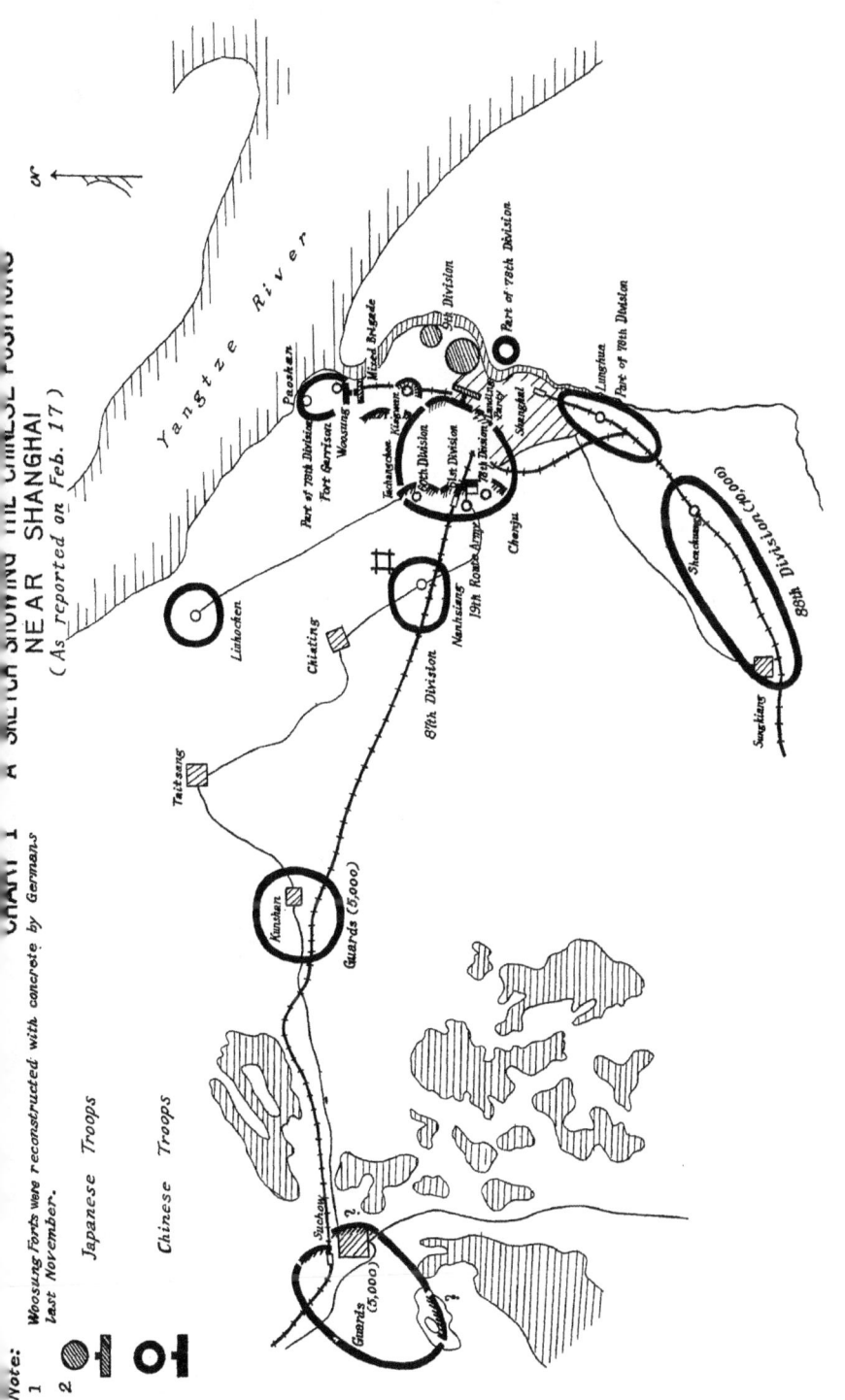

CHART II
A SKETCH SHOWING THE CHINESE POSITIONS NEAR SHANGHAI
(As reported on Feb. 23)

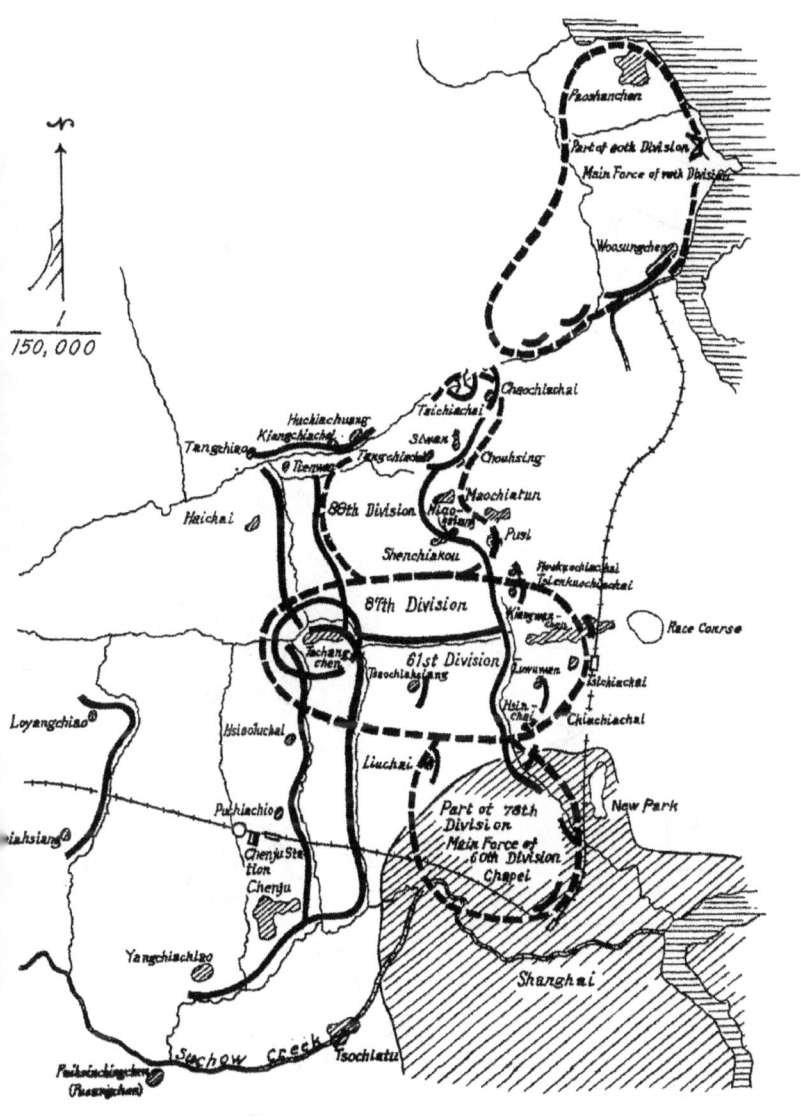

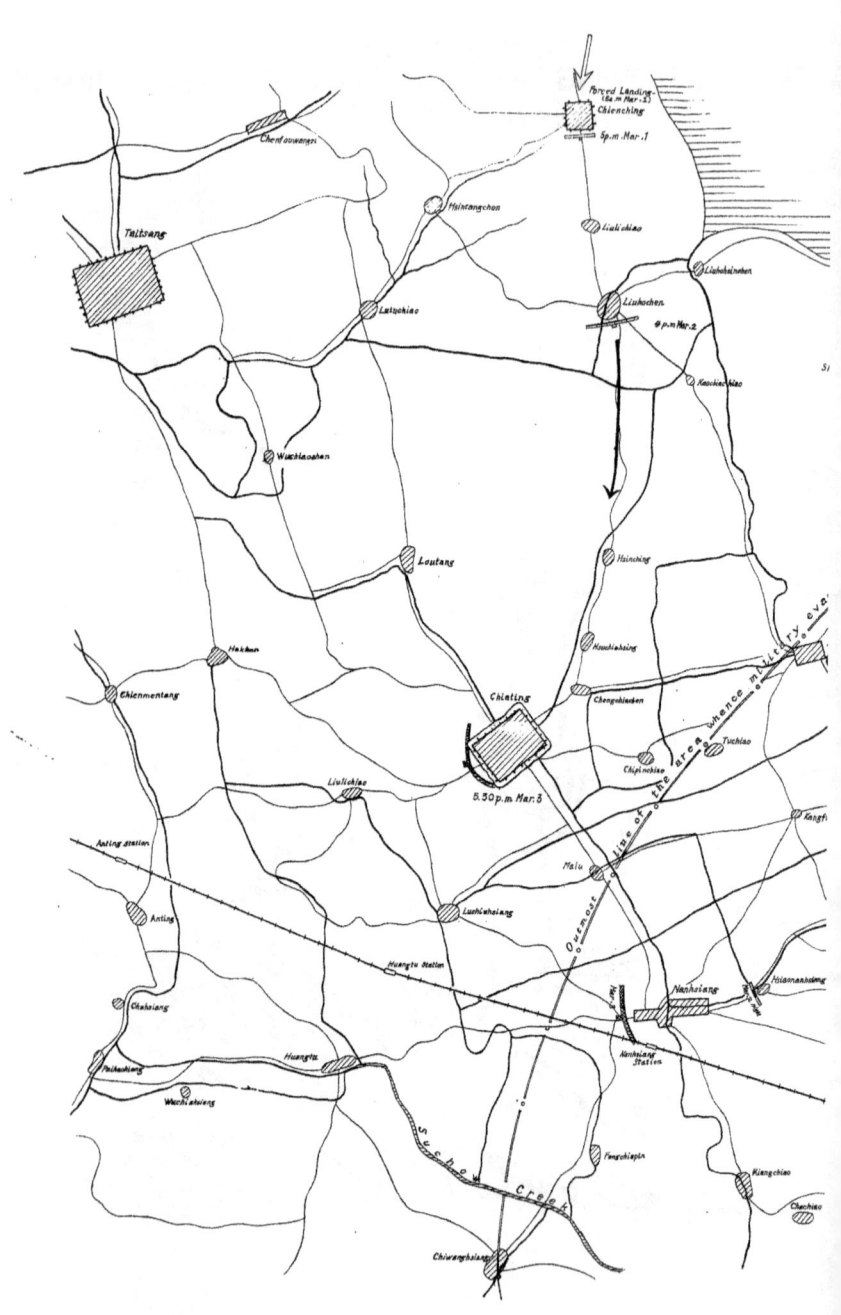

CHART III
MILITARY OPERATIONS NEAR SHANGHAI
(From Feb. 20 to Mar. 3)

THE ORIGIN AND HISTORY OF THE ANTI-JAPANESE MOVEMENT IN CHINA

CHAPTER IX

THE ORIGIN AND HISTORY OF THE ANTI-JAPANESE MOVEMENT IN CHINA

1. Introduction

The Chinese anti-foreign ideology is not of recent origin. It is simply an outgrowth of the same psychology that made the Chinese from ancient times to look down upon all outside peoples as barbarians. Anti-foreignism, however, has grown in intensity in recent times, especially since the revolution of 1911.

At the time of the Sino-Japanese war, the late Dr. Sun Yat-sen organized in Hawaii a secret society called Hing-chung Huei with the object of overthrowing the Manchu dynasty. "China," said he at the time, "has been subjected to foreign pressure since the War of Opium, and the only way to free the country from this incubus is to get rid of the Manchu regime which is so weak in its foreign policy." This marks the inauguration of the policy of "Down with the Manchus and the Foreigners," which has had such fateful consequences upon the recent history of China. The ultimate objective of the new foreignism launched under such powerful auspices was not only to raise China to a position of equality with the other countries, but to make China a Power of commanding influence in the world. In a word, it was a revival under modern garb of the traditional idea of China being the centre of the world.

The downfall of the Manchu regime having been accomplished by the revolution of 1911, anti-foreignism has since become the sole guiding principle of China's national policy. It is to the attainment of this end, that strenuous efforts are now being directed. The World War having eliminated Russia and Germany as possible objectives of China's national policy of anti-foreignism, the whole brunt of Chinese antagonism has recently been turned against Japan and England, which are most heavily interested in that country. It was England that had to suffer first, and after her it has been Japan's turn. It is interesting to notice that China's anti-Japanese movement has passed through several phases. Negative unfriendliness, which characterized the initial stage, was followed by contempt, which in turn gave way to protest, while the latest phase is marked by aggressive provocations. It was sentimental at first but grew into a conviction; it changed from sporadic to organized activities, from a local to a national movement.

It must be admitted that the anti-Japanese movement in China presents to us a most knotty problem. What shall we do about it? Can the malady be cured by the application of some diplomatic assuagement? Or will concession on our part lead to a satisfactory solution? If past experience is of any value as guidance, it must be said that neither of these remedies will be of any avail. It is true that during the initial negative stage of anti-Japanism, that is to say, prior to the emergence of the Kuomintang, concessions on our part might have had more or less favourable results. But no such result can be hoped for now that China's antagonism to Japan is active and aggressive. Concessions on our part at the present moment, so far from conciliating China, will only serve to encourage her to stiffen her attitude in the expectation of still greater concessions. So it looks as though there is no way out, unless either China abandons her anti-Japanese policy or Japan koutows before insolent China. However deeply Japan may sympathize with China's national aspirations, it goes without saying that in the present state of things in that country it will be fatal to her best interests as well as our own to please her humour. It only remains for us, therefore, to call China's attention to the serious consequences of the policy of extreme unfriendliness and hostile provocation she is pursuing toward us. It is only in this way that the relations between the two countries can be brought back into a normal condition, so that the permanent peace of Eastern Asia can be securely reestablished.

In the following pages attempts will be made to examine the guiding principles of contemporary politics and the anti-foreign education and training in China, with a view to tracing her anti-Japanese movement to its sources. Endeavours will also be made to follow the history of that movement with particular reference to the features that distinguish it from the movement applied against other Powers. Such a study, it is hoped, will present this important subject in a new aspect.

2. The Guiding Principle of Contemporary China and Anti-foreign Movement

The anti-Japanese movement which has so badly poisoned the relations between the two leading Asiatic nations, originated with the Chinese obsession about the recovery of national rights, which forms the cornerstone of China's foreign policy under the Kuomintang regime. It will, consequently, be useful to make a reference to Sun Ya-tsen's San Min Chui, which is the guiding principle of Chinese politics, and to the political platform of the Kuomintang.

1. *The San Min Chui*: The San Min Chui is the essence of Sun Yat-sen's revolutinary principles, and jointly with the Five Rights Constitution, constitutes the watchword of the Chinese revolution. Sun's convictions, ideas and aspirations concerning the national revolution are all embodied in it.

The three principles enunciated by Sun Yat-sen, consist of the principle of nationalism, the principle of popular rights, and the principle of people's livelihood. Reference will be made here only to the principle of nationalism, which is closely connected with the policy of anti-foreignism. The principle of nationalism supplied a guiding principle for the national revolution. This section of Sun's book also deals with the practical procedures for achieving the independence of the Han people. Much emphasis is laid upon their emancipation internally and externally.

Internally, a strong plea is made for the unity of all peoples in China, who shall be entitled to equal rights without any discrimination in all political, economic and social matters. United and emancipated as just mentioned, they should, it is pointed out, by their combined efforts create such a strong nation as may be fit to take a proud position side by side with the Powers of the world. As for the external policy, Sun urges that the Chinese nation should endeavour to brush aside all illegal and unreasonable oppressions imposed by foreign Powers and thereby emancipate China from the position of semi-colony into which she has been reduced by foreign arrogance. With a view to calling forth such national consciousness, recourse is had to the use of slogans like "Down with Imperialism" and "the Abolition of Unequal Treaties."

On this subject it is further stated as follows: "The principle of nationalism insists, above any thing else, upon the removal of all forms of imperialistic invasions, irrespective of the classes of people affected. For example, unless the principle of nationalism prevails in economic circles, the domestic industry will never be able to free itself from the baneful influence of foreign economic oppression. Or again, if the labour world should be devoid of nationalistic consciousness, the ignorant workers will be enslaved by imperialistic influences, with the result that our present militarists will combine with domestic and foreign capitalists in sucking our very blood. Therefore the war of national emancipation is to be fought in the interest of the masses, and its motto should be 'Oppostion to Imperialism'."

(2) *The Principles and Foreign Policy of the Kuomintang*: The principles of the Kuomintang are identical with those enunciated in Sun Yat-sen's "San Min Chui." The party considers these principles to be indispensable for the salvation of the country. The Republic of China established upon the basis of the principles of the " San Min Chui " and the provisions of the Five Powers Constitution, the party aims at (1) the assurance of livelihood for the masses, (2) the establishment of popular rights, and (3) the carrying out of the principle of nationalism. The party at the same time aims at revising the treaties with the foreign Powers, with a view to securing the country's independence upon the basis of perfect international equality. According to an official statement issued on January 10, 1923, the

Kuomintang's foreign policy includes the following items:

(a) All unequal treaties and agreements, such, for instance, as the consular jurisdiction, the control of the Customs by foreigners, and all other political powers exercised by foreigners, and which infringe upon China's sovereignty, shall be abolished, and their place be taken by treaties of mutual equality.

(b) China shall give the most favoured nation treatment to any country that voluntarily offers to give up all special privileges it enjoys in China or that agrees to the abolition of such treaties as may encroach upon China's sovereignty. China shall give Russia a specially favoured treatment.

(c) All treaties concluded between China and foreign Powers and which are deemed inimical to China's interests, shall be revised.

(d) The foreign debts owed by China shall be speedily paid back within limits not injurious to China's political or economic interests.

(e) The people of China shall be free from all obligations in regard to the foreign loans contracted by irresponsible governments, such, for instance, as the Government which functioned at Peiping under a President who owed his election to corrupt means.

(f) A conference of the delegates representing the business organizations in the various provinces shall be convened, with a view to providing the ways and means of repaying the foreign loans.

Chen Kung-po is a well-known and influential left-wing leader of the Kuomintang, and his writings form an invaluable source of information concerning the inner life and aspirations of that party. Here we shall confine ourselves to quoting only such passages as may throw light upon the inner story of the origin of China's anti-Japanese movement. In his work on "The Principles and Practice of Political Reorganization," he discusses China's foreign relations as follows:

"The World War has ushered in a new epoch in the relations of the foreign Powers toward China. Prior to that war, the countries that influenced China by means of force were England, Germany, France, America, Japan and Russia. But now those that can materially influence China's revolution, are only four, namely, England, America, Japan and Russia. Moreover, England failed in her policy of butchery, and has ever since pursued a conciliatory policy toward China. As for America, her interests in China are confined to 70 million yuan worth of imports into this country, so that her policy is comparatively moderate, her chief concern being to have the door kept open. It is quite different with Japan. She considers our revolution as a fatal blow to her, for in the event of our revolution proving a success, she would lose her acquired rights not only in the three Eastern Provinces but in Shantung also. But that will not be the worst. Korea and Formosa will become independent, and further, apart from being a fatal blow to her economic independence, it may even render the preservation of her Imperial dynasty problematical. Lastly, the Soviet Union, in view of the Far Eastern policy of the Comintern, is very anxious to extend the Bolshevik influence and rob China of her political powers by utilizing the Chinese Communists. We thus see that both Japan and Russia pursue a vigorous policy toward China, while the British and American policy is weak.........

"But for the moment the imperialistic objectives before us are Japan and England. We should make Japan the main object of our offensives for the present, reserving a defensive attitude for England and trying to make America preserve a neutral policy toward us. As for Soviet Russia, we should make it our object to restore relations with her on the common ground of anti-imperialistic aspirations, on condition that she shall strictly abstain from communistic propaganda.

"In short, imperialism is unalterably determined upon frustrating a successful accomplishment of our revolution, while the Comintern is also committed to a similar line of action, its wish being to let the Communist party gain political powers in China. In order to assure the success of our revolution and the continuance of the Kuomintang, it is necessary for us to build up a new International based on the principles of 'San Min.' Diplomacy is a kind of warfare in peace time, and it must not be forgotten that the organization of the new

International will be the surest means of laying a foundation for our revolution. To put it in one word, what we have got to do are

"(a) To set up a new International of the oppressed peoples in the shortest possible time, and

"(b) To form an alliance with all the oppressed classes in Europe and America."

Discussing the military problems of Revolutionary China, the same Chinese writer says as follows:

"Finally we are confronted with the necessity of formulating a newly reconstructed plan of our foreign military policy. A national defence must be based upon a well-defined objective, but we fail to discover any such objective in the military policy of the Nanking Government. For instance, the National Military Reorganization Conference merely decided upon the delimitation of six Reorganization Areas, and it entirely failed to designate any objective for our national defence.

"We consider the Japanese imperialism as the objective for our national defence. Unless the Japanese imperialism is successfully disposed of, our revolution will be doomed to a failure. We, therefore, consider it important that the following points should be decided upon:

"(a) North of the Yellow River, our military establishment should be planned according to an offensive strategy, while south of that river defence should be the main consideration. The directions of our strategic lines, should be from the north to the south and from the east to the west.

"(b) In consideration of the fundamental principle of our national strategy mentioned above, our first line of importance should be the three Eastern Provinces, and the Provinces of Hopei, Shantung, Kiangsu, Chekiang, Fukien and Kuangtung. As for the remaining Provinces, they will only be needed for the second and third lines of national defence.

"(c) As for the defence of the coastline, considerations of time and financial requirements make it impossible for us to build the needed warships within a period of ten years. It will, consequently, be necessary for the present to concentrate our attention upon the construction of submarine boats and aereal planes."

From what has been remarked above, some light, we hope, has been shed upon the ideas and sentiments that are moulding China's political development. These ideas and sentiments, viewed in conjuction with China's deep-seated attitude of hostility to and contempt of other peoples subsisting from the beginning of history, make it easy for us to understand how deep and strong is the sentiment of anti-Japanism among the Chinese people. There are people who think that, if Japan agreed to China's demands for a commercial treaty on the basis of absolute equality, the abolition of extraterritoriality, the recognition of customs autonomy, and the abandonment of rights of coasting trade and of navigating inland waters, the immediate result would be the restoration of friendship between the two countries. Nobody who knows the ideas lying deep in the hearts of the Chinese people and who bears in mind the guiding principles of the Kuomintang, will be prepared to agree with such a light-hearted view of the situation.

3. Education and Training in Anti-foreign Movement

Appreciating the value of popular education and training as a means of securing the success of the anti-foreign movement, the Kuomintang is directing its attention in this direction on a conspicuous scale. Its endeavours in this respect take various forms, but tne most important are the inculcation of anti-foreign, especially anti-Japanese, ideas and sentiments in schools and colleges, and the training of the masses in public demonstrations. These methods will be briefly described in the following paragraphs.

1. *Anti-foreign (Particularly anti-Japanese) Education:* Since the San Min Chui Revolution, the Kuomintang has devoted a great deal of efforts to the teaching of the San Min principles to the people as the most efficient means of developing its party strength. Particular effort has been made to instil into the minds of people the idea of recovering national rights in accordance with the principle of nationalism. In this way it has become

possible to make use of very concrete objectives upon the subject of nationalistic spirit. By the time the Kuomintang forces advanced into the Yangtze-valley, the ground had been fairly well prepared, so that the cry of national rights recovery spread like the wildfire. England succumbed to it, and attention has since been chiefly directed against Japan, recourse being had to a most intensive cultivation of anti-Japanese sentiment through the medium of school education. This has been carried out so efficiently that the impressionable minds of Chinese young men and women and children are now filled with hostile feelings against Japan.

The educational institutions throughout China are, by Government orders, teaching San Min principles and other ideas sponsored by the Kuomintang. The text-books contain lessons on the so-called unequal treaties, foreign imperialistic oppressions, the recovery of rights and privileges. Considerable skill is noticed in the way these pernicious lessons are prepared. In the majority of cases, Japan is represented as the worst offender in oppressing China. The more serious of the offences Japan is accused of are politico-military invasions, economic encroachments, the pressure of over-population, and cultural invasion.

In the field of politico-military invasions, the claim is made for the abolition of the "unequal" treaties, and strong criticisms are offered concerning the Treaty of Shimonoseki, the settlement of the Boxer trouble, and the negotiations of the so-called

Twenty-one Demands. At the same time a strong demand is made for the recovery of Loo Choo (Okinawa), Formosa, Korea and the Leased Territory of Kwantung. Prominence is given to the observance as National Humiliation Days of May 4 (Peking affair), May 9 (the signing of the Twenty-one Demands treaty) and May 30 (Shanghai affair). Attention is also called to the importance of arresting Japan's advance in Manchuria and Mongolia, the Tsinan affair is bitterly criticised, and the abolitian of consular jurisdiction is strongly advocated.

As for the economic invasions, they are said to follow military invasions, and they are stated to be more dreadful than forcible invasions. An eloquent plea is made for the recovery of customs autonomy. Complaints are also made of the enormous losses China is alleged to suffer on account of the investment loans, taxation in the settlements, the right of aerial navigation, the maintenance of post offices, and the carrying on of special enterprises by the Japanese such as railways, mines, and cotton spinning industry. By way of reprisal, the severence of economic relations with Japan through the boycott of Japanese imports is advocated. Strong appeal is necessarily made for the purchase of Chinese made goods in preference to those imported from Japan.

With regard to the problem of population, it is stated that Japan pursues a policy of territorial invasion in order to relieve the congestion of population in her small area. Japan is blamed for incursion into Manchuria and Mongolia, and Shantung. Much sympathy is professed for the Koreans and Formosans, who are instigated to form a federation of minorities.

Finally in connection with the cultural invasion, it is maintained that foreign enterprise in education and religious propagation has injurious effects upon the minds of the Chinese people, because such enterprise is really intended for transplanting of imperialistic influences. It is, therefore, argued that all the establishments connected with the enterprise in question should be handed over to the Chinese. For the same reason, Japan's cultural work in China is branded as an illegal cultural invasion.

An examination of the text-books on anti-foreign education reveals the fact that their authors never hesitate to repudiate the logical sequence of historical events whenever it is unfavourable to their arguments, while they acknowledge its truth when by so doing they can strengthen their arguments. They in effect show little compunction in distorting historical truth. They ignore altogether wrong doings on the part of their country, confining their attention only to alleged persecutions by foreign nations. In this way Chinese children and youths are nurtured on a dangerous diet of one-sided accusations of the most misleading tendency. One cannot help shuddering when one thinks the consequences of such a system of eduction upon the relations between Japan and China.

2. *Training in Anti-foreign Mass Movement:* Apart from the anti-foreign and anti-Japanese education in class-room, every encouragement is given to fostering the movement by taking advantage of memorial days and other occasions when students gather together in large numbers. On such occasions, speeches by instructors and students are largely on subjects connected with anti-foreignism.

Propagandists are also sent out from the Kuomintang headquarters to the factories under foreign management to talk on the question of boycotting foreign made goods and instigate strikes. These propagandists very often organize factory hands into societies under their control for the purpose of creating an anti-foreign atmosphere. Kuomintang delegates are also attached to the armies, charged with the duty of giving political instructions to the men according to the principles of the San Min doctorine. The tenor of such instructions is decidedly anti-foreign.

Another noticeable method of training the masses in anti-foreign demonstrations, is the observance of the so-called National Humiliation Days. The people at large are required to observe these days as National Holidays. These days commemorate the occasions when China was subjected to humiliating treatment at the hands of foreign nations. The object of commemorating these dates is to keep their unpleasant memories ever fresh in the minds of the people in order to stimulate the hatred of foreign nations. On these days, care is taken to organize parades by students and workers, and lecture meetings are organized, where addresses of a highly inflammatory character are made. Dangerously anti-foreign posters are exhibited at all busy quarters. The one object kept in all these activities is to incite and foster anti-foreign feelings by means of highly distorted explanations of the particular historical events commemorated.

The more important of these Commemoration Days are:

Day	Event Commemorated
January 3	Recovery by force of the British concession at Hankow, 1917.
May 3	Tsinan affair, 1928.
May 4	The Student Demonstration at Peiping, 1919.
May 9	Approval of "21 Demands," 1915.
May 30	Collision of Chinese students with foreign police at Shanghai, 1925.
	Beside those mentioned above, there are several other events listed for commemoration. Among them are the British-Chinese conflict at Shamien, Canton, 1925, the alleged British massacre at Wan-hsien, 1925, and the humiliating settlement of the Boxer trouble, 1901.

3. History of Anti-Japanese Movement

A national characteristic of Chinese people, is to be meek like sheep to the strong but overbearing like despots to the weak. It is this trait in the Chinese character that forms the basic principle of the Chinese boycott of Japanese goods. In other words, the Chinese argue in this way: "Japan is deficient in raw materials, for which she has to look to China, and at the same time it is to China she has to export her manufactures." So arguing, the Chinese convince themselves that they have us at their mercy, and consequently they proceed to boycotting our goods whenever they want us to behave. But they fail to realize that, although their trade with us amounts to 40 percent of their total foreign trade, our trade with them represents only 20 percent of our foreign trade.

The application of boycott against our goods was carried out for the first time in connection with the steamship Tatsu Maru affair in 1908. It has since been repeated several times during the past 24 years. It has always been resorted to in relation to some political events, like, for instance, the negotiation of the "Twenty-one Demands" or military expeditions into China. It is thus obvious that boycott has always been resorted to by China as an instrument of national policy.

Arranging them in chronological order, mention may be made of the more important of these anti-Japanese boycotts. It will be observed that a steady improvement has taken place in their size and technique.

1. *Tatsu Maru Affair:* On February 5, 1908, the Japanese steamship Tatsu Maru was seized and her cargo confiscated by a Chinese gunboat at Canton on suspicion of smuggling arms. The matter was vigorously taken up by the Japanese Government, with the result that it was settled by

an apology by the Chinese Government on five points. Japan's strong attitude as well as the Chinese Government's inefficiency angered the Chinese people who started a boycott against Japanese goods, which, starting at Canton, finally assumed almost nation-wide dimensions. It was continued for over eight months from March to November in 1908.

2. *The Antung-Mukden Railway Affair:* On August 8, 1909, Japan notified China that she had decided to rebuild the railway between Antung and Mukden, in virtue of the Peking treaty of 1905, and obtained China's consent to an Agreement consisting of five articles. A movement in opposition to this Agreement was started by the Chinese students in Japan. It gathered strength in the three Eastern Provinces in the form of a boycott of Japanese goods. The boycott spread to North China, where it acquired great strength under the patronage of the educational institutions and the officialdom. It finally became almost nation-wide. In response to a strong protest from Japan, the Governor-General of Manchuria issued an ordinance prohibiting the boycott. It had its effect, and the boycott which had started in August subsided in October.

3. *The "Twenty-one Demands":* On May 25, 1915, the treaty of the so-called Twenty-one Demands concerning South Manchuria and Inner Eastern Mongolia was concluded. Japan's attitude in negotiating this treaty aroused a strong hostile

movement throughout Middle and South China. The incident was utilized by the Southern Government in its opposition to the Northern Government. The result was that the boycott lasted for nearly eight months.

4. *Paris Peace Conference:* In January, 1919, the Chinese Delegation to the peace conference at Paris, tried, with America's support, to get the Kiaochow concession, Shantung Railway and other interests Japan had wrested from German hands, restored to her direct from the Peace Conference. But at the session of April 30, it was decided that all matters concerning Shantung should be settled by direct negotiations between Japan and China. The receipt of this news in China was a signal for the initiation of a double-headed agitation, that is to say, an anti-Japanese boycott on the one hand, and on the other hand the denunciation of the Tuan Cabinet, especially the new Communication clique, and other politicians friendly to Japan.

On May 4 a large body of students in Peking, numbering several thousands, attacked the residence of Tsao Ju-lin who was considered to be the leader of the pro-Japanese group. At the same time Japanese goods were piled up in the streets of Peking and burned. The anti-Japanese movement, which had spread to Shanghai, Canton and other large cities throughout the country, acquired a fresh impetus on May 9, the National Humiliation Day (on account of the signing of the Treaty of the Twenty-one Demands). In June the movement lost much of its fire, as Tsao Ju-lin and the other pro-Japanese officials were dismissed, but it again acquired a new momentum in July by the return of the Chinese delegates from Paris. It was not until April, 1920, that it finally died out.

Because this movement lasted for a year, the students felt a new confidence in their own power. They sanctified it by calling it a patriotic or a cultural agitation. In carrying on this movement, the students received help and assistance from foreign missionaries, while the other Powers regarded Japan's discomfiture with pleasure. In this way the balance of Powers vis-a-vis China was completely disturbed, which naturally in turn added much to the violence of China's anti-Japanese movement. It is also worth remarking that the movement in question incidentally served to open the eyes of the Chinese leaders to the fact that the condition of their country's relations with the Powers was far from satisfactory. The feelings of insecurity and dissatisfaction thereby engendered naturally disposed the Chinese people to adopt an attitude of hostility to the outside Powers in general.

5. *Agitation for the Recovery of Dairen and Port Arthur:* At the Washington Conference in 1921–1922, the treaty status of the leased territory of Kwantung and of the South Manchuria Railway was reaffirmed. But Japan had to give up her preferential position in Manchuria, and as if that was not enough, she had to sign on January 30, 1922, a treaty for the rendition of Shantung. Such whole-

sale concessions on her part only resulted in China's increased contempt for her, and side by side with the growing spread of the ideas of freedom and equality among the Chinese people, the anti-Japanese movement in China acquired increasing strength.

On August 17, President Li issued a statement concerning the recovery of Port Arthur and Dairen, which roused a widespread response in China. On November 1, the National Congress voted that the treaty of the Twenty-one Demands was null and void, and called upon the Government to demand the restitution of Port Arthur. On March 19, 1923, the Peking Government made a formal demand upon the Japanese Government for the restitution of Port Arthur and Dairen, a demand which was rejected by Japan four days later. The immediate result was a widespread anti-Japanese movement in various parts of China. It is a noteworthy fact that the slogan " the economic boycott of Japan " was used for the first time. The boycott of Japanese goods lasted till August, 1923.

6. *May 30 Trouble of 1925:* So far the anti-foreign agitations had been chiefly engineered and conducted by students without much outside guidance. Consequently, these agitations, though at times violent, lacked persistency. But about 1921 a special current in China's thought life turned it into a general anti-foreign movement. In other words what had been more or less vague and sporadic became organized and centralised. The new thought current which produced this remarkable change in the

movement was the idea of communistic revolution. In 1923 the Kuomintang definitely adopted the policy of a close association with the Soviet Union and decided upon accepting the communistic principles. Sun Yat-sen maintained that there was no essential antagonism between communion and the principle of the mass life enunciated in his San Min Chui. As the result of this open affiliation with the Soviet Union, labour movement spread in China like a wildfire, and the valour and efficiency shown by labour organizations was a source of new inspiration to the student movement.

It was in a social atmosphere like this that the historic episode now known as the May 30 Affair took place at Shanghai in 1925. It will be recalled that during a demonstration in connection with the strike of Chinese operatives at a local Japanese cotton mill, a group of students came into collision with the municipal police of the International Settlement at Nanking Road, resulting in the death of a number of students. This led to a general strike at Shanghai on June 1, followed by anti-foreign demonstrations at Peking, Hankow, Canton and other cities. Especially disastrous was the one at Canton on June 23, when a collision occurred at Shameen between Cadets of the Hwangpu Military School and the British settlement garrison, resulting in over 140 casualties. Taking advantage of the unfortunate situation thus created, Lian Chung-kai, chief of the industrial workers' department of the Kuomintang, acting in cooperation with Borodin and

Chen Tu-hsiu, started an economic crusade against Great Britain and Japan. At Hongkong the agitation was conducted through the Chinese Strike Committee (organized upon Soviet pattern), the men going on strike reaching the formidable number of 200,000. On July 21, the Chinese hands at the Japanese Cotton Mills at Tsingtao went on strike, while at Tientsin the Yutai Cotton Mill was attacked by a mob on August 11. Throughout this period Manchuria also was a scene of violent anti-Japanese demonstrations which were effectively fanned by the Chinese officials who issued repeated instructions for the persecution of Japanese and Korean residents. It was only in October that the anti-Japanese movement subsided.

The following year, when Chiang Kai-shek succeeded in July in getting as far as Hankow in his war of crusade against the northern warlords, fresh international troubles occurred there, which led to an anti-foreign agitation of a most virulent character with Great Britain as its chief objective. Most of the British settlements along the Yangtze were recovered by China, and as a price of the cessation of this movement, the foreign Powers gave a tacit recognition of the illegal taxation of $2\frac{1}{2}$ percent, thus creating a precedent for treaty infringement with impunity. England had to send to Shanghai an army of 17,000 men for the protection of her vested interests there. But the coming into power of a Labour Cabinet led to a more weakened policy toward China, which instead of mitigating the bitterness of the anti-British movement has only been productive of contrary results.

The Communist party, as is evident from what has been remarked above, dominated the thought world of China and directed practical movements of various kinds for six years since 1921. On April 16, 1927, the Kuomintang repudiated its connection with that party by a coup d'etat at Shanghai, and adopted a more moderate policy. But it cannot so easily shake off the leftish ideas and tendencies it had acquired under the Communist tuition. Moreover, consideration of party interests makes it stick with greater vigour to those Communist slogans which appeal to the anti-foreign sentiment of the Chinese, such, for example, like the cries of "Down with imperialism" and "Away with the unequal treaties." The Kuomintang's attitude on these questions is so uncompromising that it insists on a one-sided termination of the existing treaties in case their revision in a way satisfactory to it is not otherwise practicable. It is an attitude hardly compatible with the principle of international faith.

7. *Kuo Sung-ling affair of 1925*: On November 23, 1925, Kuo Sung-ling raised a standard of revolt against Chang Tso-lin at Lanchow, and by December 1 he had passed Shanhaikwan and continued his march upon Mukden. Order and peace in Manchuria being thus threatened, our garrison there had to be strengthened. This led to anti-Japanese agitations in various parts of China. Anti-Japanese manifestoes were distributed throughout the country from the

— 214 —

headquarters of the Anti-Japanese Association at Shanghai. The anti-Japanese boycott was most virulent at Tientsin and Changsha, where it lasted until April, 1926. In Manchuria itself, the local authorities took steps to suppress all forms of anti-Japanese agitations, but the students conducted demonstrations at various places.

8. *Expedition to Shantung, 1927:* The year 1927 witnessed a series of regrettable incidents. On March 24, our Consulate at Nanking was attacked by the Southern revolutionary troops, who committed almost every form of atrocity. The Consul and some of his staff were killed or wounded, and the honour and dignity of the Empire was completely trampled under. On April 2, a collision between a sailor from a Japanese warship and a Chinese mob at Hankow, led to the invasion of our settlement there by infuriated mobs. The situation became serious enough to make it necessary to ask for a landing party for the protection of the Japanese residents.

On May 29, the Chinese at Linkiang, on the northern bank of the Yalu, a place opened for foreign trade, objected to the entry of our Consul's party to take up their post there, and set fire to the Consulate building, razing it to the ground.

About the same time, or more correctly on May 28, Japan despatched a military force to Shantung, because the northward expedition of the southern revolutionary army threatened to disturb peace and order to the imminent danger to Japanese lives and property.

The Kuomintang headquarters at once engineered a country-wide agitation against Japan. Not only the party, but the various Government organs, including the police department, openly took active parts in it. The Kuomintang headquarters at Nanking issued on June 7 the celebrated Manifesto of 15 points, which the provincial headquarters were ordered at once to carry out. The 15 points are as follows:

"(1) We are opposed to the invasion of China by the Japanese militarists.

"(2) We are opposed to Japan's military expedition to Shantung.

"(3) The Japanese militarists have followed the example set by the British imperialists.

"(4) China's rights of freedom and equality do not go hand in hand with the Japanese imperialists.

"(5) Down with the Japanese imperialists who assist the Manchurian militarists.

"(6) Eliminate the Manchurian militarists who ask for Japanese help.

"(7) Turn out Japan from Shantung.

"(8) We call upon the people of Japan to oppose the militarists who have sent troops to Shantung.

"(9) Down with the Japanese imperialism that disturbs the peace of the world.

"(10) Japan's military expedition to Shantung exposes her imperialism.

"(11) Those who send troops to China are imperialists.

"(12) Japan's military expedition to Shantung is an obstacle to China's revolution.

"(13) Enforce economic boycott against the imperialists of Japan.

"(14) The militarists being supporters of imperialism, they are doomed to extinction.

"(15) Why does Japan consort with imperialism?"

The provincial Kuomintang issued instructions on the following points in July the same year:

"(1) Enforcement of economic boycott against Japan.

"(2) Alliance with oppressed minorities like the Koreans, the Formosans, the Loo Choo (Okinawa) people, the Annamites, etc.

"(3) Demolition of the combined front by the British, Japanese and American imperialism.

"(4) Extension of the counter-propaganda against the Japanese invasion of North China.

"(5) Interruption of the Japanese trade with other nations. (By means of alliance with foreign seamen, and sympathetic strikes throughout the world.)

"(6) Helping the Japanese colonies like Korea, Formosa and Loo Choo to liberate themselves from the Japanese dominancy.

"(7) Down with Chang Tso-lin."

Of the above mentioned items, particularly noteworthy is that relating to the prevention of concerted action between Japan and Great Britain. It is interesting to notice that the Chinese concentrate their attention upon these two Powers having the largest interests in China. As for the rest of the Powers, the Chinese are well aware that there is little chance of combined action among them, as their interests in China are divergent. They therefore plan to deal separately with Britain and Japan, hoping thereby to dispose of them more easily. Another point worth noticing is that these instructions as a whole are conspicuously marked by a Communistic flavour.

9. *Secong Shantung Expedition:* In the spring of 1928 the Nanking Government's army sent on an expedition against Peking, steadily pushed northward, and the commotion caused thereby threatened peace and order along the Shantung Railway and the vicinity of Tsinan. Consequently, with a view to protecting the lives and property of the Japanese residents on the spot, the Imperial Government despatched troops to the regions in question toward the end of April. On May 3, the Southern Chinese troops commenced looting, and our forces had no alternative but to fight them. The result was the so-called Tsinan Incident.

When Japan despatched the second expedition to Shantung, China protested against it on the various grounds such as the violation of international law, encroachment upon territorial rights and so forth. In this way she tried from the start to stir up an anti-Japanese agitation among her people. The Tsinan Incident added fuel to the fire of the anti-Japanese agitation thus started. On the National Humiliation Day commemorated on May 4, violent anti-Japanese demonstrations took place at Chinkiang, Ichang and other Yangtze ports. The Nanking Government took advantage of the situation to renounce the Sino-Japanese Commercial Treaty, and try a compromise with the Mukden authorities. These actions on the part of the Nanking Government added greatly to the bitterness of feeling against Japan. The anti-Japanese movement, with Shanghai as its headquarters, now spread to the whole of the Yangtze basin, the provinces of Kwantung and Fukien in the south and to Kirin in the north. It continued till May, 1929.

Various features about the anti-Japanese agitation just mentioned are worth notice. (1) It was far better organized than any previous agitations; (2) it was openly directed by the Government; (3) there was the Communist influence at the back of it; and (4) it was powerfully assisted by the cry for "the use of domestic goods."

10. *Attack upon Chinese in Korea, 1931:* In 1931 the persecution of the Korean farmers at Wangpaoshan in Manchuria by Chinese officials and farmers, led to collisions between Chinese and Koreans in Korea. The result was a fresh anti-Japanese movement under the leadership of the Kuomintang headquarters of Shanghai. On July

15, a communication was sent out to the different parts of the country in the name of the Anti-Japanese Merchants' Association of Shanghai, urging a wholesale economic rupture with Japan—a suggestion, which, it is needless to say, was regarded as an order from the Kuomintang, and which was, consequently, widely acted upon. The Imperial Government having brought this to the notice of the Nanking Government, the latter promised to stop the movement. But that was only a pretence; in reality the Nanking Government gave encouragement to the movement, which accordingly increased in its extent and intensity and continued till the outbreak of the Manchurian incident.

In starting and fanning the anti-Japanese movement, the Kuomintang and the press of China resorted to all sorts of unfounded allegations. For instance, the Kuomintang headquarters of Shanghai stated in a manifesto thus: "The attack upon Chinese residents in Korea did not proceed from the real intentions of the Korean people. The latter were simply victims of Japanese instigation, so that, far from regarding the Koreans with enmity and anger, they should be regarded with pity and sympathy. Standing on the common battle ground of the oppressed peoples, we should try to call forth their revolutionary consciousness against imperialism, to the end that we may have them as our comrades in our long and heroic struggle for existence against Japan." Similarly in a message issued by the propaganda section of the same headquarters, the Chinese people are urged "to arouse the revolutionary spirit of the Koreans, so that they shall join our people in an anti-imperialistic fight against Japan." It will not be difficult for anybody to discern the red hands of Communist agitators in these attempts to stir up Korean revolts against us.

11. *Since the Manchurian Trouble, 1932:* Upon the outbreak of the Manchurian trouble, the anti-Japanese agitations in various parts of China received a strong impetus. These agitations were conducted under the well-ordered guidance of the Anti-Japanese National Salvation Society. Acts of violence against Japanese residents became more and more frequent all over China. The National Salvation Society not only enforced the prohibition of the sale and distribution of Japanese goods, but compelled the repudiation of all existing contracts, the stoppage of all transactions with the Japanese, and the strike of all Chinese in Japanese service. In short, it was a complete severance of economic relations with Japan that the National Salvation Society demanded. In order to secure an efficient execution of all these plans, recourse was had to a forcible inspection of stores, intimidations and all sorts of violent sanctions. Even sentences of death were meted out to rebellious spirits. In these and other ways, not only the freedom of our people to reside and trade in China were seriously interfered with, but even their right of subsistence was denied them. It was in short a warfare without

recourse to actual hostilities. It was something not essentially different from a severance of relations between the two countries.

As a matter of fact, our Consulate at Chungking, Chengchow, Chengtu and Hankow had to be evacuated, together with our residents, because it became impossible to attend to business in safety. Brutal assaults upon our people grew frequent at all important centres like Shanghai, Hankow, Tientsin, Canton, Hongkong and so forth.

The Imperial Government repeatedly requested the central and provincial authorities of China to exercise proper control over the anti-Japanese agitations. But the National Government of China never showed itself willing to comply with our request. On the contrary, it was inclined to regard these illegal activities of its people and officials as expressions of patriotic sentiment, and encourage such activities. Anti-Japanese agitations grew more and more violent. From Canton, Tsingtao, Foochow and other places came reports of Japanese residents murdered, Japanese officials insulted, and the Japanese Imperial family abused by Chinese journals. Provocative activities were most frequent in Shanghai, where the climax was reached on January 18, 1932, by the murderous assault upon a party of Buddhist priests of the Nichiren sect, killing one of them and more or less seriously wounding the others. This incident enraged the Japanese residents to the limit. It was while feeling thus ran high among the Japanese that the fire was opened by the Chinese troops upon the Japanese landing party in a very provocative manner. Thus was started the Shanghai affair, which has eventually led to the despatch of military forces. The hostile sentiment still running very high among the Chinese, the situation does not warrant any optimistic view.

The anti-Japanese agitations mentioned above may be tabulated for purposes of easy reference as follows:—

No.	Year	Occasion	Regions affected	Duration Months
1	1908	"Tatsu Maru" Affair	South China	8
2	1909	Reconstruction of Mukden-Antung Railway	Manchuria	3
3	1915	"21 Demands"	All China	6
4	1919	Shantung Problem	All China and S. Seas	8
5	1923	Port Arthur and Dairen recovery agitation	N. and M. China	5
6	1925	Shanghai Affair	All China	5
7	1926	Kuo Sung-lin Affair	N. and M. China	5
8	1927	First Shantung Expedition	M. and S. China	5
9	1928	Tsinan Affair	M. and S. China and S. Seas	13
10	1931	Korean Affair	All China	—
11	1931	Manchurian Emergency	N. M. and S. China and S. Seas	—

5. Observations upon Anti-Japanese Agitations

1. *Anti-Japanese Sentiment Deep-rooted:* China's anti-Japanese movements are really not of a temporary nature, but they are fundamentally the outcome of

the deep-rooted traditionary sentiment of anti-foreignism. Of late, especially since the revolution of 1911, they have been organized into systematic state activities for the purpose of realising the basic objectives of the revolutionary diplomacy, such as the abolition of unequal treaties and the repudiation of imperialism. These agitations are thus deep-rooted in their origin and are carried out with a determined spirit. Unless the Kuomintang changes its fundamental policies or it ceases to exist, there is no hope of these state controlled agitations being stopped. When we remember that all children and youth in school are systematically taught and trained in anti-Japanism, we cannot but help shuddering to think of consequences of such education upon the future relations between Japan and China.

2. *Anti-Japanese Agitation as an Instrument of National Policy:* Anti-Japanese agitations in China are instruments of national policy conducted under the direct or indirect supervision of the Kuomintang, which, under the existing system of government in China, it is difficult to dissociate from the Administration. These agitations can never be regarded in the same light as activites conducted by individual free will. They not only contravene the letter and spirit of the existing treaty provisions between Japan and China, but they are contrary to the ideas of justice and friendliness. They are acts of hostility without the use of military force; they are more treacherous than open warfare.

Anti-Japanese agitations, as is obvious from

what has been stated in the preceding chapter, are started in connection with political or diplomatic questions, such, for instance, as the negotiations of the 21 Demands treaties or the despatch of military expeditions, the object kept in view being to bring pressure upon Japan's economic interests and thereby facilitate the carrying out of national policies.

3. *Motives not Always Clean:* These agitations being started in connection with politico-diplomatic questions, the Chinese pretend that they are nothing but expressions of patriotism. But when closely scrutinized, it will be found that the motives behind them are in many cases far from clean, as in the cases described below:

(a) Disgruntled Chinese policticians or hostile militarists instigate students and ruffians to start anti-Japanese agitations, ostensibly for patriotic objects, but really to further their political interests at home or abroad.

(b) A small group of Chinese capitalists engineer a boycott of Japanese goods, with a view to getting the better of their Japanese competitors and disposing their stock at enhanced prices.

(c) Other nationals are not slow to take advantage of these agitations for creating a profitable market for their own national goods.

4. *Anti-Japanese Agitations as a Trade:* A successful conduct of these agitations not only benefits ambitious young men as an aid for a rise in their social standing but brings them no small

amount of pecuniary profits. No wonder, then, that an increasing number of young people join these agitations to get honour and profits. As a matter of fact the conduct of an anti-Japanese agitation has become a trade and profession. It would require strenuous exertions on the part of the Government to extirpate so lucrative a profession. It will, therefore, most probably continue to attract to it a large number of ambitious young men.

5. *Duration of Anti-Japanese Agitations:* As may have been noticed from the table printed on a preceding page, anti-Japanese boycotts have not lasted very long. They have, in the past, come to an end after a few months or at the most about a year. The reason is, because the stock of the necessaries of life imported from Japan soon gets exhausted and the Chinese themselves begin to feel the pinch. But the boycott of Japanese goods is now inevitably accompanied by a movement for the encouragement of domestic manufactures. In addition to this, the method of the party control over anti-Japanese boycotts are being steadily improved, so that it is not safe to conclude that the duration of boycotts will not increase.

6. *Intensification of Boycotts:* Reference has so far been made only to the anti-Japanese boycotts of periodic durations. It must not be inferred therefrom that anti-Japanese boycotts will always be periodic affairs. Anti-Japanese organizations have become permanent institutions, and as a boycott has become a profitable trade, the pressure

brought to bear on the resident Japanese is growing more and more unbearable. The sufferings occasioned are beyond the power of the pen to describe. The spread of an anti-Japanese movement, it must be remembered, virtually deprives the resident Japanese not only of the freedom of residence and trade, but of the very right to live. It is, indeed, an act of inhumanity of far reaching consequences.

7. *Boycott and Third Parties:* It is China's time-honoured policy to play one power against another or, to use another hackneyed Chinese expression, to make friends with distant powers and attack near neighbours. Even today essentially the same policy is resorted to by Chinese whenever she finds herself confronted by international trouble. So long as there are third parties making gestures which may be interpreted as favourable to China, anti-foreign movements will never be eradicated in that country. It seems likely that all the Powers with important relations with her are fated one after another to be victimized by this historic diplomacy of China.

8. *Centre of Anti-Japanese Movements:* From the table mentioned elsewhere, it may have been observed that anti-Japanese movements have so far been mainly confined to China proper, particularly Middle and South China. In other words, they are most frequent where the Kuomintang influences are strong, whereas in Manchuria, which is comparatively free from such influences, anti-Japanese

movements formerly seldom took place, and in the rare cases where they did occur they have never been of a virulent character. This is of great significance in view of the fact that contentious problems have always been of frequent occurrence in Manchuria. But the sitution changed when Chang Hsueh-liang came upon the scene. Under his ill-omened regime, matters grew steadily worse until at last the climax was reached in the Mukden incident which led to the present Manchurian situation.

9. *Anti-Japanese Movement and Communism:* The communist revolutionary ideology which was introduced into China during the days of alliance with Soviet Russia, has permeated the party consciousness of the Kuomintang. It expresses itself conspicuously in the slogans of "down with imperialism" and "abolish unequal treaties." Its influence is particularly felt along the whole line of the anti-Japanese movement. The principle of communism which aims at demolishing capitalism and establishing in its stead a proletarian dictatorship possesses a delicate bond of sympathy with peoples struggling to free themselves from the yoke of an imperialistic state. The Comintern, as a matter of fact, is concentrating its energy on its attempts to utilize the anti-foreign psychology of the Chinese people for the purpose of attaining its own ends. In any case, it is impossible not to be struck by the presence of a communistic taint in the anti-Japanese movement.

10. *China is not a Law Ruled State:* For a

private organization like the Anti-Japanese Association to impose punishments upon individuals according to regulations not recognized by the law of the land, is tantamount to repudiating the authority of the state. The Anti-Japanese Association, for instance, compels merchants to boycott Japanese goods, and in case they refuse to obey its orders, they are subject to most cruel punishments in addition to the confiscation of the goods dealt in. Against such cruel and lawless actions on the part of private organizations, there is no security of person or property. Such an anarchic condition in China inevitably lowers her credit among nations, and forms a serious impediment to the attainment of her object in regard to the recovery of foreign settlements, and the abolition of the consular jurisdiction. The existence of conditions like that in China is a source of no small disappointment to those who sympathize with her nationalistic aspirations.

11. *Anti-Japanese Movement and Japanese Military Prowess:* It is a historical fact that localities with memories of Japanese military prowess are as a rule free from anti-Japanese movement. For instance, at Tsinan in Shantung where people still retain a vivid impression of the heroic achievements of the 6th Division in 1928 there has not been witnessed any serious attempts at boycotting Japanese goods in connection with the present Manchurian crisis. On the other hand, the anti-Japanese movement has been very strong in the

Yangtze valley, where the people as a whole have never had an opportunity of personally witnessing the might of Japanese army and consequently feel contempt for Japan.

12. *The Results of Anti-Japanese Boycott:* An anti-Japanese boycott is accompanied by a decrease of exports to China, a decline in the shipping trade, and a blow to Japanese enterprises in China. What demands special attention on our part in connection with a boycott, is the fact that it is nowadays accompanied by a movement for the encouragement of domestic manufactures. It seems important for our business world to make strenuous efforts to recover the lost ground when the boycott is over, by producing goods which in price and quality surpass Chinese commodities. It is scarcely necessary to add that it will be unwise for our business men to rely too much upon political settlements through governmental machinery.

13. *Stoppage of Boycott and Resumption of Sino-Japanese Negotiations:* The cessation of the economic boycott against Japan, should precede the resumption of negotiations for restoring the Sino-Japanese relations to a normal condition. In order to secure a definite cessation of the boycott, it will be necessary for China to abolish the anti-Japanese education and permanently interdict anti-Japanese movement. In other words, either the Kuomintang should reconstruct its party platform, or the Chinese people should undermine the Kuomintang and free themselves from the evils of the dictatorship of that party.

SUPPLEMENT

Introductory Note

The object of this Supplement is to furnish in a convenient form reference material in connection with the investigation of the subject dealt with in the text of the present pamphlet. It has been considered advisable to list only the more important of the incidents that have taken place during the past few years.

Considerable difficulty has been experienced in collecting necessary material. The compilers regret that material for the year 1931 is particularly incomplete. It may, however, be interesting to remark that the anti-Japanese movement had by that year become so widespread and at the same time so cleverly interwoven into the daily life of Chinese people that it is very hard to single out anti-Japanese actions from the general run of normal Chinese doings.

Illegal Actions Committed Against Japan in China

(*June 1925—October 1931*)

No.	Date		Region
1	June 2, '25.	Mob attacked Japanese Volunteers at Shanghai and looted Japanese residences.	Middle China
2	„ 4, '25.	Mob broke into Japanese cotton spinning mill at Shanghai and committed violence.	„
3	„ 7, '25.	Anti-Japanese students looted a Japanese hotel at Chungking.	„
4	„ 11, '25.	Mob destroyed 8 Japanese shops at Hankow, one Japanese being killed.	„
5	„ 12, '25.	20 Chinese soldiers assaulted a Japanese police officer in the railway zone near Tsaohokou on the Antung-Mukden railway.	Manchuria
6	„ 13, '25.	Thousands of Chinese forces moved into the British Concession at Kiukiang and destroyed and looted the Japanese Consulate and other places.	Middle China
7	„ 15, '25.	Mob committed violence in Chungking.	„
8	„ 18, '25.	Mob threw stones upon the Japanese Consulate in Chungking and committed violence.	„
9	„ 21, '25.	Japanese residents in Canton were shot to death and plundered.	South China
10	„ 22, '25.	A Japanese was assaulted at Wuhu by Chinese coolies on strike.	Middle China

No.	Date		Region
11	June 23, '25.	Anti-foreign agitators assaulted the Customs at Ningpo.	Middle China
12	„ 24, '25.	Coolies at Wuhu under pretention of anti-foreign movement looted and committed violence.	„
13	„ 25, '25.	Mob assaulted the Japanese Consulate at Chungking.	„
14	„ 26, '25.	Chinese soldiers and workmen assaulted Japanese naval men in Chungking.	„
15	July 1, '25	Anti-Japanese agitators in Swatow looted and committed violence.	South China
16	„ 2, '25.	Chinese soldiers raided Japanese residences at Tsinan and committed violence.	North China
17	„ 8, '25.	Members of the National Revenge Society at Changsha interfered with coaling and victualling a Japanese warship.	Middle China
18	„ 14, '25.	Coolies assaulted a Japanese subject at Wuhu.	„
19	„ 15, '25.	Japanese merchants in Nanking had their goods seized.	„
20	„ 15, '25.	Japanese merchants were assaulted in Nanking.	„
21	„ 21, '25.	A Japanese physician was assaulted in Nanking.	„
22	„ 24, '25.	Coolies at Mawei, on intimidation by students, went on strike to bring landing and loading of ships to a standstill.	South China
23	Aug. 11, '25.	Chinese workmen assaulted the Yutai Cotton Spinning Mill at Tientsin, destroying machinery, etc.	North China
24	„ 19, '25.	Chinese students sank a Japanese boat at Foochow	South China

No.	Date		Region
25	Sept. 12, '25.	Chinese military guards at Tsinan unlawfully broke into Japanese residences.	North China
26	Oct. 18, '25.	The Mukden army at Chenkiang placed a Japanese boat under detention.	Middle China
27	„ 31, '25.	Soldiers belonging to General Yang Sen unlawfully boarded a Japanese ship at Wanhsien.	„
28	Nov. 14, '25.	The Chinese naval authorities at Shanghai issued an order prohibiting nightly movement of foreign shipping.	„
29	„ 18, '25.	General San Chuang-fang ordered seizure of the Salt Gabelle in Shanghai.	„
30	Dec. 7, '25.	Japanese were plundered in Chinchow by soldiers of the Mukden army.	North China
31	„ 12, '25.	Sergeant Namba was taken prisoner by Chinese soldiers while repairing telegraph line at Yangtsun, and killed after imprisonment.	„
32	„ 15, '25.	The strikers in Canton subjected a Japanese boat to a search.	South China
33	„ 20, '25.	The Nationalist army cut off the Japanese telegraph line near Tangku.	North China
34	„ 23, '25.	The Japanese destroyer "Tsuta" was fired upon below Tientsin.	„
35	„ 25, '25.	Students in Nanking, having passed a resolution against the Japanese military expedition in Manchuria, interfered with Japanese employing horse carriages and rikisha.	Middle China
36	„ 26, '25.	Students in Nanking threatened to attack the Japanese Consulate.	„

No.	Date		Region
37	Jan. 1, '26.	The Japanese Consulate at Changsha was demanded to take down the national flag.	Middle China
38	„ 13, '26.	The Japanese shipping at Swatow were deprived of labour for handling cargo.	South China
39	„ 27, '26.	Sergeant Tanaka was arrested by Chinese soldiers while repairing the telegraph line at Changli.	North China
40	Feb. 10, '26.	The Nationalist army dropped a bomb upon a Japanese steamship off Taku.	„
41	„ 16, '26.	The Japanese steamship "Tokei Maru" was detained by strikers of Canton.	South China
42	„ 22, '26.	On account of strikers seizing goods landed from ships, the Canton Customs announced its closing.	„
43	„ 22, '26.	The National Avenge Society of Changsha began boycotting Japanese goods.	Middle China
44	„ 28, '26.	A workman employed by a Shanghai cotton spinning mill was assaulted and killed by strikers.	„
45	Mar. 3, '26.	The telegraph line laid by the Japanese army was cut off between Lanchow and Tangshan.	North China
46	„ 8, '26.	General Yeh Kai-hsin's army opened fire on a Japanese steamship proceeding down stream near Hsiangtan, causing it to stop.	Middle China
47	„ 9, '26.	The Nationalist Army blockaded the Taku water-way.	North China
48	„ 12, '26.	The Nationalist Army began to inspect Japanese merchant marine at Taku.	„

No.	Date		Region
49	Mar. 12, '26.	The National Army at Taku opened fire on a Japanese destroyer.	North China
50	,, 25, '26.	Anti-Japanese agitators in Changsha, in course of a demonstration, broke into the Japanese Consulate and committed violence.	Middle China
51	,, 28, '26.	The Japanese steamship "Genko Maru" was fired upon by Chinese soldiers at Yochow.	,,
52	Apr. 8, '26.	A bomb was thrown into the Japanese Consulate-General at Shanghai.	,,
53	,, 9, '26.	At Wanhsien harbour dues, and trade protection tax were unlawfully imposed, with also orders for loans for military expense.	,,
54	,, —, '26.	Beginning this month all Japanese shipping plying on the Chungking line were ordered to transport Chinese soldiers free of charge.	,,
55	,, 24, '26.	A steam launch belonging to Tai Sheng Chang was interned at Yochow.	,,
56	,, 28, '26.	Anti-Japanese agitators broke into the Japanese Consulate-General at Chengtu and committed violence.	,,
57	May 9, '26.	A Japanese civilian resident at Hweili was shot and killed by a Chinese soldier.	North China
58	,, 29, '26.	A mutiny occurring at Chulu, Fengtien Province, Japanese residences were looted.	Manchuria
59	,, 30, '26.	Crowds, observing the anniversary of "The May 30th Incident" in Shanghai, flowed into Nanking Road and assaulted trams and motorcars.	Middle China

No.	Date		Region
60	June 5, '26.	Workmen committed violence at the Naigai Cotton Spinning Mill, Shanghai.	Middle China
61	,, 22, '26.	A Chinese boat hired by the Japanese gunboat "Toba" was plundered at Wanhsien.	,,
62	,, 24, '26.	Workmen committed violence at the Naigai Cotton Spinning Mill, Shanghai.	,,
63	,, 25, '26.	Chinese soldiers boarded the Japanese steamship "Unyo Maru" at Chungking, demanding to be carried free of charge.	,,
64	July 12, '26.	The steamboat "Ashido Maru" belonging to the firm of Tai Sheng Chang was fired upon by Chinese soldiers near Changsha.	,,
65	,, 12, '26.	The Japanese steamship "Kogen Maru" was fired upon on the lower Yangtze.	,,
66	,, 26, '26.	The same steamship was subjected to inspection by Chinese military men at Hsiangyin.	,,
67	Aug. 2, '26.	The Japanese steamship "Unyo Maru" was fired upon at Wanhsien.	,,
68	,, 3, '26.	The army under General Tang Sheng-chih issued an order restricting the traffic of foreign shipping on the Yangtze river.	,,
69	,, 10, '26.	A second notice was given for restriction of the traffic of foreign shipping on the Yangtze river.	,,
70	,, 20, '26.	The Japanese gunboat "Sumida" was fired upon below Yingtien.	,,
71	,, 23, '26.	The Japanese steamship "Ryobu Maru" was fired upon while moving downstream from Changsha.	,,

No.	Date		Region
72	Aug. 24, '26.	The Japanese steamship "Genko Maru" was fired upon at Hsinti.	Middle China
73	„ 25, '26.	The Japanese steamship "Daikichi Maru" was subjected to inspection at Chenglingchi.	„
74	„ 25, '26.	The commander of the Southern army at Yochow issued a notice restricting water traffic at Chenglingchi.	„
75	„ 26, '26.	Notice was given of mines having been laid on the Changsha route.	„
76	Sept. 4, '26.	The Japanese steamship "Nanyo Maru" was fired upon near Huangchow.	„
77	„ 5, '26.	The Provincial Government of Honan issued a notice restricting traffic on the Changsha line.	„
78	„ 8, '26.	The Japanese gunboat "Katada" was fired upon near Hanyang.	„
79	„ 9, '26.	The Japanese steamship "Gakuyo Maru" was fired upon near Huangchow.	„
80	„ 9, '25.	The Canton Strikers' Association began to inspect ships' log-books and fine them for having entered Hongkong.	South China
81	„ 15, '26.	A bomb was brought into the Japanese Consulate-General at Shanghai.	Middle China
82	„ 16, '26.	The Southern Army issued a notice restricting river traffic with a view to blockading Wuchang.	„
83	„ 16, '26.	The Southern Army at Hankow began to inspect postal correspondence.	„
84	„ 16, '26.	The Cantonese Army issued a notice restricting the entry of foreign shipping into Swatow.	South China

— 238 —

No.	Date		Region
85	Sept. 17, '26.	The Southern Army issued a notice restricting water traffic in the direction of Chenglingchi.	Middle China
86	„ 17, '26.	The Japanese steamship "Daikichi Maru" was fired upon at Chenglingchi.	„
87	„ 18, '26.	Chen Kung-po, the Commercial Commissioner of the Nanking Government, demanded all foreign vessels to leave Hankow.	„
88	„ 18, '26.	Ships began to be inspected at Liuchiamiao.	„
89	„ 19, '26.	Japanese ships were fired upon near Hanyang.	„
90	„ 21, '26.	The anti-Northern expeditionary army issued a notice of inspection of shipping both above and below Hankow.	„
91	„ 21, '26.	The Japanese steamship "Taikyo Maru" was fired upon at Wuchang.	„
92	„ 29, '26.	The Japanese steamship "Rozan Maru" was fired on by a Chinese warship near Whangpoo, Canton.	South China
93	Oct. 2, '26.	The Japanese steamship "Hoyo Maru" was fired on below Huangchow.	Middle China
94	„ 2, '26.	The Japanese steamship "Shoko Maru" was fired on above Hanyang.	„
95	„ 2, '26.	The Japanese steamship "Zuiyo Maru" was fired on before the mooring place at Huangchow.	„
96	„ 4, '26.	The Japanese steamship "Shoko Maru" was fired upon from the side of Hanyang.	„
97	„ 5, '26.	The Japanese steamship "Taikyo Maru" was fired on above Hanyang.	„

No.	Date		Region
98	Oct. 7, '26.	The Japanese steamship "Buyo Maru" was fired on near Hanyang from the side of Wuchang.	Middle China
99	,, 7, '26.	The Japanese steamship "Genko Maru" was fired on between Wuchang and Hanyang.	,,
100	,, 8, '26.	The Japanese steamship "Taikyo Maru" was fired on near Hanyang.	,,
101	,, 9, '26.	The Japanese steamship "Genko Maru" was fired on at the shore of Hanyang.	,,
102	,, 11, '26.	The Japanese steamship "Daitei Maru" was fired on from the left side of the river 8 miles below Tayeh.	,,
103	,, 11, '26.	Diplomatic Commissioner Chen Kung-po of Hankow notified restriction of river traffic near Wuchang and Hankow.	,,
104	,, 12, '26.	The Japanese steamships "Toyoura Maru" and "Hoyo Maru" were fired upon at Chichow.	,,
105	,, 12, '26.	The Japanese steamship "Zuiyo Maru" was fired on near Tienchiachen.	,,
106	,, 13, '26.	The Japanese steamship "Kasuga Maru" was fired on at Tienchiachen.	,,
107	,, 5, '26.	The Nationalist Government at Canton notified imposition of an unlawful tax of 2.5 percent on all imports.	South China
108	,, 15, '26.	The Japanese steamship "Kiyo Maru" was fired on at Chungchow.	Middle China
109	,, 24, '26.	The Japanese gunboat "Ataka" was fired on at Chenglingchi.	,,
110	,, 9, '26.	Official notice was issued prohibiting river traffic in the region of Chenglingchi.	,,

No.	Date		Region
111	Nov. 18, '26.	The Japanese steamship "Shoko Maru" was caused to stop by gun fire about 45 miles below Changsha and was demanded to pay $15,000. The captain was then carried off as prisoner.	Middle China
112	Dec. 14, '26.	About 20 soldiers of the Szechuan Army broke into the Nisshin Steamship Company at Ichang.	”
113	” 17, '26.	Bluejacket Katada was shot dead at Ichang by soldiers of the Southern Army.	”
114	” 19, '26.	The Chinese troops at Chuangte demanded the Japanese residents to pay for military expense.	”
115	” 28, '26.	A Japanese resident at Hankow was carried off by Chinese bandits.	”
116	Jan. 7, '27.	Armed police men and students at Hankow entered the Japanese Concession and committed violence.	”
117	” 12, '27.	The Peking Government declared imposition of a 2.5 percent super-tax by the Chinese Customs.	North China
118	” 13, '27.	The Mukden authorities notified imposition outside the open port of double and consumption taxes.	”
119	” 14, '27.	Kiukiang began to levy a super-tax of 2.5 percent.	Middle China
120	” 24, '27.	Armed Chinese soldiers unlawfully boarded the Japanese steamship "Shoko Maru" at Shasi.	”
121	Feb. 1, '27.	Changsha began to levy a 2.5 percent super-tax.	”

No.	Date		Region
122	Feb. 1, '27.	Chinese military troops tried unlawfully to board the Japanese steamship "Buryo Maru" at Ichang.	,,
123	,, 5, '27.	The Southern Army notified renewal of inspection of ships at Chenglingchi.	,,
124	,, 5, '27.	Kiukiang began to levy an additional tax for use of the wharf.	Middle China
125	,, 9, '27.	The Japanese steamship "Shoko Maru" was fired upon by Chinese soldiers below Ichang.	,,
126	,, 10, '27.	The Japanese steamship "Katsuragi Maru" was subjected by threat to inspection near Nanking.	,,
127	,, 11, '27.	A super-tax began to be compulsorily exacted at Tientsin	North China
128	,, 14, '27.	Chinese soldiers caused themselves to be carried free of charge between Kiukiang and Hankow by the Japanese steamship "Daikichi Maru"	,,
129	,, 17, '27.	Chinese soldiers boarded the Japanese steamship "Joyo Maru" for unpaid passage between Kiukiang and Hankow.	,,
130	,, 19, '27.	The General Industrial Association of Shanghai began to strike.	,,
131	,, 20, '27.	Chinese soldiers boarded the Japanese steamship "Joyo Maru" for free transportation between Kiukiang and Hankow.	,,
132	,, 22, '27.	Chinese soldiers boarded the Japanese steamship "Hoyo Maru" for free transportation between Kiukinag and Hankow.	,,
133	,, 24, '27.	Restriction was notified of navigation at Woosung.	,,

No.	Date		Region
134	Mar. 5, '27.	The Japanese steamship "Nanyo Maru" was fired on by the Southern Army above Tatung.	North China
135	„ 9, '27.	The Japanese steamships "Buryo Maru" and "Tairyo Maru" were forced at the point of arms to take Chinese soldiers aboard at Ichang.	„
136	„ 10, '27.	The Japanese steamship "Nanyo Maru" was fired on about 7 miles below Wuhu.	„
137	„ 11, '27.	The Hankow authorities declared imposition of an unlawful tax.	Middle China
138	„ 12, 27.	Armed police men tried to carry off an employe of the Japanese Consulate-General at Hankow.	„
139	„ 17, '27.	A Japanese naval officer was carried off by Chinese soldiers at Putung.	„
140	„ 18, '27.	Attempt was made by Chinese soldiers to intern the Japanese steamship "Dairi Maru" at Chenkiang.	„
141	„ 22, '27.	Japanese residences in Hankow were assaulted by mob.	„
142	„ 22, '27.	The steam launch belonging to the Japanese destroyer "Amatsukaze" was fired on at Woosung by plain-clothed soldiers.	„
143	„ 22, '27.	Plain-clothed Chinese soldiers committed violence at the Toyoda Cotton Spinning Company, Shanghai.	„
144	„ 24, '27.	A number of soldiers of the Southern Army assaulted the Japanese Consulate at Nanking, committing unspeakable atrocities and killing some Japanese.	„
145	„ 24, '27.	Soldiers of the Southern Army looted the hulk of the Nisshin Kisen Kaisha at Nanking.	„

No.	Date		Region
146	Apr. 3, '27.	Chinese mob broke into the Japanese Concession in Hankow.	Middle China
147	„ 6, '27.	Anti-Japanese movement broke out in Changsha.	„
148	„ 7, '27.	Plain-clothed Chinese soldiers fired on Japanese sentinels at Shanghai.	„
149	„ 11, '27.	Chinese workmen raided the Japanese Consulate and residences in the Concession at Suchow, looting at places.	„
150	„ 15, '27.	The Chinese military at Tientsin subjected the Japanese steamship "Choan Maru" to inspection.	North China
151	„ 17, '27.	The Japanese destroyer No. 10 was fired on near Nanking by Chinese soldiers.	Middle China
152	„ 18, '27.	The Japanese steamship "Daitoku Maru" was fired on by Chinese soldiers below Chenkiang.	„
153	„ 18, '27.	The Chinese Diplomatic Commissioners in Shanghai requested Japan, Britain and America to stop the navigation of their warships and merchant marine on the Yangtze.	
154	„ 25, '27.	The farm of Toa Kangyo Koshi, a Japanese company at Hsinminhsien, Fengtien Province, was raided by Chinese mob.	Manchuria
155	„ 27, '27.	A Korean police inspector was beaten by mob at Maoerhshan.	„
156	„ 27, '27.	Order was issued restricting entry of foreign ships into the port of Amoy.	South China
157	„ 30, '27.	Order was issued restricting entry of foreign shipping into Woosung.	Middle China

No.	Date		Region
158	May 1, '27.	The Japanese consulate was assaulted by Chinese mob.	South China
159	" 7, '27.	The Japanese destroyer "Hasu" and "Yomogi" of the 28th flotilla, with the aide-de-camp to His Majesty aboard, was fired upon below Chenkiang by the Southern Army.	Middle China
160	" 8, '27.	The Kirin Army at Shanhaikwan pulled down the notices posted by the Japanese army.	North China
161	" 10, '27.	A motor ship belonging to a Formosan native was attacked by Chinese pirates off Swatow.	South China
162	" 11, '27.	The Japanese gunboat "Toba" was fired on by the Southern Army about 5 miles above Chenkiang.	Middle China
163	" 12, '27.	The Japanese gunboat "Sumida" was fired on by the Southern Army about 8 miles above Chenkiang.	"
164	" 13, '27.	The Chinese Naval Command at Shanghai caused anti-Japanese agitations concerning the repairs ordered on a man-of-war of the Mukden Government at the South Manchuria Railway Company's dockyard.	"
165	" 14, '27.	A Chinese warship demonstrated off Lungkou to intimidate Japanese fishing craft.	North China
166	" 17, '27.	The Japanese destroyer "Momo" was fired on while mooring at Chenkiang.	Middle China
167	" 22, '27.	The Japanese 24th destroyer flotilla was fired on by both Northern and Southern Armies while passing off the Kiangyin forts.	"
168	June 6, '27.	Chinese soldiers forced themselves aboard a Japanese ship at Haichow.	"

No.	Date		Region
169	June 7, '27.	Routed soldiers of General Sun Chuang-fang commandeered a Japanese ship at Haichow.	Middle China
170	„ 9, '27.	Japanese residents at Haichow were plundered.	„
171	„ 10, '27.	The Japanese steamship "Kokai Maru" was plundered at Haichow by the Southern Army.	„
172	„ 10, '27.	The Japanese steamship "Hoyo Maru" was fired on by the Southern Army below Tayeh.	„
173	„ 14, '27.	Chinese soldiers tried to force themselves aboard a Japanese steamship at Wuhu.	„
174	„ 22, '27.	Five Chinese soldiers boarded the Japanese steamship "Zuiyo Maru" at Chenkiang without payment.	„
175	„ 29, '27.	Anti-Japanese mass meeting was held at Woosung, accompanied by some acts of violence by Chinese.	„
176	„ 29, '27.	The Japanese steamships "Unyo Maru" and "Kiyo Maru" were fired on by Chinese soldiers at Ichang.	„
177	„ —, '27.	The Mukden authorities applied pressure upon "Seikyo Jiho," a Japanese owned newspaper.	Manchuria
178	July 1, '27.	The Japanese steamship "Gakuyo Maru" was fired on above Ichang.	Middle China
179	„ 1, '27.	The Nanking Government declared imposition of special super-taxes.	„
180	„ 9, '27.	Chinese soldiers broke into a Japanese owned building at Ichang.	„
181	„ 11, '27.	The Anti-Japanese Boycott Commission in Shanghai interfered with transportation of Japanese merchandise.	„

No.	Date		Region
182	July 12, '27.	A Japanese gendarme at the Tientsin railway station was fired on by Chinese soldiers.	North China
183	„ 12, '27.	The Japanese steamship "Taikyo Maru" was fired on 7 miles below Ichang.	Middle China
184	„ 15, '27.	Chinese civilians and soldiers threw stones at police men of the Executive Committee of the International Settlement.	„
185	„ 17, '27.	Notice was given of inspection to be made of shipping at Anking.	„
186	„ 17, '27.	Notice was issued restricting river traffic between Kiukiang and Matang.	Middle China
187	„ 19, '27.	A Sino-Japanese military clash at Tsinan.	North China
188	„ 20, '27.	Japanese bluejackets had a clash with Chinese rickshaw coolies at Tsingtao.	„
189	„ 20, '27.	Chinese soldiers boarded the Japanese steamship "Taikyo Maru" at Hankow without payment.	Middle China
190	„ 22, '27.	The Southern Army issued notice of inspection to be made of all shipping at Ichang.	„
191	„ 24, '27.	Officials of the Salt Gabelle at Ichang, accompanied by armed Chinese soldiers, inspected a Japanese steamship.	„
192	Aug. 8, '27.	The captain of the Japanese steamship "Hirao Maru" was carried off at Haichow.	„
193	„ 9, '27.	Chinese soldiers forced themselves aboard the Japanese steamship "Dairi Maru" at Kiukiang.	„

— 247 —

No.	Date		Region
194	Aug. 10, '27.	The captain and members of the crew of the Japanese steamship "Hirao Maru" were carried off at Haichow.	Middle China
195	„ 20, '27.	The Japanese steamship "Gakuyo Maru" was prohibited navigation at Chenkiang by the Southern Army.	„
196	„ 22, '27.	The Japanese steamships "Daitei Maru" and "Gessan Maru" were fired upon about 6 miles above Chenkiang.	
197	„ 23, '27.	Workmen at the Penchihu coal mines started anti-Japanese agitations.	Manchuria
198	„ 24, '27.	A steamship belonging to a Formosan native was unlawfully stopped by a Chinese man-of-war at Swatow.	South China
199	„ 24, '27.	The Japanese steamships "Jyoyo Maru" and "Miyoshi Maru" were fired upon about 5 miles above Wuhu.	Middle China
200	„ 26, '27.	The Japanese destroyer "Kashi" and the hospital ship "Kasado Maru" were fired upon about 2 miles above Nanking.	„
201	„ 27, '27.	Chinese soldiers broke into the office of the Nihon Kinkai Yusen at Wuhu.	„
202	„ 28, '27.	Armed police men at Chungking interfered with cargo work for the Nisshin Kisen ships.	„
203	„ 29, '27.	The Japanese steamship "Jyoyo Maru" was fired on at the upper end of Bar Pheasant.	„
204	Sept. —, '27.	Beginning this month illegal action began to be directed against the Nanchang-Kiukiang Railway and the Hang Yeh Ping Mining Company.	„

No.	Date		Region
205	Sept. 1, '27.	The Japanese destroyer "Hinoki" was fired on at Chunglungchow.	Middle China
206	" 4, '27.	Anti-Japanese agitations started in Mukden on a very large scale, causing more than 120 cases of violence before they were ended on Sept. 14.	Manchuria
207	" 4, '27.	The Japanese destroyer "Hinoki" was fired on below Hsiasanshan Island.	Middle China
208	" 4, '27.	The steamship "Tensan Maru" of the Mitsui firm was fired on at Hsiasanshan Island.	"
209	" 11, '27.	Chinese police men of Mukden committed violence against a Japanese police officer.	Manchuria
210	" 12, '27.	The 18th destroyer flotilla of the Imperial Navy was fired on below Woosung.	Middle China
211	" 12, '27.	Chinese mob threw stones at Japanese police officers in Mukden.	Manchuria
212	" 13, '27.	Two Japanese passengers aboard the Japanese steamship "Otaka Maru" were carried off by bandits at Haichow.	Middle China
213	" 14, '27.	Japanese shops at Shihchiachuang were plundered.	North China
214	" 21, '27.	Chang Tsung-chang seized the Salt Gabelle at Chefoo.	"
215	" 21, '27.	Chinese soldiers fired on and wounded a Japanese sentinel at Hankow.	"
216	" 24, '27.	A member of the Japanese naval landing party at Shanghai was detained by the Chinese police.	"
217	" 26, '27.	The Japanese steamship "Jyoyo Maru" was subjected to inspection at Shanghai.	"

No.	Date		Region
218	Sept. 28, '27.	A member of the Japanese landing party at Swatow was fired on with revolver by a Chinese soldier.	South China
219	" 28, '27.	The Japanese steamship "Gakuyo Maru" was subjected to inspection at Shanghai.	Middle China
220	Oct. —, '27.	Beginning in October pressure was continually brought to bear upon the Koreans in the provinces of Fengtien and Kirin.	Manchuria
221	" 5, '27.	The Japanese steamship "Kiyo Maru" was fired on at Ichang.	Middle China
222	" 10, '27.	General Chang Tsung-chang ordered the Sino-Japanese firm of Lu Tai Kungsu to supply coal for Chinese war vessels.	North China
223	" 22, '27.	The Japanese steamships "Joyo Maru," "Niitaka Maru" and "Icho Maru" were fired on above Tichiang.	Middle China
224	" 22, '27.	Discussions were made concerning restriction of the Yangtze navigation about Tichiang and Tungling.	Middle China
225	" 25, '27.	The Nisshin Kisen Kaisha steamship "Choyo Maru" was fired on at Kweichow.	"
226	" 27, '27.	The Japanese steamship "Hokuto Maru" was visited by bandits at Maanshan for blackmail.	"
227	" 28, '27.	The "Kiyo Maru" and "Unyo Maru" were fired on at Ichang.	"
228	" 29, '27.	The steamship "Hoyo Maru" was fired on at Matouchen.	"
229	" 30, '27.	The steamship "Nanyo Maru" was fired on at Wuhsueh.	"
230	Nov. 1, '27.	The steamship "Taikyo Maru" was fired on at Ichang and Shasi.	"

No.	Date		Region
231	Nov. 5, '27.	Japanese nationals were arrested at Tangshan by Mukden soldiers.	North China
232	„ 6, '27.	The steamship "Choyo Maru" was fired on at Wanliu.	Middle China
233	„ 7, '27.	The Japanese gunboat "Katada" was fired on about 30 miles above Shasi.	„
234	„ 8, '27.	The steamship "Unyo Maru" was fired on at Foushih.	„
235	„ 10, '27.	The steamships "Tensan Maru" and "Daini Daishin Maru" were fired on near Tienchiachen.	„
236	„ 10, '27.	The Japanese destroyer "Urakaze" was fired on at Tienchiachen.	„
237	„ 12, '27.	The destroyer "Urakaze" was fired on at Chichow.	„
238	„ 14, '27.	The steamship "Nanyo Maru" was fired on near the breakwater of Woosung.	„
239	„ 14, '27.	Soldiers of the Szechuan army broke into Japanese residences at Shasi.	„
240	„ 16, '27.	Chinese soldiers unlawfully boarded the Nisshin Kisen Kaisha steamship "Matsu Maru" at Shasi.	„
241	„ 17, '27.	Orders were issued for inspection of merchant ships at Chenglingchi and Yochow, and also for restriction of navigation.	„
242	„ 17, '27.	Notice was given of restriction of navigation on the Whangpoo at Canton.	South China
243	„ 18, '27.	Three Japanese vessels were fired upon on their entry into the Whangpoo at Canton.	„

No.	Date		Region
244	Nov. 20, '27.	The Nisshin Kisen Kaisha steamship "Take Maru" was fired on near Hankow.	Middle China
245	" 20, '27.	The Nisshin Kisen Kaisha steamship "Tairyo Maru" was fired on near Hankow.	"
246	" 20, '27.	The Nisshin Kisen Kaisha steamship "Choyo Maru" was fired on at Hantsui.	"
247	" 20, '27.	The tug boat of the Mitsui firm was fired on at Paotaochow.	"
248	" 22, '27.	Restriction was made of navigation at Humen, Canton.	South China
249	" 23, '27.	The Nanking Government declared abrogation of the "unequal" treaties.	Middle China
250	" 23, '27.	Chinese mob fired on Japanese soldiers.	"
251	" 24, '27.	The Japanese steamship "Torai Maru" was unlawfully taxed at Tsingtao.	North China
252	" 24, '27.	Victualling the Japanese warship at Changsha was interfered with.	Middle China
253	Dec. 2, '27.	A steamship belonging to the firm of Tai Sheng Chang was attacked by bandits at Nanhuchow.	"
254	" 2, '27.	Chinese troops attempted to force their passage through the Japanese concession at Hankow.	"
255	" 7, '27.	A Japanese boat was detained off Haichow by General Chen Lu's Army.	"
256	" 9, '27.	Notice was given of restriction of navigation between Chenglingchi and Yochow.	"
257	" 14, '27.	The Nisshin Kisen Kaisha steamship "Zuiyo Maru" was unlawfully stopped off Woosung.	"

— 252 —

No.	Date		Region
258	Dec. 15, '27.	The Nisshin Kisen Kaisha steamship "Karyo Maru" was fired on at Ichang.	Middle China
259	„ 16, '27.	The agitations against the Koreans in Manchuria began to show greater activity.	Manchuria
260	„ 16, '27.	Officials of the Ichang Customs tried to examine members of the crew of the Nisshin Kisen Kaisha steamship "Buyo Maru."	Middle China
261	„ 19, '27.	The steamship "Tairyo Maru" was unlawfully subjected to inspection at Ichang by Chinese soldiers.	„
262	„ 30, '27.	Passage to the Nisshin hulk at Shasi was blocked by bandits.	„
263	Jan. 1, '28.	The Japanese steamship "Shin Oki Maru" was subjected to unlawful inspection on her entry into Haichow.	„
264	„ 2, '28.	The steamship "Daini Oki Maru" was unlawfully inspected at Haichow.	„
265	„ 3, '28.	The steamship "Toan Maru" was unlawfully inspected on her entry into Haichow.	„
266	3, '28.	The Nisshin Kisen Kaisha steamship "Kashiwa Maru" was fired on at Chienlihsien.	„
267	„ 11, '28.	The Japanese national flag was insulted at Harbin.	Manchuria
268	„ 13, '28.	The Nisshin Kisen Kaisha steamships "Toyo Maru," "Genko Maru" and "Kashiwa Maru" were fired on at Shasi.	Middle China
269	„ 22, '28.	The Nisshin Kisen Kaisha steamships "Buyo Maru" and "Shoko Maru" were fired on at Paotaochow.	„
270	„ 26, '28.	Chinese soldiers broke into Japanese residences at Changsha.	„

— 253 —

No.	Date		Region
271	Jan. 29, '28.	The Nisshin Kisen Kaisha steamship "Karyo Maru" was fired on above Ichang.	Middle China
272	Feb. —, '28.	The Japanese nationals resident along the southern branch of the Chinese Eastern Railway were ordered to evacuate.	Manchuria
273	,, 2, '28.	The Nisshin Kisen Kaisha steamship "Ume Maru" was fired on in the upper reaches of the Yangtze.	Middle China
274	,, 3, '28.	The Nisshin Kisen Kaisha steamships "Toyo Maru" and "Genko Maru" were fired on near Hsiachewan.	,,
275	,, 27, '28.	The Nisshin Kisen Kaisha steamship "Karyo Maru" was fired on while proceeding up the river from Ichang.	,,
276	Mar. 5, '28.	The Nisshin Kisen Kaisha steamship "Buyo Maru" was fired on at Ichang.	,,
277	,, 5, '28.	Anti-Japanese agitations began at Amoy.	South China
278	,, 5, '28.	Officials of the Bureau of Public Peace in Shanghai caused the wharf of the Han Yeh Pin to be closed.	Middle China
279	,, 7, '28.	A Chinese lighter was found flying the Japanese national flag near Taipankou in the middle section of the Yangtze river.	,,
280	,, 10, '28.	Chinese coolies assaulted a Japanese naval man at Kiukiang.	,,
281	,, 12, '28.	The Nisshin Kisen Kaisha steamship "Nanyo Maru" was fired on at Wuhsueh.	,,
282	,, 14, '28.	The Nisshin Kisen Kaisha steamship "Kayo Maru" was fired on near Ichang.	,,

No.	Date		Region
283	Mar. 15, '28,	A steam launch belonging to the firm of Tai Sheng Chang was attacked by bandits near Lulinhsin.	Middle China
284	" 17, '28.	The Nisshin Kisen Kaisha steamship "Kayo Maru" was fired on at Fenghsianghsia while proceeding from Ichang to Chungking.	"
285	" 24, '28.	The Nisshin Kisen Kaisha steamship "Kayo Maru" was fired on in the lower Yangtze while proceeding to Ichang.	"
286	" 26, '28.	The Nisshin Kisen Kaisha steamship "Toyo Maru" and "Taikyo Maru" were fired on while proceeding to Ichang.	"
287	" 27, '28.	A Chinese police boat interfered with unloading work of the Japanese steamship "Hozan Maru."	South China
288	Apr. 6, '28.	The Nisshin Kisen Kaisha steamships "Buyo Maru" and "Matsu Maru" were fired on while proceeding to Ichang.	Middle China
289	" 9, '28.	The Nisshin Kisen Kaisha steamship "Kashiwa Maru," on her way down from Hankow, was subjected to inspection above Woosung.	"
290	" 10, '28.	Chinese soldiers interfered with business at Japanese shops in Huoshanling, a town east of Changchun.	Manchuria
291	" 11, '28.	The rolling stock of the Taonan-Angangchi Railway was transferred to the Mukden-Hailung Railway.	"
292	" 14, '28.	The Chinese authorities caused the telephone between Harbin and Changchun to be cut off.	"

— 255 —

No.	Date		Region
293	Apr. 15, '28.	The Nisshin Kisen Kaisha steamship "Kayo Maru" was fired on while proceeding up the Yangtze to Chungking.	Middle China
294	„ 21, '28.	A Japanese ship was seized by the Southern Army at Haichow.	„
295	„ 29, '28.	Soldiers of the Northern Army in route looted Japanese warehouses at Tsinan.	North China
296	May 4, '28.	The Japanese troops trying to stop the looting at Tsinan by soldiers of the Southern Army met with armed resistance.	„
297	„ 8, '28.	The Japanese landing force in Shanghai was fired on by Chinese.	Middle China
298	„ 8, '28.	Armed conflict again took place at Tsinan between Japanese and Chinese forces.	North China
299	„ 10, '28.	Japanese residents at Shitouchengtze, Kirin Province, were demanded to evacuate.	Manchuria
300	„ 11, '28.	Provisions for the Japanese destroyer "Yanagi," moored at Wuhu, were seized by the Anti-Japanese Society.	Middle China
301	„ 12, '28.	Students of the Chekiang University at Hangchow committed violence against a Japanese police officer.	„
302	„ 13, '28.	The Nisshin Kisen steamship "Hoyo Maru" was unlawfully inspected at Woosung.	„
303	„ 14, '28.	Anti-Japanese agitations in Peking began to be active over the Tsinan incident.	North China
304	„ 14, '28.	Chinese custom-house brokers in Shanghai stopped handling Japanese goods.	Middle China
305	„ 15, '28.	The Chinese military prohibited steamship navigation at Fouchow, Szechuan Province.	„

No.	Date		Region
306	May 19, '28.	Chinese students in Hongkong assaulted Japanese shops.	South China
307	„ 19, '28.	Bandits assaulted the Japanese guard station at Odo, Kokai-gun, Chosen.	Manchuria
308	„ 25, '28.	A party of Japanese nationals, while proceeding up the river Yalu, was attacked by 60 bandits about 3 miles below Antung on the Korean side. Lieutenant Wakabayashi was taken away as prisoner.	„
309	„ 25, '28.	A Japanese military aeroplane was fired on by Chinese soldiers at Laiwu, Shantung Province.	North China
310	„ 27, '28.	A Japanese merchant in Wanhsien, Szechuan Province, was assaulted by bandits.	Middle China
311	„ 29, '28.	The Nisshin Kisen Kaisha steamship "Unyo Maru" was fired on.	„
312	June 1, '28.	The Cantonese Government enforced unlawful taxation.	South China
313	„ 2, '28.	The steamship "Kiyo Maru" was fired on above Fouchow while going on the upper Yangtze.	Middle China
314	„ 6, '28.	A bandit force, about 1500 strong, attacked a squad of Japanese telegraph engineers at work at Huangchipu on the Kiaochow-Tsinan Railway.	North China
315	„ 6, '28.	Chinese police men fired on the Japanese garrion force at Tungkou on the Yalu.	Manchuria
316	„ 8, '28.	A Chinese attack was made at the Military Arsenal in Tsinan under guard of Japanese troops.	North China
317	„ 9, '28.	The Japanese warships "Maki," and "Soya" were fired on by Gen. Yung Gen-pei's Army near Suchwangtze at the mouth of the Paiho.	„

No.	Date		Region
318	June 11, '28.	The destroyer "Maki" was fired on by the Southern army while proceeding up the Paiho.	North China
319	„ 11, '28.	The maintenance department of the Antung-Mukden Railway at Chikwanshan was attacked by bandits.	Manchuria
320	„ 11, '28.	The destroyer "Maki" was fired on by the Southern army on the Paiho.	North China
321	„ 11, '28.	A Japanese steamship was fired on without provocation.	„
322	„ 11, '28.	A Japanese steamship was prohibited to unload cargo at Wanhsien.	Middle China
323	„ 12, '28.	A Japanese merchant was thrown a bomb at in Mukden.	Manchuria
324	„ 12, '28.	The destroyers "Kuwa" and "Maki" were fired on without provocation by the Northern army on the Paiho.	North China
325	„ 13, '28.	The destroyer "Kuwa" was fired on by the Northern army on the Paiho.	„
326	„ 13, '28.	Japanese merchants in Shanghai had their cotton goods seized by Chinese soldiers.	Middle China
327	„ 15, '28.	Unpaid Chinese passengers forced themselves aboard the Japanese steamship "Daitei Maru" at Nanking.	„
328	„ 20, '28.	Alcohol was unlawfully taxed at Tsingtao.	North China
329	„ 25, '28.	A Japanese sentinel was fired on at Tsinan by plain-clothed Chinese soldiers.	„
330	„ 25, '28.	Anti-Japanese agitators in Hankow began to inspect Japanese merchandise.	Middle China

No.	Date		Region
331	June 26, '28.	The Japanese military train was attacked by bandits at Tsinan.	North China
332	,, 26, '28.	3000 coal miners at Tsuchuan went on strike.	,,
333	,, 27, '28.	Chinese soldiers at Shanhaikwan committed violence against a Japanese.	,,
334	,, 27, '28.	A Japanese was fired on at Kuyeh by a Chinese soldier of the Mukden army and robbed of his money.	,,
335	,, 29, '28.	A Japanese sentinel was fired on at Tsinan by plain-clothed Chinese soldiers.	,,
336	,, 30, '28.	The Japanese firm of Chinpei Kungsu at Haichow was destroyed, some property being carried off.	Middle China
337	July —, '28.	Early this month anti-Japanese armed police men in Amoy began to interfere with Japanese business, seizing merchandise in many cases.	South China
338	,, 3, '28.	The steamship "Kiyo Maru" was fired on at Chungking.	Middle China
339	,, 7, '28.	The Nationalist Government declared abrogation of the "unequal" treaties and enforcement of emergency laws."	,,
340	,, 7, '28.	Anti-Japanese inspectors in Shanghai began to show activity.	,,
341	,, 10, '28.	A section of the Kiaochow-Tsinan Railway was destroyed by explosion.	North China
342	,, 11, '28.	Armed police men in Amoy interfered with the Japanese ships hiring sampans.	South China

No.	Date		Region
343	July 15, '28.	Unpaid Chinese passengers forced themselves aboard a Japanese steamship at Nanking.	Middle Chinn
344	„ 20, '28.	A clash occurred between Chinese and Japanese soldiers at Chouyangchi, Shantung Province.	North China
345	„ 27, '28.	Bandits, making their appearances near Choutsun, engaged Japanese troops in action.	„
346	Aug. 5, '28.	Japanese soldiers were unlawfully detained near Chunliangcheng.	„
347	„ 5, '28.	A large number of Chinese coolies, emboldened by their numerical superiority, attacked Japanese gendarmes at Tientsin.	„
348	„ 7, '28.	Japanese residents at Jichao, Shantung Province, were put under arrest.	„
349	„ 10, '28.	The Shanghai branch of the Kuomintang published its second collection of anti-Japanese songs.	Middle China
350	„ 11, '28.	Chinese military officers forced themselves abaord a Japanese steamship at Amoy.	South China
351	„ 12, '28.	Japanese residences were looted between Tayeh and Kiukiang.	Middle China
352	„ 20, '28.	Japanese shipping at Chungkiang were refused labour to handle cargo.	
353	„ 20, '28.	The Anti-Japanese Society of Swatow began to interfere with Japanese business and inspect postal matters.	South China
354	„ 22, '28.	The Japanese ship "Joyo Maru" was looted by bandits while going up from Kiukiang to Tayeh.	Middle China

No.	Date		Region
355	Aug. 22, '28.	Japanese sentinels were fired on at Tsingtao.	North China
356	,, 26, '28.	Chinese authorities at Tientsin announced illegal taxation.	,,
357	,, 30, '28.	The Anti-Japanese Association of Wuhu seized drugs at a Japanese pharmacist's.	Middle China
358	Sept. 1, '28.	The Japanese steamship "Kaiyo Maru" was fired on at Tengchow, Shantung, by Chinese soldiers.	North China
359	,, 5, '28.	The Shanghai Temporary Legislative Council unlawfully noticed application of emergency laws.	Middle China
360	,, 13, '28.	The Anti-Japanese Society in Foochow interfered with hiring of sampans for Japanese ships.	South China
361	,, 18, '28.	The Japanese steamship "Unyo Maru" was fired upon while streaming down from Chungking.	Middle China
362	,, 18, '28.	The Japanese steamships "Kiyo Maru" and "Choyo Maru" were fired upon in the upper Yangtze.	,,
363	,, 22, '28.	The Chekiang Province published anti-Japanese songs.	,,
364	,, 29, '28.	The Anti-Japanese Society in Swatow took under its charge all sampans used by Japanese ships.	South China
365	Oct. 1, '28.	An unlawful surtax was imposed in Tientsin.	North China
366	,, 2, '28.	Passage of Japanese troops was obstructed at Tangku.	,,
367	,, 6, '28.	Members of the Anti-Japanese Society of Shanghai detained Japanese goods.	Middle China
368	,, 9, '28.	Lighters of Japanese merchants of Tientsin were unlawfully requisitioned.	North China

No.	Date		Region
369	Oct. —, '28.	In middle October Japanese merchants in Mukden were demanded by Anti-Japanese Society to evacuate.	Manchuria
370	„ 13, '28.	Anti-Japanese Society in Shanghai seized Japanese goods.	Middle China
371	„ 15, '28.	The Anti-Japanese Association of Shanghai seized Japanese goods.	„
372	„ 16, '28.	The Anti-Japanese Association of Shanghai seized Japanese goods.	„
373	„ 20, '28.	Anti-Japanese mob seized Japanese merchandise.	„
374	„ 24, '28.	Members of the Anti-Japanese Association of Shanghai seized cotton cloth from Japanese shops, and tore down the Japanese national flag.	„
375	„ 25, '28.	The Anti-Japanese Association of Shanghai seized Japanese goods.	„
376	„ 29, '28.	Japanese residents at Shihchiachuang were unlawfully demanded to evacuate.	North China
377	„ 29, '28.	The Anti-Japanese Association of Shanghai seized cotton cloth of Japanese merchants.	Middle China
378	Nov. 2, '28.	Members of the Anti-Japanese Association of Foochow destroyed Japanese merchandise.	South China
379	„ 7, '28.	Discussion was made as to the recovery of the Shantung Lutai Kungsu at Tsingtao.	North China
330	„ 11, '28.	The Japanese national flag was insulted at Antung.	Manchuria
381	„ 12, '28.	The Nisshin Kisen Kaisha tugboat "Matsu Maru" was fired upon on the Yangtze.	Middle China
382	„ 14, '28.	The Nisshin Kisen Kaisha tugboat "Himeshima Maru" was fired on at Changmatao in the middle Yangtze region.	„

No.	Date		Region
383	Oct. 15, '28.	The Nationalist Government announced recovery of the right of supervising the Salt Gabelle.	All China
384	,, 16, '28.	The Anti-Japanese Society of Peking imposed unlawful taxes on Japanese merchandise.	North China
385	Nov. 23, '28.	Rights of the Radio Station at Shuangchiao, Nanking, were infringed upon.	Middle China
386	,, 24, '28.	The Nanking Government, in view of the Tsinan affair, issued to all provinces an order for economic severance with Japan.	All China
387	,, 25, '28.	The Anti-Japanese Society of Peking confiscated Japanese merchandise.	North China
388	,, 26, '28.	The Chinese army took possession of the Salt Gabelle office at Chefoo.	,,
389	Dec. 9, '28.	Interference was made with the business of Japanese merchants at Tiehling.	Manchuria
390	,, 10, '28.	The Anti-Japanese Society of Ichang interfered with labour to handle cargo for the Nisshin Kisen Kaisha ships.	Middle China
391	,, 10, '28.	Employees of Japanese firms at Mukden were unlawfully arrested.	Manchuria
392	,, 15, '28.	Anti-Japanese meeting was held in Peking. A plain-clothed Japanese gendarme was assaulted and later carried off.	North China
393	,, 17, '28.	The machinegun carriage of the Japanese landing party at Hankow clashed with Chinese rickshaws, causing damage and casualties on either side.	Middle China
394	,, 20, '28.	General Liu Hsiang's army laid mines below Chungking.	,,
395	,, 28, '28.	Wuhu bandits looted the home of a comprador in the employ of the Kinkai Yusen Kaisha.	,,

No.	Date		Region
396	Jan. 1, '29.	The Wuhan Government declared transference of the 1st and 2nd Special Districts of Hankow to the charge of the Wuhan Municipal Executive Committee.	Middle China
397	„ 9, '29.	Upon the avowed ground of trouble with Chinese rickshaw men an anti-Japanese strike was started in Hankow. Armed police men blockaded the Japanese concession against food supply.	„
398	„ 10, '29.	The second day of anti-Japanese disturbances in Hankow.	„
399	„ 10, '29.	Agitations in Changsha became more violent, Japanese merchandise being seized.	„
400	„ —, '29.	In mid January the Nationalist Government declared its control of the Nanchang - Kiukiang Railway.	„
401	„ 11, '29.	The third day of anti-Japanese disturbances in Hankow.	„
402	„ 11, '29.	The Anti-Japanese Association of Nanking decided on an anti-Japanese boycott.	„
403	„ 12, '29.	The fourth day of anti-Japanese disturbances in Hankow.	„
404	„ 13, '29.	The 5th day of anti-Japanese disturbances in Hankow.	„
405	„ 14, '29.	The 6th day of anti-Japanese disturbances in Hankow.	„
406	„ 14, '29.	Inspired by anti-Japanese disturbances in Hankow, the Anti-Japanese Societies of Kiukiang and Shasi began to be active.	„
407	„ 14, '29.	Voices began to be raised for recovery of the Japanese Concession at Chungking.	„
408	„ 15, '29.	The 7th day of anti-Japanese disturbances in Hankow.	„
409	„ 17, '29.	The 9th day of anti-Japanese disturbances in Hankow.	„

No.	Date		Region
410	Jan. 17, '29.	The Mayor of Peiping started the movement to recover the districts about the Japanese Legation.	North China
411	,, 18, '29.	The 10th day of anti-Japanese disturbances in Hankow.	Middle China
412	,, 20, '29.	The National Anti-Japanese Association of Nanking passed an anti-Japanese resolution.	,,
413	,, 21, '29.	The 13th day of anti-Japanese disturbances in Hankow.	,,
414	,, 24, '29.	The 16th day of anti-Japanese disturbances in Hankow.	,,
415	,, 24, '29.	The Anti-Japanese Society of Kiukiang began to move in sympathy with the anti-Japanese agitations in Hankow.	,,
416	,, 25, '29.	Japanese shops at Lungkow were looted by the army of General Liu Chen-nien.	North China
417	,, 27, '29.	The Anti-Japanese Society of Changsha proposed anti-Japanese movements, in view of the Hankow affairs.	Middle China
418	,, —, '29.	In late January the Korean farmers at Kuantien, Fengtien Province, were subjected to unlawful taxation.	Manchuria
419	,, 30, '29.	The 7th Factory of the Naigai Cotton Spinning Mill at Shanghai went on strike.	Middle China
420	Feb. 1, '29.	The Customs Headquarters in Shanghai ordered the Custom House in Dairen to impose a super-tax of 2.5 percent.	Manchuria
421	,, 1, '29.	The 24th day of anti-Japanese disturbances in Hankow.	Middle China
422	,, 2, '29.	The 25th day of anti-Japanese disturbances in Hankow.	,,

No.	Date		Region
423	Feb. 2, '29.	The Anti-Japanese Association of Shanghai seized Japanese merchandise.	Middle China
424	,, 2, '29.	The Custom House of Dairen gave notice of an unlawful supertax.	Manchuria
425	,, 3, '29.	The workers of the Naigai Cotton Spinning Mill went on strike.	Middle China
426	,, 4, '29.	The 27th day of anti-Japanese disturbances in Hankow.	,,
427	,, 6, '29.	The Anti-Japanese Society of Wuhu obstructed food supply to Japanese warships.	,,
428	,, 8, '29.	The Ssupingkai-Taonan Railway manoeuvred to drive away the Japanese managing director.	Manchuria
429	,, 10, '29.	The 33rd day of anti-Japanese disturbances in Hankow.	Middle China
430	,, 10, '29.	Japanese merchants in Foochow were looted by members of the Anti-Japanese Society.	South China
431	,, 12, '29.	Japanese nationals were wounded by Chinese soldiers at Shanhaikwan.	North China
432	,, 14, '29.	The Anti-Japanese Society of Nanking inspected and sealed up Japanese goods.	Middle China
433	,, 15, '29.	The Anti-Japanese Society of Chengchow passed the resolution to drive away the Japanese residents, enforcing a boycott of Japanese goods.	,,
434	,, 15, '29.	The Anti-Japanese Society of Nanking sealed up Japanese merchandise.	,,
435	,, 16, '29.	Soldiers of the Peace Guards of Tientsin fired on the Japanese soldiers in manoeuvre.	North China

No.	Date		Region
436	Feb. 16, '29.	The workers of the Japanese cotton mills at Woosung went on strike.	Middle China
437	„ 18, '29.	The Military Administrative Office prohibited issue of military passes for foreigners for inland travel.	„
438	„ 19, '29.	Chinese officials in Imienpo unlawfully appropriated themselves with money and goods.	Manchuria
439	„ 21, '29.	Chinese police men in the Legation districts in Peking began to strike.	North China
440	„ 23, '29.	The Anti-Japanese Society of Ichang prohibited labour to handle cargo for the Nisshin Kisen Kaisha ships.	Middle China
441	„ 25, '27.	Anti-Japanese mob in Hankow, on the 48th day of their continued disturbances, attacked Japanese sentinels.	„
442	„ 26, '29.	On the 49th day of the anti-Japanese disturbances in Hankow armed police men attacked the Japanese police.	„
443	„ 27, '29.	Cases in Mukden of pressure being applied to expel the Japanese.	Manchuria
444	„ 28, '29.	On the 51st day of the anti-Japanese disturbances in Hankow armed Chinese police men attacked the Japanese police.	Middle China
445	Mar. 1, '29.	Antung Province promulgated illegal custom duties.	Manchuria
446	„ 1, '29.	The Nationalist Government ordered the Han Yeh Ping Kungsu, the Sino-Japanese company, to turn over all its property to the Liquidation Committee.	Middle China

No.	Date		Region
447	Mar. 2, '29.	The Japanese steamship "Ryuhei Maru," while mooring at Tengchow, was illegally subjected to inspection.	North China
448	,, 4, '29.	Anti-Japanese agitators in Wuhu paraded in demonstration.	Middle China
449	,, 7, '29.	The Koreans at Chiaotou were demanded to evacuate.	Manchuria
450	,, 7, '29.	The Chinese warship moored at Tengchow illegally subjected the Japanese steamship "Takamatsu Maru" to inspection.	North China
451	,, 8, '29.	On the 59th day of the anti-Japanese disturbances in Hankow the Japanese landing party had a clash with the armed Chinese police.	Middle China
452	,, 8, '29.	Illegal taxation was enforced in Chefoo.	North China
453	,, 8, '29.	The Anti-Japanese Society of Wuhu compulsorily inventoried Japanese merchandise in local stock.	Middle China
454	,, 10, '29.	Mining work of sulphur-ore at Tsaohokou, Fengtien Province, was obstructed.	Manchuria
455	,, 13, '29.	Greater frequencies of seizing and looting Japanese merchandise by the Anti-Japanese Association of Shanghai.	Middle China
456	,, 13, '29.	A Japanese was assaulted by Chinese soldiers at Sanfenkou.	Manchuria
457	,, 14, '29.	A Japanese steamship was illegally subjected to inspection at Lungkou.	North China
458	,, 14, '29.	The Japanese steamship "Shinanokawa Maru" was all but inspected by a Chinese warship off Tengchow.	,,

No.	Date		Region
459	Mar. 15, '29.	The neutral zone between Japanese and Chinese armies was invaded by the Mukden army.	Manchuria
460	„ 17, '29.	The 68th day of anti-Japanese disturbances in Hankow.	Middle China
461	„ 17, '29.	Attempts were made at Tunhua to drive off the Japanese by obstruction of their business.	Manchuria
462	„ 19, '29.	The Anti-Japanese Society of Wuhu passed an anti-Japanese resolution.	Middle China
463	„ 20, '29.	Interference was made with digging of clay at Wuhutsui, Fuhsien, Fengtien Province.	Manchuria
464	„ 20, '29.	Japanese women and children, in view of the increasing pressure being applied by the Chinese, sought refuge in Hsiakwan.	Middle China
465	„ 20, '29.	Japanese merchandise was illegally seized at Antung.	Manchuria
466	„ 20, '29.	Notice was given of inspection to be made of merchant ships at Woosung.	Middle China
467	„ 22, '29.	The Kaho Cotton Spinning Mill at Woosung, in view of its workers' impending strike, closed down.	„
468	„ 24, '29.	Attempt was made to recover land outside Mukden from possession of the South Manchuria Railway Company.	Manchuria
469	Apr. 1, '29.	The Koreans in China Town of Harbin were demanded to evacuate.	„
470	„ 3, '29.	Illegal inspection of ships by Chinese in the lower Yangtze became increasingly frequent.	Middle China
471	„ 4, '29.	The charter for coal mining at Penchihu was cancelled.	Manchuria

No.	Date		Region
472	Apr. 4, '29.	The 86th day of anti-Japanese disturbances in Hankow.	Middle China
473	„ 7, '29.	With settlement of the Tsinan affair the Nationalist Government issued an order dissolving anti-Japanese societies.	All China
474	„ 8, '29.	Anti-Japanese disturbances in Hankow came to an end.	Middle China
475	„ 10, '29.	Attempts were made in Taonan to expel the Japanese by obstructing their business.	Manchuria
476	„ 13, '29.	The Anti-Japanese Society of Foochow committed violence against Japanese merchants.	South China
477	„ 13, '29.	The anti-Japanese Association of Canton changed its name as National Salvation Society.	„
478	„ 19, '29.	Paymaster Ifuji was fired at in Tsinan.	North China
479	„ 19, '29.	The Nisshin Kisen Kaisha steamship "Baiyo Maru" was fired on near Shasi.	South China
480	„ 20, '29.	Interference was offered in Mukden with transportation of Japanese goods.	Manchuria
481	„ 21, '29.	Japanese merchandise was illegally seized in Mukden.	„
482	„ 23, '29.	Chinese soldiers unlawfully boarded a Japanese steamship at Tengchow, Shantung Province.	North China
483	„ 24, '29.	A Japanese steamship was illegally inspected at Chefoo.	„
484	„ 26, '29.	Japanese merchants in Mukden were obstructed in business.	Manchuria
485	„ 28, '29.	The gunboat "Hira" was fired on while moving downstream from Ichang.	Middle China

No.	Date		Region
486	Apr. 28, '29.	The Chinese made an illegal demand as a condition for settlement of the rickisha affair in Hankow.	Middle China
487	„ 29, '29.	The gunboat "Hira" was fired on by Chinese soldiers at Itu.	
488	„ 29, '29.	Cases in Mukden of Japanese business obstructed, transportation of goods interefered with, and merchandise confiscated.	Manchuria
489	May 2, '29.	The Nanking and Hankow affairs were settled.	Middle China
490	„ 3, '29.	Three Japanese soldiers were fired at in Tsinan.	North China
491	„ 4, '29.	The Anti-Japanese Society of Hankow seized Japanese merchandise.	Middle China
492	„ 7, '29.	The Diplomatic Committee of Hankow demanded the Japanese landing party to withdraw itself.	„
493	„ 9, '29.	Soldiers and students of Foochow, in observance of the anniversary of the "May 9th Incident," held a mass meeting.	South China
494	„ 9, '29.	The Japanese farm at Kungtaipu, a suburb of Mukden, was raided by mob.	Manchuria
495	„ 9, '29.	The National Salvation Society of Foochow made seizure of Japanese merchandise.	South China
496	„ 13, '29.	Anti-Japanese agitation starting in Wanhsien the Nisshin Kisen Kaisha steamships found no labour to handle cargo.	Middle China
497	„ 14, '29.	The Anti-Japanese Society of Ningte confiscated Japanese goods.	„

No.	Date		Region
498	May 15, '29.	Though the time limit for the construction of the Kirin-Hueining Railway and the Changchun-Talai Railway expired, work was not started.	Manchuria
499	,, 16, '29.	Anti-Japanese goods inspectors at Hankow put Chinese in Japanese service in confinement.	Middle China
500	,, 18, '29.	The Anti-Japanese Society of Nanking made dealers in Japanese merchandise prisoners and had them carried through the streets.	,,
501	,, 24, '29.	Workers at the Naigai Cotton Spinning Mill at Tsingtao went on strike.	North China
502	,, 24, '29.	Japanese fishing craft were illegally inspected off Lungkou.	,,
503	,, 25, '29.	Japanese troops while manoeuvreing outside Mukden were fired on by Chinese police.	Manchuria
504	,, 26, '29.	Japanese non-commissioned and police officers were assaulted by Chinese police outside the city of Mukden.	,,
505	,, 26, '29.	Chinese warships interfered with Japanese fishing off Lungkou.	North China
506	,, 28, '29.	The Cantonese Government restricted navigation of foreign warships on the Szikiang.	South China
507	,, 28, '29.	The steamship "Taikichi Maru" was fired on at Huangchow.	Middle China
508	June 2, '29.	A Japanese was killed in Tsinan.	North China
509	,, 2, '29.	A Chinese warship intererfered with Japanese fishing near Tsinwangtao.	,,

No.	Date		Region
510	June 6, '29.	A national anti-Japanese mass meeting was held in Shanghai and resolved to carry through the original anti-Japanese plans.	Middle China
511	,, 9, '29.	A Japanese soldier of the Shanhaikwan garrison was assaulted.	North China
512	,, 10, '29.	The Chinese authorities at Chientao declared recovery of the right of education and applied pressure upon 28 subsidiary schools and 207 private schools in those regions.	Manchuria
513	,, 13, '29.	Chinese police in Harbin committed violence against Japanese police officers.	,,
514	,, 13, '29.	Boycott of Japanese goods went on in Foochow.	South China
515	,, 27, '29.	The Chinese authorities showed their determination to force a railway through the Sakakibara farm in a suburb of Mukden.	Manchuria
516	,, 27, '29.	The Nationalist Government made propositon for abolition of Japan's cultural institutions in China.	Middle China
517	July 1, '29.	The Anti-Japanese Society of Tsinan made a resolution of five points for economic severance with Japan.	North China
518	,, 6, '29.	The rickisha affair in Hankow was settled.	Middle China
519	,, 8, '29.	The Anti-Japanese Society of Hankow made decision to strive for abrogation of unequal treaties.	,,
520	,, 8, '29.	The Bureau of Home Affairs in Shanghai imposed illegal postal rates.	,,
521	,, 10, '29.	The workers of the Toa Hemp Dressing Company at Shanghai went on a go-slow strike.	,,

No.	Date		Region
522	July 10, '29.	The Government of Kirin ordered the governor of Enkihsien to drive away the Korean farmers.	Manchuria
523	„ 10, '29.	The Kuomingtang headquarters issued a secret order to carry on anti-Japanese agitations.	Middle China
524	„ 11, '29.	The National Association for Encouraging Repudiation of Japanese Contracts settled on its anti-Japanese commemoration badge.	„
525	„ 12, '29.	In view of the increasingly disturbing situation as regards the local Industrial Association the Japanese cotton spinning mills decided to close.	North China
526	„ 13, '29.	The Mayor of Shanghai declared unconditional recovery of roads outside the official demarcation lines.	Middle China
527	„ 22, '29.	The Japanese factories in Tsingtao were all closed.	North China
528	„ 22, '29.	The Anti-Japanese Society of Changsha went on confiscating Japanese goods.	Middle China
529	„ 26, '29.	A tugboat belonging to the firm of Tai Sheng Chang was looted by Chinese soldiers near Changsha.	„
530	„ 31, '29.	Official notice of inspection of foreign shipping at Foochow.	South China
531	Aug. 1, '29.	At Wanhsien, Szechuan Province, an additional tax of 2.5 per cent began to be imposed.	Middle China
532	„ 4, '29.	A Japanese national was detained at Changtu by Chinese officials.	Manchuria
533	„ 4, '29.	Armed Chinese police made economic blockade against the Japanese factories in Tsingtao.	North China

— 274 —

No.	Date		Region
534	Aug. 5, '29.	At Chungking the Japanese steamship "Unyo Maru" was all but subjected to inspection on her entry into the harbour.	Middle China
535	" 6, '29.	The Diplomatic Society of Four Eastern Provinces at Mukden made decision concerning an anti-Japanese agitation.	Manchuria
536	" 6, '29.	Soldiers of the Independent Railway Guards were attacked while patrolling.	"
537	" 22, '29.	The Kuomingtang headquarters issued a secret order to branches in all cities to renew the anti-Japanese movement.	Middle China
538	" 22, '29.	"The Nichi Nichi Shimbun" and "Junten Jiho," Japanese owned dailies, had their outgoing mail stopped without notice.	"
539	" 30, '29.	Japanese troops manoeuvring near Shoushanpu were fired upon by the Chinese Public Peace Guards.	Manchuria
540	Sept. 7, '19.	The movement for recovery of the navigation right was started in Shanghai.	Middle China
541	" 10, '29.	The Finance Ministry of the Kiangsu Government notified an illegal taxation.	"
542	" 10, '29.	Labour trouble at Tsuchuan coal mine in Szechuan Province became worse.	North China
543	" 13, '29.	Japanese troops manoeuvring near Changchun were fired upon by Chinese police men.	Manchuria
544	" 16, '29.	Japanese factories at Tsingtao were closed.	North China
545	" 21, '29.	The Japanese steamship "Dehli Maru" on her way to Hongkong from Swatow was looted.	South China

— 275 —

No.	Date		Region
546	Sept. 23, '29.	Chinese police men fired upon Japanese soldiers at Tieling.	Manchuria
547	,, 27, '29.	The Board of Commerce of Hutan, Changsha, Hunan decided to resume boycotting Japanese goods.	South China
548	,, 30, '29.	In view of the Tieling trouble, the Diplomatic Association of Mukden decided upon anti-Japanese agitations.	Manchuria
549	Oct. 3, '29.	The Nanking Government's delegate in Harbin encouraged anti-Japanese boycotts.	,,
550	,, 4, '29.	Regarding the Tieling trouble, the Kuomintang of Peiping made anti-Japanese decisions.	North China
551	,, 4, '29.	The National Diplomatic Association of Mukden brought pressure upon the newspapers of Japanese affiliations.	Manchuria
552	,, 6, '29.	Chinese policemen fired upon Japanese troops manoeuvring near Lishan.	,,
553	,, 6, '29.	Inspired by the Tieling trouble the Diplomatic Association of Mukden raised its voice for recovery of Port Arthur and Dairen.	,,
554	,, 8, '29.	The Japanese steamship "Unyo Maru" was attacked by Chinese bandits at Wanhsien.	Middle China
555	,, 23, '29.	The Japanese steamship "Daitei Maru" was fired upon while steaming down from Hankow.	,,
556	,, 17, '29.	The Japanese steamship "Tenchi" was subjected to inspection at the Miaotao Islands.	North China
557	,, 29, '29.	A Japanese newspaper office was attacked in Shanghai.	Middle China

No.	Date		Region
558	Oct. 30, '29.	Protest was made against movement up the Paiho beyond the port district of Tientsin.	North China
559	Nov. 2, '29.	Illegal taxes were imposed in Tientsin.	”
560	” 5, '29.	Chinese soldiers broke into a Japanese factory in Chengchow.	”
561	” 5, '29.	A Japanese ship was fired upon at Fowchow.	Middle China
562	” 5, '29.	Japanese soldiers on guard at Tangkangtze were attacked by bandits.	Manchuria
563	” —, '29.	Early this month the Shanghai Temporary Legislative Council, on its reelection, excluded Japanese.	Middle China
564	” 9, '29.	Chinese destructed without notice the embankment at the Sakakibara Farm outside Mukden.	Manchuria
565	” 20, '29.	The local Kuomintang headquarters of Tsingtao detained and examined postal matters of Japanese nationals.	North China
566	” 20, '29.	A band of 1,000 workmen broke into the Shikata Cotton Mill in Tsingtao and committed violence.	”
567	” 21, '29.	The Canton Government notified the blockade of the Sikiang.	South China
568	” 29, '29.	The Shantung Provincial Government projected to recover the Lutai Kungsu.	North China
569	Dec. 5, '29.	The Japanese gunboat "Katada" was fired upon below Ichang.	Middle China
570	” 19, '29.	A Japanese steamship was fired upon below Hsiangchi.	”
571	” 21, '29.	Chinese soldiers unlawfully boarded a Japanese ship at Hankow.	”

No.	Date		Region
572	Dec. 21, '29.	Pressure was applied on a Japanese owned newspaper in Shantung.	North China
573	,, 29, '29.	Pressure was applied on "Junten Jiho."	,,
574	Jan. 1, '30.	A steamship belonging to the Nisshin Kisen was fired upon while anchoring at Chenglingchi.	Middle China
575	,, 13, '30.	The movement for recovering the Japanese concession was started in Chungking.	,,
576	,, 24, '30.	A steamship belonging to the Nisshin Kisen was fired upon at Chikianghsien below Ichang.	,,
577	,, 26, '30.	A steamship belonging to the Nisshin Kisen was fired upon above Tiaokwankou.	,,
578	Feb. 14, 30.	The Japanese steamship "Ume Maru" was fired upon while moving up to Changsha.	,,
579	,, —, 30.	A Japanese police officer was killed by Chinese police guards at Hsilinho in Chientao.	Manchuria
580	,, 19, '30.	The pilots of the upper Yangtze went on strike.	Middle China
581	,, 27, '30.	Protest was made against the Shale Oil Plant at Fushun.	Manchuria
582	Mar. 8, '30.	The Japanese steamship "Shinyo Maru" was fired upon below Shasi.	Middle China
583	,, 19, '30.	The Japanese steamship "Kashiwa Maru" was fired upon between Chenglingchi and Shasi.	,,
584	,, 27, '30.	The Canton customs prohibited sailing of the Japanese steamship "Times Maru" as if by order of the Nanking Government.	South China

No.	Date		Region
585	Mar. 30, '30.	The Kuomintang headquarters in Shanghai made propaganda against the entry of the 1st Torpedo-boat Flotilla of the Imperial Navy.	Middle China
586	„ 31, '30.	The Japanese newspaper "Junten Jiho" was discontinued under the pressure of Chinese authorites and local Kuomingtang.	North China
587	Apr. 5, '30.	Students and mob carried out anti-Japanese and British demonstrations in Nanking.	Middle China
588	„ —, 30.	Officials of the Chinese Public Peace Bureau attacked the Japanese police office at Talatze in Chientao.	Manchuria
589	May 1, '30.	Japanese fishing-boats were plundered off Haichow.	Middle China
590	„ 3, '30.	Outdoor lectures were given at many places in the Chientao districts for commemoration of the "May 3 Affair" (Tsinan Affair).	Manchuria
591	„ 3, '30.	A Japanese liaison officer in Chientao was assaulted by Chinese police men.	„
592	„ 21, '30.	The Japanese steamship "Toyo Maru" was fired upon above Chenglingchi.	Middle China
593	„ 22, '30.	The Japanese steamship "Gakuyo Maru" was fired upon above Wuhsueh.	„
594	June 5, '30.	Wounded Chinese soldiers committed violence in Nanking.	„
595	„ 13, '30.	Tayeh was occupied by Chinese bandits, the transportation of ore being brought to a standstill. Japanese gunboats and merchant ships were fired on.	„

No.	Date		Region
596	June 15, '30.	Students of the Fukuoka Commercial School were attacked by Chinese soldiers at Suchow.	Middle China
597	„ 16, '30.	The Japanese steamship "Nagate Maru" was imposed on a double-tax in Shanghai.	„
598	„ 21. '30.	The Japanese steamship "Banyo Maru" was attacked by bandits near the mouth of the Laowhang-ho.	„
599	„ 27, '30.	The Japanese Consulate in Changsha was set on fire and Japanese shops were plundered.	„
600	Sept. —, '30.	A monument erected in Hsiungyen-hsien in memory of the Russo-Japanese War was destroyed.	„
601	Oct. 6, '30.	Japanese police officers were fired upon by Chinese police men at Lungtsun.	Manchuria
602	„ 11, '30.	Japanese soldiers manoeuvring near the North Barracks in Mukden were fired upon by Chinese sentinels.	„
603	„ 10, '30.	A Japanese national was carried off near Whangtien, Fukien Province.	South China
604	Nov. 28, '30.	The Japanese consular police office in Taonan was demanded to evacuate.	Manchuria
605	Dec. 5, '30.	The Diplomatic Association of Liaoning Province started the movement for removal of the Japanese monument of the Russo-Japanese War.	
606	„ 19, '30.	The Tumentze Self-Protection Party killed a Korean.	„
607	„ 6, '30.	The Chenju Radio Plant began operation.	Middle China

No.	Date		Region
608	Dec. 19, '30.	The leader of the Tumentze self-protection guards having killed members of a Korean family at Yenkihsien, in Chiento, charged it against bandits.	Manchuria
609	Feb. 2, '31.	Chinese natives placed stones on the track of the Antung-Mukden line to interfere with traffic.	,,
610	Mar. 11, 31.	Mayor Wu Tieh-cheng, speaking under the title of "The Four Eastern Provinces under invasion of Japan and Soviet Russia", gave a sensational anti-Japanese lecture at the Communicational Association.	Middle China
611	,, 20, .31.	The Public Peace Bureau at Harbin secretly ordered the police under its control to drive the Japanese and Korean residents away from Harbin and Puchiatien.	Manchuria
612	Apr. 5, '31.	The general meeting of the Liaoning Provincial Diplomatic Association decided upon plans against "unlawful Japanese actions," and on an anti-Japanese boycott.	,,
613	,, 5-8, '31.	The Diplomatic Association of Liaoning Province decided upon the following :— (1) Strong foreign policy against Japan; (2) Plans for resisting against Japan; (3) Anti-Japanese boycott; (4) Policy against the railways owned by Japanese; (5) Anti-Japanese economic severance.	,,
614	,, 20, '31.	A Kuomintang newspaper in Anhui Province printed an insulting article on the birth of a princess to the Imperial Family.	Middle China
615	,, —, '31.	The Mukden Government authorities ordered, prohibiting the press to print telegraphic communications sent by "Rengo."	Manchuria

No.	Date		Region
616	May —, '31.	Chinese police men interfered with the whole operation of the coal factories maintained by Japanese in Penchihu.	Manchuria
617	„ —, '31.	Women and children of a family from Toyama Prefecture, Japan, living in Mukden, were beaten and outraged by many Chinese police men.	„
618	„ 24, '31.	Attempts were made to expel Korean farmers from Santao-kow, north of Changchun.	„
619	June —, '31.	A band of Chinese police men forced into the Railway Zone in Changchun and assaulted a Japanese police officer.	„
620	„ 3, '31.	The construction work of Toa Kangyo Kungsu farm in Tung-liao was obstructed by the local Chinese police.	„
621	„ 13, '13.	Chinese soldiers made a bodily search of a Japanese merchant woman while passing a street in Chinchow.	„
622	„ 15, '31.	Chinese stoned Japanese school children.	„
623	„ —, '31.	A member of the Shikoku Natives' Association in Wafang-tien was assaulted by the local Chinese peace guards.	„
624	„ —, '31.	The Tax Bureau of Liaoning Province prohibited Chinese Special Products Traders' Union to deal with Japanese.	„
625	„ 12, '31.	The Public Peace Bureau of Open-Port in Mukden seized silver "tayang" currency transported by Japanese.	„
626	„ —, '31.	On the day of "Nyang-nyang" festival at Michenshan, Tashih-chiao, several Chinese peace guards assaulted a Japanese police man.	„

No.	Date		Region
627	June —, '31.	The Japanese shop "Meiji Yoko" in Harbin was looted.	Manchuria
628	,, 23, '31.	The local Chinese peace guards assaulted and outraged a Japanese old woman living at Kengchuangtze, in Haichenghsien.	,,
629	July 1, '31.	Chinese farmers, numbering about 500, interfered with the irrigation work of Korean farmers, having a clash with Japanese police officers.	,,
630	,, 1, '31.	Captain Nakamura and party were shot to death and burnt up by local Chinese regular soldiers near Suokungyehfu.	,,
631	,, 4, '31.	The O.S.K. steamship "Koshi Maru" was fired upon by Chinese bandits 2 mils above Whangpu while steaming up to Canton.	South China
632	,, 4, '31.	Students of a Korean school in Harbin were assaulted by Chinese students, one being wounded.	Manchuria
633	,, 5, '31.	40 Koreans were persecuted by Chinese land-owners in Suihua.	,,
634	,, 6, '31.	Korean farmers near Taolaichao on the Southern Branch of the Chinese Eastern Railway were ordered by the local Chinese authorities to evacuate.	,,
635	,, 7, '31.	Chinese farmers destroyed the irrigation water-ways of the paddy-fields worked by Koreans near Suihua in Heilungkiang Province.	,,
636	,, 7, '31.	Japanese patrols were attacked by Chinese bandits north of Taochiatun.	,,
637	,, 7, '31.	Students of the Korean school in Harbin were assaulted by Chinese students.	,,

No.	Date		Region
638	July 8, '31.	The Kuomintang in Tientsin decided upon anti-Japanese agitations on the ground of Japanese instigation being behind the anti-Chinese riots in Penyang.	North China
639	„ 9, '31.	The mass meeting of Students' Associations of Harbin decided upon anti-Japanese propaganda and economic rupture.	Manchuria
640	„ 10, '31.	Chang Tso-hsiang issued anti-Korean instructions.	„
641	„ 11, '31.	The central Kuomintang headquarters issued a secret order to local branches for boycotting Japanese goods.	Middle China
642	„ 12, '31.	The central Kuomintang headquarters in Nanking issued an instruction to the party branch in Shanghai sanctioning anti-Japanese agitations.	„
643	„ 12, '31.	A Japanese gendarme was assaulted in Chinese Town of Changchun.	Manchuria
644	„ 12, '31.	1,000 Chinese made anti-Japanese demonstrations in Tunhua in agitation over the Wanpaoshan and Penyang incidents.	„
645	„ 13, '31.	Chinese Merchants' Anti-Japanese Conference issued a manifesto upon the anti-Japanese economic rupture.	Middle China
646	„ 14, '31.	A patrol of the Japanese Railway Guards was carried off by Chinese police men near Whangkutun on the Peiping-Mukden Railway.	Manchuria
647	„ 15, '31.	Chinese Merchants' Anti-Japanese Conference declared that they "should always go on with the anti-Japanese economic rupture in the spirit of calm fortitude."	Middle China

No.	Date		Region
648	July 15, '31.	An anti-Japanese mass meeting was held under the auspices of the Kuomintang in Tientsin.	North China
649	„ 17, '31.	Regarding Wanpaoshan and Penyang incidents, the Kuomintang in Nanking telegraphed throughout the country, informing of its decision on anti-Japanese economic rupture.	Middle China
650	„ 19, '31.	All Province Commercial and Industrial Association of Hupei and the Commercial Council of Hankow and Wuchang jointly decided upon anti-Japanese economic rupture.	„
651	„ 20, '31.	Japanese goods were subjected to inspection and confiscated at Ningpo port in Cheking Province.	„
652	„ 22, '31.	The Commercial Council of Hankow prohibited Chinese merchants to make contracts for buying Japanese goods.	„
653	„ 22, '31.	Anti-Japanese mass meeting was held in Nanking.	„
654	„ 23, '31.	Japanese goods were subjected to inspection and confiscated at Putung, Chapei and South City of Shanghai.	„
655	„ 24, '31.	Chinese Merchants' Anti-Japanese Conference made seizure of Japanese goods at South City, Chapei and Putung of Shanghai.	„
656	„ 30, '31.	The Kuomintang headquarters in Hupei Province organized the Anti-Japanese Society and decided upon anti-Japanese agitations.	„
657	Aug. 5, '31.	A Japanese soldier on guard at Haicheng Station was shot at by a Chinese.	Manchuria

No.	Date		Region
658	Aug. 8, '31.	A patrol of the Penchihu Railway Guards was assaulted by Chinese near Shichiaotze.	Manchuria
659	„ 11, '31.	An inspector of the Anti-Japanese Society in Shanghai detained goods being transported from a Japanese steamship.	Middle Chi
660	„ 14, '31.	Protest was made against manoeuvres of Japanese engineers at Liutotao, east of Chingyuan.	Manchuria
661	„ 17, '31.	Chinese decided against sale of vegetables to the 4th regiment at Changchun.	„
662	„ 21, '31.	Reconstruction work of a school building at Takangtze in Chientao was promptly interfered with by Chinese.	„
663	Sept. 4, '31.	The train carrying the President of the South Manchuria Railway Company and his party was attacked by bandits between Kirin and Tunhua.	„
664	„ 5, '31.	Japanese residents in Chungking were obstructed in buying daily necessities.	Middle Ch
665	„ 5, '31.	Provisions for the Japanese gun-boat and the steamship "Unyo Maru" were confiscated by Anti-Japanese Society while in transit in Chungking.	„
666	„ 9, '31.	Rolling stock of the South Manchuria Railway Company was raided by Chinese near Hushihtai north of Mukden.	Manchuri
667	„ 14, '31.	Japanese patrols were attacked by local bandits north of Ssupingkai, one being killed.	„
668	„ 18, '31.	Chinese regular soldiers destroyed the South Manchuria Railway track at Liutianghu, north of Mukden.	„

No.	Date		Region
669	Sept. 20, '31.	A Chinese resolution was made in Peiping that Japanese instructors should voluntarily resign.	North China
670	,, 21, '31.	The Metropolitan Pressmen's Society was inaugurated at the Kuomintang headquarters in Nanking in support of the anti-Japanese diplomacy, demonstrations also being made.	Middle China
671	,, 22, '31.	A mass meeting of delegates of all sections of community was held under the auspices of the Shanghai Anti-Japanese Society.	,,
672	,, 22, '31.	Posters urging action against the Japanese Imperialism and advocating friendship with Soviet Union were distributed to all branches of the Kuomintang in Shanghai.	,,
673	,, 22, '31.	Resolution was made by the Anti-Japanese Society in Changsha to force the Chinese in Japanese employment to go on strike.	,,
674	,, 23, '31.	Threatening and abusive message was addressed to the Japaness Consulate in Foochow.	South China
675	,, 24, '31.	The Students' Anti-Japanese Society in Shanghai made outdoor speeches and demonstrations at Chinese Town and Chapei.	Middle China
676	,, 24, '31.	Anti-Japanese demonstration was made in Canton.	South China
677	,, 25, '31.	4,000 men attended the citizens' mass meeting in Suchow.	Middle China
678	,, 25, '31.	The Kuomintang in Hangchow telegraphed to the Central Government, requesting that they should declare an economic severance and their non-responsibility for protection of the Japanese in the same event.	,,

No.	Date		Region
679	Sept. 25, '31.	Citizens' mass meeting was held in Wuhu under the auspices of the local Kuomintang when a more active anti-Japanese movement was decided upon.	Middle China
680	„ 25, '31.	Anti-Japanese citizens' mass meeting was held in Chengchow to intensify the anti-Japanese feeling.	„
681	„ 25, '31.	Demonstrations were made in Changsha under the auspices of the local Anti-Japanese Society.	„
682	„ 25, '31.	The Chungking Anti-Japanese Society issued an order to stop coal supply for Japanese ships.	„
683	„ 25, '31.	Japanese residents were subjected to violence and persecution in broad daylight at Hongkong.	South China
684	„ 25, '31.	More daring cases of intimdation and persecution against the Chinese employed by Japanese firms.	Middle China
685	„ 26, '31.	Labour was strictly prohibited by the Kuomintang in Amoy-hsien to handle cargo for Japanese ships.	South China
686	„ 26, '31.	A Japanese family was assaulted by Chinese at Kiulung, six being killed and two wounded.	
687	„ 26, '31.	The Anti-Japanese Society in Shanghai decided upon rejection of Japan's consolation gifts for flood victims and made other anti-Japanese decisions.	Middle China
688	„ 27, '31.	9 cases of Japanese in Singapore being assaulted by Chinese.	Strait Settlement

No.	Date		Region
689	Sept. 28, '31.	The Kuomintang headquarters in Suchow, by order from the central headquarters, disbanded Chinese Merchants' Anti-Japanese Association and organized instead the Anti-Japanese National Salvation Society.	Middle China
690	„ 28, '31.	The Kuomintang in Chungking raised money for the "national salvation fund."	„
691	„ 28, '31.	Chinese soldiers carried off a Japanese at Haichow.	„
692	„ 28, '31.	Citizens' mass meeting in Peiping decided upon anti-Japanese economic rupture and seizure of Japanese goods.	North China
693	„ 29, '31.	Cotton cloth owned by Japanese was plundered in Shanghai while in transit.	Middle China
694	Oct. 1, '31.	Compredors and clerks employed by Japanese in Shanghai were forced to resign.	„
695	„ 1, '31.	New transactions with Japanese were stopped in Shanghai.	„
696	„ 1, '31.	Labour was prohibited to handle cargo for Japanese ships in Swatow.	South China
697	„ 1, '31.	An anti-Japanese demonstration was held at Chuangte, Japanese being obstructed in business.	Middle China
698	„ 3, '31.	The Chinese authorities in Yunnan seized telegrams for the Japanese Consulate, mob throwing stones at Japanese shops.	South China
699	„ 4, '31.	Two Japanese women of a Shanghai cotton mill were assaulted by Chinese with bamboo sticks.	Middle China

No.	Date		Region
700	Oct. 4, '31.	Japanese were attacked by a party of Chinese soldiers and mob in Whangpo.	Middle China
701	„ 5, '31.	Cases of non or delayed delivery of mail for Japanese residents in Shanghai and bad service of the telephone exchange for Japanese.	Middle China
702	„ 6, '31.	Inspectors of the Anti-Japanese Society in Shanghai inspected packages from Japan at the Central Post Office.	„
703	„ 7, '31.	One roll of newspaper of the Japanese firm, "Bunshin Yoko," in Shanghai, was seized with the carriage while in transit.	„
704.	„ 9, '31.	Cases in Ichang of stoning primary school, living quarters for employees of the Nisshin Kisen Kaisha, Naval Club and Japanese Consulate.	„
705	„ 10, '31.	2 gendarmes of the Japanese Garrison in Tientsin were assaulted by Chinese soldiers and robbed of their personal effects.	North China
706	„ 10, '31.	8 Japanese were subjected to violence and plundered near the entrance to the S.M.R. wharf in Shanghai.	„
707	„ 10, '31.	Fire was set to the annex to the Japanese Naval Club in Ichang.	Middle China
708	„ 10, '31.	A case of shooting a revolver on the police office in the Japanese Concession in Chungking.	„
709	„ 11, '31.	A Japanese toy merchant in Shanghai had his shop cleaned out by members of the Anti-Japanese Society.	„

No.	Date		Region
710	Oct. 11, '31.	A Japanese police officer of the Executive Council of the International Settlement was stoned and wounded, while engaged in tearing off anti-Japanese posters.	Middle China
711	,, 11, '31.	O.S.K. and N.K.K. ships were refused labour for handling cargo in Chungking.	,,
712	,, 14, '31.	A collision took place between Chinese mob and the Japanese tearing off anti-Japanese posters on North Szechuan Road and other places in Shanghai.	,,
713	,, 18, '31.	A bomb was thrown into a building over the postern gate of the Japanes Consulate at Kulanghsu near Amoy.	South China

APPENDICES

APPENDICES

		PAGE
JAPAN AND CHINA IN MANCHURIA	*Hugh Byas*	293
JAPAN IN TRANSITION	*Frazier Hunt*	303
THE WAR MINISTER SPEAKS CONCERNING CHINA AND MANCHURIA		311

APPENDIX I

JAPAN AND CHINA IN MANCHURIA

(The following clear and well-informed presentation of a neutral observer's views on the Manchurian problem was broadcast by Mr. Hugh Byas, the able staff correspondent in Japan of the *Times* of London and of New York, on December 2, 1931)

There is an English saying that the onlooker sees most of the game and when JOAK asked a foreigner to speak on this question they wanted to know how the present dispute looked to a neutral observer.

The dispute started with an attack on the South Manchuria Railway by Chinese soldiers. The attack caused little damage and, if relations between the two countries had been normal, it might have been soon settled. But if you will allow me another English saying, "It is the last straw that breaks the camel's back." The incident of September 18 came on top of a long series of acts in which Japanese rights had been attacked. The Japanese Government determined to have a show-down and clear up the situation.

The attack on the railway was the work of Chinese soldiers. Japanese troops are stationed in Manchuria for the protection of the railway, and it was their duty to resist it. The employment of troops created a danger of war and therefore the League of Nations intervened because it has the duty of preventing war, and a purely local question became a matter of concern to the whole world.

The first question which occurs to a neutral observer is: How does Japan come to be in Manchuria?

Forty years ago Manchuria was a kind of No Man's Land without railroads, with few towns, with a small population. The making of the Trans-Siberian railway by Russia suddenly brought this No Man's Land right in the track of the expanding Russian Empire. Railways were laid across the wilderness. What had been remote and unknown was brought near. Russia began to absorb Manchuria.

You know what happened. After the war with China in 1894 Japan obtained the Kwantung peninsula where Dairen and Port Arthur now stand. The famous triple intervention of Russia, France and Germany compelled Japan to give up the rights she had gained. Shortly afterwards Russia, with cynicism which we will hope belongs to the past, seized the Kwantung peninsula for herself. She carried the Trans-Siberian railway through Manchuria in a straight line, and she built another line southwards to Dairen, where she created a Russian port and she made Port Arthur the most powerful fortress in Asia.

Nations do not build great fortresses in other people's countries. Manchuria was No Man's Land no longer. The Russian eagle had taken Manchuria very firmly in her claws. It had become a dependeney of the Russian Empire, developed by Russian railways, defended by Russian armies.

Every schoolboy knows what followed. The Russian

war was fought and won. Port Arthur was redeemed from Russia by the blood of 80,000 Japanese soldiers. It is now a harmless summer resort, a place of peace, its guns which had been aimed at Japan were no longer needed. All that is history.

The point I wish to emphasize is perfectly clear yet continually forgotten. Japan did not take Manchuria from China. Manchuria has ceased to belong to China. The rights Japan gained in Manchuria were acquired from Russia in a war which Japan with a clear conscience can say was a war of self defence.

With Japan established in Manchuria by a perfectly clear title, not as the dispossessor of China but as victor over Russia, the history of modern Manchuria begins. It is a history of the building up of a state by railways. Manchuria today is what the Middle West of America was 50 years ago. It is one of the few regions left in the world where a great and fertile territory remains to be opened up. Sixty or seventy years ago the states of the Middle West were mostly wilderness, inhabited by herds of buffalo and wandering tribes of Indians. Great waves of immigration from Europe and the eastern part of America flowed over them and they were inhabited and settled. Fields and farms cover the lands where the buffalo roamed, and hundreds of peaceful cities have been founded.

Manchuria is such a region in its earliest stage. One does not easily realize its size and potential importance. Manchuria is three times larger than Japan —Manchuria, 363,000 square miles, Japan 147,000—

twice as large as California, four times larger than the British Isles, twice larger than Germany. It is a land of natural beauty with mountains and forests, great rivers and fertile plains. Two mountain ranges traverse the country. There is no Fuji, but there are many regions resembling the Japanese Alps. The climate in winter is very cold but healthy. It has unlimited coal beds. The soil is as fertile as that of Canada. It is a land deserving of peace and good government, and if peace and good government were granted it would become the home of a great nation.

Thirty years ago the population of Manchuria was under five millions. Today it approaches thirty millions. Immigrants with their families have been going in at the rate of nearly a million a year. Unlike the United States and Canada and Australia which drew their immigrants from distant lands across great oceans, Manchuria is being peopled from the overflowing reservoir of China. They go direct by road, rail and steamer. The poorest travel steerage and walk the rest of the way. Manchuria has in recent years been China's land of promise, the way of escape of the northern Chinese masses from war, tyranny, banditry, floods and famine. The population is hardy and poor, well suited for pioneering. Its increase is probably unparalleled in history. Twenty years from now the population of Manchuria may easily be 50 millions: by the end of the century 100 millions. Manchuria is a nation in the making.

It is being made by railroads. More than 5,000 miles of railway have been laid in Manchuria in 30 years, while little more than 3,000 miles have been laid in the whole vast territory of China Proper in 50 years.

In China at intervals some war lord commandeers the railway for his troops, interrupts ordinary commercial traffic for weeks or months, takes the engines and cars with him when he retires. Track and rolling stock deteriorate, railway revenues are seized by the war lords for their own purposes. Interest on capital is unpaid and funds for development cannot be raised.

In South Manchuria under Japanese control the picture is exactly the opposite. The main line has been modernized; rolling stock has been increased to three times its original capacity; branch lines have been pushed out into fertile virgin territory carrying settlers to the land and opening the markets of the world to their produce. Largely through the development work of the S. M. R., the neglected areas of the country have been opened to cultivation. The arable land under crops has risen from 17 million acres in 1907 to 31 million acres; trade has increased from 52 million taels to 679 millions a year.

You may ask why I go into this history which should be known to the world. I am answering the question which as a neutral observer I was bound to put: What right has Japan in Manchuria and what is she doing there? we have seen that she has a moral and legal right to the position in Manchuria which she claims, and she has not used her power in a selfish manner for the exclusion of Chinese.

What bearing has this record upon the present dispute? The incident of September 18 is of very little importance. It was only the spark that caused the fire. It is of almost no importance compared with the long and deliberate disregard of Japanese rights. The real question at issue is whether Japan is to remain in Manchuria, or whether, after having developed the country to its present stage, she is to be squeezed out, her position undermined, her rights withered away.

The action of the League of Nations and of the United States at Geneva and Paris is not due to any desire to hamper Japan but to the new spirit of modern diplomacy which seeks to prevent war and to solve international disputes by peaceful means. Japan is a foundation member of the League of Nations. She is respected as the greatest stabilising influence in the Far East. It is certain that the League of Nations will never take any steps which would limit Japan's rights in Manchuria. The League has been formed by agreement between the nations of the world to prevent war, and that is all that it is trying to do.

It is in this case more to China's benefit than Japan's that war should be prevented, for war could only mean a humiliating defeat for the Chinese armies. But peace is also the true interest of Japan, which does not seek to conquer her neighbouring people of China but to live in harmony with them and continue to lead the way, along with them, in the economic development of Manchuria.

It now seems certain that war will be prevented and that before long Japan and China will settle down to discuss their future relations in Manchuria. That brings me to my last question: What is to be the future of Manchuria?

Opinion in other countries has supposed that the action of the Japanese army in Manchuria would lead to annexation, or to a protectorate, or at least that Japan would demand new concessions and privileges. A writer in the *New York Times*, Herbert Bayard Swope, has advocated that Japan should annex Manchuria. "Is it not better," he says, "to have that vast country open to commerce instead of to famine: open to industry instead of looting; open to peace instead of unrest."

But that is not Japan's policy, as I understand it. At the commencement of the military operations the foreign minister, Baron Shidehara, told the world that Japan would make no new demands upon China and simply required fulfilment of existing treaties.

That implies that Japan intends to continue her civilising role not as the ruler and administrator of Manchuria but as a partner or a fellow shareholder with the Chinese in the development of that country. In this Japan has the support of the world. There is no opposition on the part of any foreign country, certainly not England or America, in both of which countries there is nothing but admiration for the work Japan has done in Manchuria.

It cannot be denied that annexation by Japan would give the 30 million peaceful Chinese people who dwell in Manchuria better government than they have received from their successive war lords, yet annexation is not Japanese policy, and for very good reasons.

Manchuria is No Man's Land no longer. It is a great Chinese state. There were some seven million Chinese in Manchuria when Japan went there but there are 30 millions today. The objection to the annexation of Manchuria is that it would make Japan responsible for the government of 30 million Chinese. The population of Manchuria has decided its destiny. It can never be anything but a Chinese state.

From those facts it is clear that Japan should continue along the lines fixed by circumstances—economic development in the co-operation with the Chinese. If the Chinese were less blinded by the anti-Japanese propaganda which has been created by the Kuomintang in its own political interests, would see that Japanese development is in the true interests of China.

But it is not in the true interests of either China Proper or Manchuria that Manchuria should be dragged into the vicious circle of Chinese civil war. The real root of the present trouble is that in recent years Manchurian resources have been wasted on the upkeep of huge armies which have been thrown into China's civil war politics sometimes on one side and sometimes on the other. Currency has been debased and population impoverished, so that the Manchurian war lords might play a part in China. That is not fair either to the Chinese or to the Manchurians. Japan is determined to stop that, and it is in the interests of civilization and of China herself that it should be stopped.

Join with me for a moment in looking beyond the present dispute which will pass away and in a few years be forgotten. What is to be the future of Manchuria? By the end of the present century the Japanese leases of Kwantung and the South Manchuria Railway will expire. Manchuria, with the strong hand of Japan keeping peace and security, will then be a nation of 100 million Chinese.

The leases of Chinese territory, like the railway troops and extraterritoriality, are temporary expedients made necessary by China's helpless and disordered conditions. As conditions improve these arrangements will become obsolete. In an orderly country with a strong government, foreign troops will not be necessary to preserve foreign rights. Ties of trade and mutual interests will take their place. If it can be avoided, it is not desirable that Japan should take the burden of governing 30 million Chinese. The aim of Japanese policy must be the development of commercial relations so valuable to both countries that the end of the leases will not interrupt them. The Chinese and the Japanese alike have everything to gain by co-operation. The more railways that are built the better, but they must be economically planned to develop the country, and not simply to compete with the S.M.R. and divert trade from Dairen.

With peace and order secured, Manchuria will continue to be a land of promise for the Chinese— the Middle West of the Chinese republic. Chinese labour will continue to flow in, Chinese and Japanese investments will alike be profitable. Japanese capital and enterprise will reap rich and well deserved rewards. The more that Japanese enterprise develops in Manchuria the wealthier will Manchuria become. The expanding population of Manchuria and its increasing prosperity will create a market for Japanese goods, and Manchuria will prosper by producing the food and raw material required by Japan. My last word therefore to you is to look beyond the quarrels and disputes of the present moment and work for a future of harmony and co-operation with the Chinese people in Manchuria.

APPENDIX II

JAPAN IN TRANSITION

(Broadcast to America by Mr. Frazier Hunt, special Correspondent for the International News Service, on June 2, 1932.)

Hello Japan, good-morning America, or I suppose I should say good-afternoon America. You see it is 7.45 Saturday morning here in Tokyo and I have just finished my bacon and eggs and my copy of the "Japan Advertiser."

We are having exciting times here in Japan. History is being made. Japan is going through one of the most remarkable transitions in its long life. To many it is a political upheaval, a silent transformation—the ending of certain corrupt, inefficient and unfair elements in the political, economic and social life of the nation, and the coming of a new hope to the people of Japan.

There is a demand everywhere for change, for this recasting of values. Government officials, business men, leaders in the professions, writers, social workers, farmers, military people, and the youth of Japan all reiterate in one way or other this call for a new deal—a new deal internationally and a new deal internally. All are interested, but it is the youth whose protest is the most vivid and the most dramatic.

At 5.30 on a Sunday evening two weeks ago I was seated in a beautiful little teahouse with some Japanese friends. On a hill sloping just above us was the official residence of the Prime Minister. Suddenly, through the paper windows came the sound of shooting and frightened voices. That moment the aged Prime Minister of Japan was being shot to death.

An hour before, nine young military and naval officers and cadets met and offered a prayer and a vow: "We are about to give our lives for our country: soon our spirits will return." Quickly they entered taxicabs, bribing the chauffeurs, and were driven to the residence of the Prime Minister. Five entered by the back entrance and four by the front gate. The four pushed their way in through the front door and when two unarmed policemen tried to bar the way, one was killed and the other seriously wounded. An old woman servant rushed to the Japanese room where the Prime Minister was talking to a visitor; 'Run for your life,' she screamed, 'dangerous men are coming.' Calmly and with stoic dignity the courageous 77 year old Prime Minister, a little man, five feet three inches tall and weighing only slightly over 100 pounds, remained unmoved. "Let them come in,' he replied, 'I will talk to them.' The men were now in the room, their revolvers pointed at the Prime Minister. 'Sit down and let us talk over matters,' the Prime Minister said in ordinary tones. 'We are going to shoot you!' they cried. 'Come into the library where we can talk better': the Prime Minister parried, leading the way towards a European room. For possibly a minute he calmly answered their excited questions and accusations. By this time the group who had entered by the back door, rushed up with drawn pistols. 'Shoot him,' they cried, and then this brave little man said, 'All right, go ahead and shoot.' Half a dozen fired. One bullet grazed his temple, and a second crashed through his jaw. The old man crumpled up at their feet and they ran out. 'Call them back,' he whispered, 'there is something I want to explain to them.' His frail body was crushed, but his spirit was aflame. At midnight he died.

Immediately after this desperate deed, these nine misguided boys drove to the headquarters of the military police and there surrendered. Rightly or wrongly they had felt that anything that would awaken Japan, even the murder of an innocent man— was worth the frightful cost.

It was a Japanese writer who explained the depth of all this unrest and dissatisfaction for me: "You see," he said to me, "Japan has been going through the same economic crisis and the same questioning of modern democratic institutions, that you people in America have been going through. Our farmers who work in our rice fields, our silk cultivators and our tea growers, are in the same deplorable financial condition that I imagine your farmers in America are in. They owe more money than their land is worth; their taxes are high, and prices are low: silk growers, for instance, get one half for their cocoons that they received one year ago, and one-tenth of what they received—say ten years ago. They are discouraged, dissatisfied and weary, the city worker is much the same, and likewise men of the middle classes. While there is no such vast unemployment here as in America," he went on, "it is because our family system absorbs our city unemployed, but there is discontent and dissatisfaction in the cities. We have had many bank failures and all in all we are in the same position as American farmers and city people are in. We feel that politics is not only insufficient but in many ways corrupt. We are not sure that we have fully assimilated western political ideas. Many of our young men," he continued, "feel that Japan came into the family of nations too late to get her share of the good things of the earth. Our people are more or less bitter at what apparently is the determination of the world to hem in our growing population—to exclude it from other lands. Many of us are dissatisfied with what I suppose you might call the western economic system of capitalism. In a word," he concluded, "we want Japan to work out for herself some individual system inherent in Japanese tradition, that will do away with many of these injustices of the present day."

Everywhere one hears much this same sentiment. Millions scattered throughout the islands feel the need of some great reform, of some political and social evolution. Among certain classes it takes the form of a genuine Red movement. This is limited, however, to city workmen and groups of radical young college students. There is no real leadership in this left wing, and much of its popularity exists because it is prohibited. But everywhere you find some vague and indefinite hope for a new arrangement of affairs, for some system that will give greater prosperity and greater justice to the discouraged classes. Japan is not idly sitting down with folded hands, hoping some one will do something for her. All over the islands there are eager and intelligent people bravely trying to find some solution to the condition of the backward and debt ridden farmers and the city masses.

The other day I had one of the most interesting dinners in my life. My hosts were four Japanese college students. For hours we talked of the dreams and hopes of young Japan, not of college athletics, or fraternities, or jobs, or senior proms—but of Japan and her problems. Now and again we had a little language trouble—my Japanese consisting of the single word banzai—but all in all we understood each other perfectly. Here were four young men, all juniors or seniors in one of the six great Tokyo universities— belonging to what we would call ordinary middle class families; they were 20 to 22 years old, and each of them was deep in his dreams for an awakened, socially recast and spiritually inspired new Japan.

"What do you fellows want?" I asked quite bluntly. "We want a government that will not belong to any party," one of them answered, speaking for his fellow students. "We want our politics to be separated from big business and favoritism. We think that some way or other a new scheme of government and of social life can be worked out here in Japan."

"You mean some sort of state socialism?" I questioned. "Yes, something like that," he answered.

"We want equal sharing in the benefits of the important industries. We want debts to be reduced. Party governments have been unable to attempt all this: it must be done by some strong and powerful force backed by the genuine will of the people."

"A sort of Fascism," I suggested.

"Well"—he hesitated—"you understand." "Somehow or other we want to form a new machine here that will take care of our peculiar Japanese aspirations, both international and within our own country."

Now that was the average Japanese college student talking. Against this stands a great class of very moderate people, who would see Japan slowly evolve. Ideas and methods vary with the age and moderation of the person you talk with, but everywhere you do find a demand that something be done in Japan that will answer the growing unrest and dissatisfaction.

I want to repeat that Japan suffers only what the rest of the world is suffering, and I rather doubt if it is so severe as in other parts. Here, prosperity was not as exaggerated as ours in America for instance. Here there was less fantastic stock gambling and super prices, so Japan's balloon did not rise so high into the blue sky, and consequently did not have so far to fall. But she has dropped the easy money of the war days and of later years and now she is determined to try to work out some peaceful solution to her economic problems, that have become inescapably tangled up with her political problems and her social longings.

Much of it all is economic—dramatized in the price

of silk that the American market controls, but behind it all is a spiritual evolution, a moral transition. With my own eyes I have seen the great and lasting revolutions of Mexico, Soviet Russia, of China and India, and the social and political upheavals of half the world, but in many ways this is one of the most bewildering transitions of them all. Japan's unrest and dissatisfaction are the unrest and dissatisfaction of the world. The disillusionment of the whole world, over the failure of the old systems and beliefs,—the feeling that political, industrial and financial leadership has fallen down and proved inadequate in a crisis—the social unrest bred from prolonged depression—all are reflected in this beautiful land of Japan—Japan has heard the cry of an unhappy world. She is answering this cry in her own unique fashion. Her older men, her senior statesmen, are fully alive to the responsibility that they face. They are spurred on by the energy and zeal, the inspiration of the youth of Japan.

They want a new Japan to come out of this—a Japan for all. They want the benefits of the machine not to be concentrated in the pockets of selfish individuals, but to be shared by everyone.

Theirs is the dream of youth, but behind it stands the spirit of old Japan, a spirit of loyalty and sacrifice and idealism. The high spiritual side of ancient Japanese life that for almost one thousand years guided the samurai, still lives in Japan despite all impact with western civilization. It gives Japan a tradition of high morality and an idealism that is a great spiritual reservoir that is so sadly lacking in many other countries of the world. Young men here approach this crisis with the same high idealism with which they would answer a call to war. They have gone far to arouse the whole nation to its duties.

A new Cabinet has just been formed—a Nationalist Cabinet, a liberal coalition Cabinet. It has pledged its honour towards bravely starting to build the new Japan. It will do its best to cleanse the political Government of some of its taints of corruption and inefficiency. It is a part of Japan's answer to the unrest and dissatisfaction and disillusionment of the world. Behind it march the singing youth, calling for a return of the stern ancient conceptions of honour and loyalty, coupled with a modern conception of social justice and equality.

Now my time is about up, and I have only a moment to tell you that this May morning here in Tokyo is very beautiful. There are flowers everywhere and smiling, hospitable people, who dream the same dreams as all the other peoples of the world. They want a little better life for themselves, a better chance for their children and a little more happiness and comfort. And I believe that is what you folks in California and Texas and Dakota and New York, and in all the other 44 States also want.

Well, good-bye, until Mukden, Manchuria, next month.

APPENDIX III

THE WAR MINISTER SPEAKS CONCERNING CHINA AND MANCHURIA

1. Interview with "Times" Correspondent

Lieutenant-General Sadao Araki, Minister of War, granted an interview to Mr. Hugh Byas, the staff correspondent in Tokyo of the "Times" of London and New York on January 16, 1932. The conversation covered various features of the Japanese policy concerning Manchuria and Mongolia. The War Minister's answers are translated from a verbatim report in Japanese.

Question: "With the conclusion of military operations, Japan's constructive policy in Manchuria now has to be developed, and other Powers are more interested in Manchuria's future status than in past events. The following questions are asked with a view to understanding Japan's policy. What form do you expect the new government of Manchuria to take—imperial or republican?"

Answer: "I am sorry to say that I could not answer that question; it bears in part upon the question what policy Manchuria and Mongolia will follow in creating a new state, a question outside the War Minister's line. But I may venture to say this that a question of the sort should be settled by the new

Manchurian administration on the basis of popular will, and not by Japan or any other people. What I particularly wish to have you transmit to the peoples of the countries you represent, is that if a new state is brought into being in Manchuria and Mongolia as a result of China's self-destructive moves, such event should be regarded purely as an incident in the internal politics of China, with which no foreign nation should interfere. And no nation takes a clearer view of this same matter than Japan which has always adhered to the policy of non-interference in internal politics of China. What we truly want in Manchuria and Mongolia may be stated in plain terms. We want, from our unchanged motive of securing peace in the Far East, a new reign of peace established throughout those countries, where natives as well as foreign peoples may alike live in peace and security, and enjoy, through the open door policy, commercial equality and opportunity for investment. Concerning our recent military operations, we may state that we were simply compelled in self-defence. But in no instance did we go beyond such limits. And I believe that our conduct of affairs over there has been so clear and above the board that nobody with a real knowledge of the positions can doubt that that is our policy. Now as for the question what form of government may be expected in Manchuria, there seems quite a divergence of opinion even among the leaders of the new Manchurian administration. Some of them would like to see the Imperial regime restored, while others favour a republic composed of the four races—Manchurian, Mongolian, Chinese and Japanese—who inhabit the territory and deserve a measure of credit for its present development. But when all is said and done, this is a question that the Manchurian administration must decide by itself on the basis of the people's collective will. I can't make any prophecy."

Q. "If the same is to take a republican form of government, will there be a central government or simply four local provincial governments?"

A. "That is a question for the new Manchurian Government."

Q. "What will be the link, if any, between the Manchurian Government and the central government of China?"

A. "I dare say that it may be fortunate for the 30 million people of Manchuria, if the Manchurian Government dissociate itself from the central government of China. Was it not a realization of this that made the local governments of Mukden, Kirin and Heilungkiang declare their independence and break off relations with General Chang Hsueh-liang and the Nanking Government? Apart from the matter of making enquiries in historical lines, we may say that, in the light of the actual conditions in Manchuria and Mongolia during these recent years, these countries have been part of China in name but not in fact. They have existed as truly feudalistic provinces, each of them having a government of its own. The head of the government, invested with both civil and military authority, had absolute power to rule. There was no clear distinction between his private funds and the government's funds. Provincial banks at his order issued each of them inconvertible paper currency without limit. He kept personal soldiers and state soldiers and made no distinction between them. On the strength of these soldiers he abused his powers and enriched himself and indulged in pleasures. He, therefore, often imposed heavy and unreasonable taxations. These conditions became worse when the late Marshal Chang Tso-ling, not satisfied with ruling the four provinces of Manchuria, extended the fields of his ambition within the Great Wall of China. This policy was later pursued even at the cost of Japan's vested interests, finally developing into moves expressive of antagonism and contempt for Japan. Such being the case, it will be, in my opinion, for the benefit not only of the people of Manchuria but also for the peace of the whole Far East, if Manchuria remains separated from China."

Q. "What will be independent Manchuria's relations with the Japanese Government? In other words, how will you ensure that Japan's interests will be respected in future?"

A. "New independent countries, born under the conditions of modern times, must needs have in their early days a positive support of countries and peoples specially interested. You will understand this, if you study the story of the independence of Cuba or the formation of Panama, and of many other new countries formed in Europe after the great war. It is natural that Japan should support the progress and development of a government in Manchuria which is prepared to recognize and protect Japan's rights and interests and maintain friendly relations with her. Apart from the question how the new administration might be asked to ensure our interests, is it not natural at all that we should ask it to guarantee them and expect that it should do so?"

Q. "Japan's aim is to prevent Manchuria being involved again in Chinese political turmoil. Judging by past experience, that will require some power to prevent excessive armaments being built up and excessive taxation imposed. How would you expect to prevent those evils reappearing?"

A. "I share your view that Manchuria should be prevented from again being involved in China's turmoil, and my view is based on the ground I have already set forth. It is most desirable for peace in the Far East that 30 million people should be saved from China's war lords and given their freedom. It is interesting to observe that the new government in order to wipe out the influence of the former war lords, are steadily enlisting good men from the old armies in their police forces. It is also interesting to see how they disband the rest of the old armies and offer them work, in order to eliminate the evils with which their countries have been infested."

Q. "Would you favour appointing Japanese advisers to the new government?"

A. "That depends on the new government. We shall not force the employment of Japanese advisers.

If the new government wants them there is no reason why we should object."

Q. "If the unification of Japanese organs in Manchuria is effected, would the head of the new Board have special relations with the Manchurian Government?"

A. "It is generally recognized that we have in the past experienced considerable difficulty in many ways through the quadripartite system of administration we have had there. I should not be surprised, therefore, if a new organ should be worked out unifying the existing institutions. But I can't say beforehand what, in such event, the relations of the new head of the Japanese board and the head of the Manchurian Government will be. That is for the Japanese and Manchurian Governments to arrange."

Q. "The Kwantung army has invited legal, financial and industrial advisers to prepare plans for development, according to press reports. How is it proposed to have these plans carried out—by the new unified Japanese administration or the Chinese?"

A. "I have heard that experts have been invited by the Kwantung army to study various problems. The present chaotic conditions explain this step. The army, however, is interested in matters affecting itself. Details are unknown to me as there have been no discussions yet with the central authorities."

Q. "What security would you have against another period of inflated currency?"

A. "That question is out of my line. The currency question in Manchuria and Mongolia is very complicated. The province of Mukden has its own Fengpiao or Mukden notes, the province of Kirin has its own currency notes, while in Harbin we find Harbin Tayang notes in circulation. Besides, these notes are so over-issued that they are just about the value of waste paper today. The war lords printed notes recklessly to provide for their military and political expenditure and for their private investments. Nobody knows the exact amount of the currency issued. In any case, it seems obvious that the new government of Manchuria will have to attend, as one of the very first things, to the task of unifying its currency system on a sound basis of conversion, by disposing of all those worthless notes in circulation."

Q. " Would the relations of Manchuria with the Maritime Customs be altered in any way?"

A. " I am not in a position to answer that question."

Q. " Are you satisfied that an independent Manchurian Government will carry out policies satisfactory to Japan?"

A. " I have no idea."

Q. " Will there not be a risk that Japan may eventually have to annex Manchuria, or seek a mandate for its administration from the League of Nations?"

A. "There is absolutely no risk. Japan will respect treaties to the utmost."

Q. " Are you in favour of the South Manchuria Railway taking over the railways for which they have not yet paid?"

A. "As War Minister I can't answer this, but I think if the other parties are willing, the South Manchuria Railway will accept."

Q. "How would you dispose of the bandit problem?"

A. "The first step to make Manchuria and Mongolia a happy land is to wipe out the bandits, restore order and maintain local peace, by doing away with the bandits over-riding the whole territory. That is exactly what 30 million people want. But the Manchurian government at present is not strong enough to suppress them. The Kwantung army is compelled, for its own safety, to suppress them. It was for the same reason that we claimed and obtained that right at the Council of the League of Nations. But as a matter of fact, the Kwantung army, which numbers little over 20,000, has considerable difficulty to deal with the bandits who number tens of thousands and keep shifting throughout the vast country where there is little else to hamper their movement. What should be noted is that the Chinese population in Manchuria are in most part immigrants from Shantung, a fierce race, with strong anti-foreign sentiments. It was among them that the Boxer movement developed. Some bandits are used by General Chang Hsueh-liang as tools against Japan but others are reduced to banditry by poverty. The former must be suppressed. The latter will be given employment or means of support if they surrender. Many bandit gangs have lately submitted to the Japanese forces, and asked to be employed as police."

2. Interview with Associated Press Representative

Lieutenant-General Araki, Minister of War, granted interview to Mr. Howe, the staff correspondent in Tokyo of the Associated Press of America, on February 21, 1932. A series of the questions raised on the same occasion are given below with the War Minister's answers.

Question: "Will the Japanese army forces in Manchuria be permanently maintained at their present strength?"

Answer: "Japan has the right by treaty to maintain a military force in Manchuria. No doubt she will permanently maintain an armed force within the limit of the treaty agreement. But the question of maintaining the present strength depends upon the conditions of the country. It is impossible to make any prophecy now. But I may as well add that conditions in Manchuria and Mongolia have undergone such changes that it is deemed now necessary to study what may be an adequate military force to meet the changed situation over there."

Q. "What is the present strength?"

A. "There was prior to the outbreak of the trouble a railway guard of 10,400, to which a reenforcement of 11,600 has been added, making a total of approximately 22,000. Of this force a part of the special service troops has already been brought back home."

Q. "Is any further reinforcement of the army in Manchuria contemplated?"

A. "It depends entirely on the conditions over there. But some of our troops there are really overworked and played out. It looks as if something has to be done about it."

Q. "Is it planned to move another division to Korea to replace that of Lieutenant-General Muro, presently operating in Manchuria?"

A. "There is no plan of the sort at present. There is, however, a plan for moving one division from Japan to Korea, in addition to the present force of two divisions. But this plan is being considered purely from the strategic point of view, the idea being to strengthen the defence of the Peninsula and having nothing to do with the present Manchurian trouble; a point about which I hope there will be no misunderstanding. This contemplated change in our military system, however, has been postponed, not only because the budget was not passed due to the dissolution of the Diet, but also because it was thought inadvisable, in view of the present situation as respects Manchuria, Mongolia and China itself, to effect at this particular juncture any change in the system of army division or in military organization which might create wrong impressions as to the true motive. It was also thought that it would be more advisable to withhold such question of armament until it would be possible to consider it in the light of the changed conditions in Manchuria and Mongolia."

Q. "Will such points outside the South Manchuria Railway zone as Harbin, Chinchow, Kirin, Chengchiatun, Tsitsihar, Tahushan, Tungliao be permanently occupied by Japanese forces? Is there any intention of an early withdrawal of the Japanese forces within the S.M.R. zone?"

A. "We have no intention of permanent occupation. The presence of Japanese troops outside the South Manchuria Railway zone means only a temporary measure to meet the conditions brought about by the activities of disbanded soldiers, bandits and lawless gangs. In those provincial regions peace is being constantly disturbed, and, especially, the economic life of the inhabitants is virtually wrecked. Local representatives of the new administration are too weak to maintain peace. The Imperial army is being requested to suppress and dispose of those disturbers of peace. Such being the case, the Kwantung army, in consideration of its mission, is compelled to station its troops in those regions until a return of peace and order will make their presence no longer necessary."

Q. "Is there any intention of an early withdrawal of the Japanese forces from the South Manchuria Railway zone?"

A. "There is no intention of withdrawal from the railway zone. Our troops are stationed in the South Manchuria Railway zone in virtue of treaty rights. I wonder if such a question could be possible where there is a real knowledge of the positions."

Q. "Will the Japanese army continue indefinitely to protect and provide support for the autonomous provincial governments which are being established in Manchuria?"

A. "We have always been most anxious that

Manchuria and Mongolia should become a land of lasting peace. We are, therefore, most favourably disposed toward any move to further the same cause. When the new government of Manchuria is bent on establishing a good regime for the 30 million people, without prejudice to the Japanese interests, we naturally consider it nothing less than the friendly duty of a neighbour nation to render it support."

Q. " Will such police functions eventually be turned over to Chinese forces under such friendly leaders as Chang Hai-peng, Ma Chan-shan and others, many of whom already are reported to be co-operating with the Japanese forces in clearing Manchuria of bandits?"

A. " Yes. When Chang Hai-peng, Ma Chan-shan, Yu Chih-shan, Wang Tien-chung and others will place themselves under the direction of the new Manchurian Government and prove their faith in performing those police functions, without committing such atrocities as the former war lords were guilty of, those duties will no doubt be turned over to them."

Q. "Is it proposed to conduct further military operations in North Manchuria?"

A. "The Japanese military forces have made no move except in self-defence. I may also state that they will never act otherwise in the possible event of operating in North Manchuria. As a matter of fact, North Manchuria had been menaced by the activities of such men as Ting Chao and Li Tu, acting at the instigation of Chang Hsueh-liang, until their troops were driven away from the vicinity of Harbin by our Tamon division. Thus a new era of peace and order dawns in North Manchuria. If there appears no armed force to oppose our army, North Manchuria will see no more of armed clash. But even now there are soldiers of the old armies, partizans and bandits at large and active at all places, a situation that may eventually call our troops to action as a matter of necessity."

Q. "Will General Tamon's forces be confined to Harbin, or will they move east and west along the main line of the Chinese Eastern Railway or northwest toward the lower Sungari in pursuit of recalcitrant elements?"

A. "We feel that we should call to account the anti-Kirin army against which a number of things are charged; namely, the killing of an air officer of our army, massacre and outraging of Koreans, burning of their houses and also of the building of the Japanese owned newspaper *Taihoku Shimpo*, armed oppositions along the southern branch of the Chinese Eastern Railway, especially at Shuangchengpu. But we have at present no intention of making pursuit with our main force. The main force of General Tamon's division, temporarily stationed in Harbin, will attend to the safeguarding of our resident population, until peace and order will be established in North Manchuria."

Q. "Does the Minister believe there is danger of conflict with Russia growing out of Japan's occupation of Harbin and use and control of the southern branch of the Chinese Eastern Railway?"

A. "I do not believe there is any such danger.

It is very gratifying that the Soviet authorities and the Chinese Eastern Railway management, with a straightforward appreciation of the legitimacy of our military actions in North Manchuria, have consistently taken a fair attitude toward us. The revolutionary ideas of Communism are never acceptable to a country like Japan. As long as Soviet Russia will refrain from interference, with a full regard for our action, we shall never encroach upon the rights of the Chinese Eastern Railway or break in upon Russian territory. As for the allegation of instigating the White Russians, with which Soviet Russia seems most seriously concerned, it is nothing but a wild fantasy. What I should like to add is that the occupation of Harbin by our troops is only temporary one. As for the use of the southern branch of the Chinese Eastern Railway, we have a positive consent of the Soviet Government, there being no case of our men taking control of the railway, as your question seems to imply."

Q. "Does Japan propose to buy this branch?"

A. "We do not."

Q. "Does Japan desire to control the whole of the Chinese Eastern Railway?"

A. "We have never had such a desire."

Q. "What is the connection between the Japanese army and the new Government growing up in Manchuria?"

A. "We understand that the new Manchurian state aims, internally, to ensure good government to its population of 30 millions within the boundaries and, externally, to become as honourable a member as any in the family of nations, affording them equal opportunity through its open door policy. The leaders of Manchuria are devoting themselves to the creation of a new state in consonance with the general will of the people of Manchuria and Mongolia who wish for the birth of a community where they are never to be exploited, an ideal state of lasting peace. It would be an unpardonable outrage to interfere with their efforts consecrated in such a lofty cause. It is but natural that Japan should be friendly disposed toward them. And we do hope most sincerely that the new Manchurian Government will make an unhampered and sound progress toward its goal."

Q. "What part are such men as Colonel Itagaki and Colonel Doihara playing in the establishment of the new order of affairs in Manchuria?"

A. "The former belongs to the staff of the Kwantung army, while the latter is chief of the Special Service Bureau in Harbin. They are charged with no work except of purely military character."

Q. "Does the Army favour the establishment of a new unified and autonomous (or independent) state of Manchuria and Mongolia?"

A. "It does; because it is convinced that it will be a long way better than the absurdities of former militarist governments."

Q. "How far into Mongolia should such a state extend? To the borders of Outer Mongolia, which Soviet Russia dominates?"

A. "That is for the new Manchurian Government,

and not for me, to decide."

Q. "What does the Army propose to do with Fengtien-Shanhaikwan portion of the Peking-Mukden railway?"

A. "That's, too, for the new Manchurian Government; Japan should make no interference. However, it is to be expected that Japan for her part should demand the new Manchurian Government to show full respect for the existing Japanese rights relating to railways in Manchuria and Mongolia."

Q. "How soon will the railway between Tunhua (terminus of the Kirin-Tunhua Railway) and the Korean coast be built?"

A. "I can't answer. This railway or the Kirin-Huinin (Kainei) Railway is based on the rights secured by virtue of the Sino-Japanese agreement concerning Chientao concluded September 9, 1909. Japan made an advance of 10,000,000 yen in 1918. And in 1928 President Yamamoto, of the South Manchuria Railway Company, had a contract made for the construction of the railway. All those rights were trampled upon by the former military government. Prior to the outbreak of the present Manchurian trouble, the railway between Tienpaoshan and Tumen had been completed as a Sino-Japanese undertaking. From the other side or Kirin, a Chinese railway had been built between Kirin and Tunhua, leaving an intervening distance of no more than 67 miles between Tunhua and Laotoukou. In view of such fact, it will be but proper that Japan should have the new Manchurian Government recognize her rights pertaining to the same railway. With the same recognition obtained, Japan will undoubtedly set about construction of the railway. But as for the date for starting the same work, or that for its completion, nothing definite is known."

Q. "What is to become of the Chinese project for the creation of a great port at Hulutao, now under Japanese occupation?"

A. "That, too, is for the new Manchurian Government to decide and not for Japan to interfere. We at present station there a small squad of soldiers as an outpost and for the protection of the Japanese residents; but with regard to the harbour work, we have had no concern whatever, neither interfering nor applying pressure in any way. We learn that there are some 300 workmen employed, who are at present working ashore, having stopped to work in the water due to the cold weather. The work thus far completed represents about 20 percent of the whole project. According to expert opinion, it will take five more years at the present rate of progress."

Q. "What are the intentions of the Japanese army with regard to Shanghai?"

A. "The objects of the Japanese expedition to Shanghai are, as set forth in a series of official statements, to protect our nationals and their property running up into billions of yen, and also to discharge our international duties of safeguarding the International Settlement. If the Chinese side cease hostilities, or if they make no interference with our army in pursuit of such objects, we have no intention of taking armed action."

Q. "Will there be a long-time occupation of the Shanghai area by Japanese military forces?"

A. "We hope to evacuate as soon as possible. But inasmuch as our army is there in self-defence, it all depends on China. It is to be hoped that the Powers will arrive at a correct appreciation of the situation, and render assistance to the end of restoring normal conditions in the international city with the least delay."

Q. "Is the despatch of other divisions besides those already under orders for Shanghai contemplated by the War Office?"

A. "I can't tell. Future developments alone will determine."

Q. "How far is it intended to conduct operations outside Shanghai? To Soochow? To Nanking?"

A. "We have sent over our soldiers, as already explained, to do our utmost to prevent the unfortunate situation from spreading, to remove all menaces to the lives and property of our resident population as peacefully and as speedily as possible, thus restoring conditions desirable for other nationals as well. Extension of the present situation is desirable to none. If there is any one who does wish for such development, it can be none but a certain Chinese military party or the Chinese Communist party, which one as much as the other hope to draw Britain and America, and possibly others, into the trouble. Such being the truth of the matter, you will understand why the Japanese army has at present no intention to carry its action very far from Shanghai. What is certain in any event is that we must demand the Chinese army to withdraw itself to a distance sufficient to ensure safety for the international port of Shanghai. The only question is whether such arrangement may be accomplished by diplomatic negotiations or by methods of war. We do hope for the former, but it appears highly doubtful if the Nineteenth Route Army is in a mood for peaceful withdrawal."

Q. "There are rumours of a general mobilization in Japan. Is such a step contemplated?"

A. "Absolutely not. We do hope you will know such rumours for what they are really worth. We hope so, especially because we know that when such an institution as yours should give credit, without discrimination or due enquiry, for such rumours, very serious harm would be done."

Q. "What are the intentions of the Army with respect to the regions on the southern and western borders of Manchuria—the Peiping-Tientsin district and the province of Jehol?"

A. "We contemplate nothing at present."

Q. "Does the Minister believe it will be necessary to extend military operations into these regions in order to ensure peace and stability in Manchuria?"

A. "We do not believe there is any necessity."

Q. "Are the forces now in Manchuria sufficient if it becomes necessary to extend operations into these regions or into North Manchuria?"

A. "The present strength is not sufficient even as matters stand now. The Kwantung army has none the less remained content with it, seeing the existing state of affairs. No thought, in fact, of tactical difficulty has ever induced it to ask for reinforcement."

Q. "How far will the Japanese army expedition co-operate with the land forces of other Powers now stationed at Shanghai in the task of restoring and maintaining peace and order in that region?"

A. "All practical arrangements are left with the commander of the expedition. We have had it conveyed to him particularly that we expect our army to do its best to effect friendly co-operation with other Powers in a spirit of mutual help to the end of promoting orderly life and prosperity in the region of Shanghai, thus serving in the cause of peace and welfare in the Far East."

Q. "It is current gossip that the Army and especially the General Staff are attempting to exercise a military dictatorship in Japan. How far is this true? Does the Army desire to dictate the policies of the Cabinet?"

A. "A rumour of which we know nothing. However, it is our conviction that, should the peace of the Far East be endangered, international honour disregarded, and our country and people driven to the choice between life and death, then our country, especially our warlike organizations, would display such a discipline and unity as would surprise the whole world."

Q. "Owing to the censorship imposed on press messages from Japan to foreign countries, exaggerated accounts of the size and intended use of the Japanese army expedition to Shanghai are current in other countries, casting grave suspicions on Japan's motives and intentions. Some of these accounts assert Japan is sending five divisions or 100,000 men. Would it not be wise to publish definite figures? How long is the censorship to remain in force? Is it believed to be serving a useful purpose?"

A. "We have been giving out, whenever the occasion arose, an approximate number of soldiers sent out. With regard to matters of tactical significance, it is a rule with every country to withhold them from publicity as long as thought necessary. We regret very much to learn that exaggerated accounts are current abroad; but we trust that truth will become known in course of time. Such a form of propaganda as China has no scruple to conduct will, in our opinion, only prove self-disparaging, especially in an international place like Shanghai. As for the censorship of telegrams, it is outside the line of the War Ministry. We may only say this in reply that censorship at a time like the present, when war-time conditions are not to be imposed, really presents a very difficult question. We know that it will be extremely difficult to accomplish it to satisfaction. We, however, know at the same time that to have information leak out to a limited section is one thing, while to have it broadcast to all public is quite another."

3. Interview with International News Service Correspondent

On June 2, 1932, Mr. Frazier Hunt, correspondent of the International News Service of America and the *Cosmopolitan Magazine* and also representative of the National Radio Broadcast Corporation of the same country, was granted an interview by General Araki, Minister of War. Below are given a series of questions asked on the same occasion with answers by the Minister.

Question: "What is the ideal of Japan Tomorrow?"

Answer: "We now uphold, even as in the past, the fundamental principles of our nation, as lasting as its history, 'the path of Imperial rule' which is symbolized by the Three Sacred Treasures of the Imperial Family, viz. the principles of justice, benevolence and decision—a lofty ideal which we propose to have made known abroad and fully recognized at home. To know Japan one must make a study of this path of Imperial rule."

Q. "What can the Army do towards obtaining this ideal?"

A. "The Army should first incorporate itself this ideal and then, by imparting its influence to others, contribute toward its ultimate general attainment. In other words, the Imperial Army is a moral existence to serve as an implement for propagating the great principles of the path of Imperial rule; its idea is to fight only in the cause of justice and truth."

Q. "Under certain conditions would not a Fascist government be fully justified?"

A. "We know from our history that we have invariably been impartial in inviting from abroad new thoughts, new religions and new forms of culture, as shown in the cases of Buddhism, Confucianism, Christianity and others. Our nation has in each instance proved itself capable of absorbing and digesting what was imported from the outside, making it ultimately its own flesh and blood. Through such process our unique national polity has alway been even more glorified. The Fascism of Italy was a product conditioned by history, geography and environments peculiar to the Italian nation alone. In Italy it has developed under the direction of Mussolini into a polity well deserving of respect. Japan has its own principle of Imperial rule. No mind, unless misled by superficial, if not fallacious views, could ever conceive Japan turning to Fascism."

Q. "Has not the Army the right to urge and inspire a New Japan built on pure Japanese lines?"

A. "For the attainment of our national ideal, not only the Army but the whole nation should equally put forth their best effort. The Army never should concern itself directly with politics. It is our ideal that as long as the Imperial Army exists, as it does, there will be no bad statesmanship. In any event, the Imperial Army will never move except by His Majesty's order."

Q. "Is not the whole world 'soft'?"

A. "I am unable to say anything about young

people of other countries. In so far as our younger generation is concerned, I believe that something must be done to create a race of more fortitude and greater sturdiness. In fact, I am even now striving to do what I can to the same end. With regard to the way our young soldiers have acquitted themselves in both Manchuria and Shanghai, it is, as you are well aware, little short of wonder, their bravery in some instances even surpassing what was seen in our war with Russia. Display of such order of courage shows that the true spirit of our nation has been quickened to life through the Manchurian crisis."

Q. "Theodore Roosevelt believed wars were necessary for a country's spirit and for the preservation of its soul. Is not this true?"

A. "For any nation to deliberately contemplate a war, be the circumstances what they may, would be to dishonour its arms, and likewise when any nation is disposed to beg for peace, be the cost what it may, it is to commit a crime. A nation, if compelled to fight for justice, should have the courage to take up arms with a will. It is a moral obligation every nation owes to its country. What are the circumstances under which a nation finds war necessary? Any nation should maintain its rights of self-defence and self-government. Each nation must have cultural and moral missions of its own—its own soul as Mr. Roosevelt termed. When its rights of self-defence and self-government are encroached upon, and its independent existence is consequently endangered, then the nation has every moral right to wage war.

In the light of such views, we must say that Mr. Roosevelt's expression carries a measure of truth."

Q. " Has not the old system of government and economics over the whole world fallen down and proven inadequate ? "

A. " At no time of world history or at no place under the sun do we ever find an instance of universal approval of any political or economic system. It is absolutely impossible. I consider it obvious, however, that every one of us has the duty to strive steadily and constantly for improvement of our political as well as economic life."

www.ingramcontent.com/pod-product-compliance
Lightning Source LLC
Chambersburg PA
CBHW072039160426
43197CB00014B/2550